VIOLENT WORLD

JUNE $1.0

LLER SHARKS
VADE
HALLOW
ATERS
PAGE 12

CRUSHED PAGE 2

E MILLION BATTERED WIVES

S WAITING TO DIE ON DEATH ROW

STAGE FEVER MAKES YOU A TARGET

TORTURED

AMERICA'S PART
IN THE BLOODY WAR

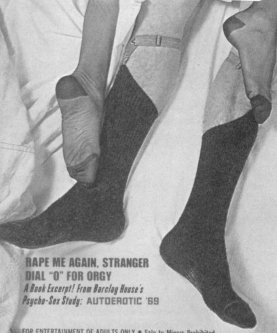

$2

RAPE ME AGAIN, STRANGER
DIAL "O" FOR ORGY
A Book Excerpt! From Barclay House's
Psycho-Sex Study: AUTOEROTIC '69

FOR ENTERTAINMENT OF ADULTS ONLY • Sale to Minors Prohibited

MOD LOVERS

NUMBER TWO / MP / $3.50

A MARQUIS MAGAZINE

A CANDID LOOK
INTO THE LIVES

SALES TO MINORS FORBIDDEN

Nymphet

NOVEMBER • $1.
49305

HE-MAN OR
SHE-MAN ?
HOW SEXY ARE YOU ?

TIPS ON HOW
TO SEDUCE
THE SHY WOMAN

FOR THE ASPIRING
CONNOISSEUR
OF THE BOSOM:
GUIDE FOR
THE BREAST LOVER

WOMEN IN CAGES:
FEMALE SEX IN
PRISON

SUPERCHICKS:
THE WOMEN WHO
PLAY ROUGH IN

HEADPRESS 18

Contents

Credits

Editor **DAVID KEREKES**

Layout **David Kerekes** & **Walt Meaties**
Front cover **Antonio Ghura**
Inside front cover **Magazines of yesteryear from the collection of Tom Brinkmann**
Back cover (*from top left, clockwise*) **Al Goldstein** (© *Screw*); *Beat Girl* (courtesy BFI); **self-portrait** (© Antonio Ghura), *Perverted Older Asians* (© Samurai Video)

contributors

DARREN ARNOLD	KNUD ROMER
BILL BABOURIS	JØRGENSON
GJ BASSETT	MARTIN JONES
ANTON BLACK	SHAUN KIMBER
TOM BRINKMANN	JAMES MARRIOTT
MIKITA BROTTMAN	WHEEZER MCTEAGUE
EUGENE CARFAX	PAN PANTZIARKA
MICHAEL CARLSON	ANTHONY PETKOVICH
RICK CAVENEY	RIK RAWLING
SIMON COLLINS	JACK SARGEANT
MARK DEUTROM	HE SAWYER
DOGGER	STEPHEN SENNITT
ANTHONY FERGUSON	JACK STEVENSON
DUKE FRETSCORCHER	PHIL TONGE
ANTONIO GHURA	MARTIN TRAFFORD
JERRY GLOVER	CHRIS VAILLANCOURT
DAVID GREENALL	JOE SCOTT WILSON
ADRIAN HORROCKS	WILL YOUDS

acknowledgements
Yves Albrechts, Gerard Alexander, bANAL pROBE, Donna Borromeo (Screw), Bill Brent (Black Books), Laura Briscall (Taschen), Poppy Z Brite, Darrell Buxton, John Carter, Sophie Cossette, Harvey Fenton (FAB Press), Claudius Fischer, Creation Books, Antonio Ghura, Katharine Gifford, Jerry Glover, Barry Hoffman, Rikki Hollywood, Buck Hotko, Dave Huxley, Arno Keks, Lesley Kerekes, Richard King (Screen Edge), Desmond Knight, Stefan Jaworzyn, Russ Kick, Craig Ledbetter (ETC), Christian Lewis (Orion Publishing), Phil Liberbaum, Walt Meaties, Medusa, Chris Mikul, Michael Moynihan, Network News, Steve Puchalski (Shock Cinema), Chris Reed (BBR), Roger Sabin, Samuria Video, David Slater, Chip Smith (Hoover Hog), Claire Thompson (Turnaround), TTA Press, Anna Vallois (Titan Books), Stephen Wilson, Stuart Wright.

The Agony and the Ecstasy of Underground Culture! Headpress 18

ISBN 1-900486-05-9

A catalogue record for this book is available from the British Library.

Headpress, 40 Rossall Avenue, Radcliffe, Manchester, M26 1JD, Great Britain
fax: +44 (0)161 796 1935
email: david.headpress@zen.co.uk

SCREW

TURNS 30

Last Battle Looms for America's First Fighting Sex Paper

JACK STEVENSON

Been to New York City lately?

The Deuce, that fabled stretch of 42nd street between 7th and 8th avenues that for decades personified the essence of New York City, is dead. The theatres have been demolished. The hustlers, whores, street peddlers and even the tourists are gone. The neon-buzzing promise of big city sin that raced the pulses of a million Iowa farmboy tourists and swirled in the air as thick as the steamed pretzel smoke and honking horns... gone. On that one long block, in a circus atmosphere doped with the aura of outlaw carnality, every segment of American society collided on jam-packed sidewalks overhung by movie theatre marquees posting their squalid, ghastly delights. And it's all over.

42nd street has become a silent, empty, shutdown monument to Mayor Rudolph Giuliani's urban clean-up campaign as the fascistic forces of moral self-righteousness try to mop up the town like a hospital hallway. Sex clubs, porn theatres, adult bookstores — all gone.

Al Goldstein: still here.

If there is anyone that represents all that mayor Giuliani hates — besides just about any black person — it is Al Goldstein, raconteur supreme, bullshitter unstoppable and publisher now for 30 years of SCREW, New York City's first crusading sex paper.

As New York's adult bookstores face certain decimation, placing SCREW's primary retail outlets — as well as its very future — in jeopardy, a look back at the irrepressible Goldstein and the attack dog he created out of cheap newsprint that put the bite on America's biggest city, might just be the last look.

3

A Jew born and raised in Brooklyn, Goldstein worked in the insurance industry until the mid-Sixties when he "dropped out" of the straight life — and things immediately got worse.

By 1968, he was at the end of his rope. He was 32, overweight, had terrible fashion sense (if period photos are anything to go on) and was on welfare after a string of part-time gigs that had run the gamut from working a stall in the 1965 World's Fair to selling his blood for cash.

Enter Jim Buckley, 24, who, after a three year stint in the Navy was now working as a typesetter for 75 bucks a week at the NEW YORK FREE PRESS, an underground paper. They both needed to make more money. They mulled over the possibilities of starting up their own underground paper since both had done some writing and Goldstein was a photographer. Buckley knew the mechanics of putting out a newspaper and brought an underground sensibility to the project. Goldstein had something special to offer, too — an inexhaustible obsession with sex. This probably sprang, as much as anything, from spending ages 14 to 24 in the ultra-repressive Fifties. In this respect the paper they would launch, SCREW, was probably more a product of the Fifties than the Sixties.

It was Buckley who suggested they put out a sex paper, "an honest sex newspaper." But it was Goldstein who would mould the content into the object of his own sweaty desires, and create a paper that he, as a shill on the street, would buy. And — at 25 cents — buy at a price he could afford.

However new in many ways it might have been, SCREW had its influences. Goldstein was greatly inspired by the courage and jagged-edged humour of Lenny Bruce. Paul Krassner's THE REALIST, which ran from 1958 to 1974 and was reprised in the Eighties as a newsletter, was another major influence. The first issues of SCREW also exhibited a penchant for the type of hairy anarcho-hippy humour that tended to the bizarre, exalted in vulgarity and at the time could also be found in the music of Frank Zappa, the antics of the Diggers and Yippies, and the movies of John Waters.

But what made SCREW different from the outset was its no-holds-barred commitment to take the sin out of sex and demystify it. (Ironically, today in the age of AIDS, that's exactly what health workers, armed with condoms and pamphlets, are doing in junior high schools.) "We don't have to... fob ourselves off as a conscientious newspaper with 'redeeming social value'," declared the publishers with revolutionary zeal in the inaugural issue.

For decades the producers of news and entertainment in America had thrown curve balls at the public when it came to issues of sex. The tabloid press and exploitation movie makers went for the hot-sell, by wrapping their wares in the sensationalism of horrific headlines and prurient come-ons that played the sex card behind a façade of guilt, shame and violence. The other approach, to which "legitimate" books, papers and films were forced to adhere by the moral watchdogs of American society, was to obfuscate sexual content in a cloud of sterilising codification. PLAYBOY magazine, founded in 1953, had taken another, no less calculated and artificial approach to sex — to translate it into a marketable lifestyle via a specific iconography; to commodify the component parts and then to franchise the end product like a burger chain. Desire into upmarket consumerism.

Sexual content could be allowed to a limited degree in film and printed matter if the overall work contained, in the fabled words of the Supreme Court, sufficient "redeeming social value". This was the sucker's game everyone had played, the game that now in this small window of opportunity in the late Sixties, a pathetic little cut-and-paste tabloid was refusing to play... to the notice of just about no one.

THE SCUM ALSO RISES screw is born

The first issue, dated November 29th, 1968, but ready to hit the streets on November 4th, was a crude melange of uneven press-on lettering and linotype text in different fonts. "How to buy sex books", "exposing a fake vagina", "SCREW reviews a beaver film" — these were some of the enticements posted on the cover which featured a girl in a bikini and Fifties style hairdo hoisting what appears to be a giant salami.

Buckley and Goldstein promised to uncover the entire world of sex for the awe-struck first-time buyer, to be "the CONSUMER REPORTS of sex" — even if they couldn't spell "dildoes". "We don't want kids to read SCREW if their folks are hung up," continued the editorial, "but we do want adults who admit they dig the same thing we do and want to cut the sham and groove on truth. It's your move now — king me! — SCREW is here!"

A publicity photo of Al Goldstein taken and circulated in the mid-Eighties.
From the collection of Jack Stevenson.

Substantial text and photoplay was given to a pair of reviews on BARBARELLA that didn't seem to be written by Buckley or Goldstein, who otherwise broadly operated under a host of transparent pseudonyms.

On page nine came a pre-Stonewall tip: "Best place for gay pick-ups, blow jobs and various perversions that feel nice is down at the boats on West Christopher street, after 9 PM. Head for the trucks and follow the crowds of participants and voyeurs. Police harass the folk but rarely run anybody in. If cops bother you, say you're 'taking a piss'."

One-liners like "Jerry Rubin and Abbie Hoffman are going steady", and "Ralph Nader is a reckless driver" were pasted up randomly through the pages.

Issue one was published in a press run of 7,000 copies at a total cost of 300 dollars, the sum of Goldstein and Buckley's combined resources. Part-time underground distributor, Archie Gordon, agreed to handle the paper, despite the fact that Gordon's wife hated it. It was a monumental disaster: 2,500 copies were destroyed and a mountain of 4,000 copies were returned to Goldstein and Buckley.

They were forced to try and distribute the first issue themselves. Goldstein had no car so he got on his bicycle. "I remember going to dealers along 8th avenue," he would recall 20 years later. "These old Jewish guys would yell at me and call me filthy and disgusting and they'd rip the papers up right in front of me." The first issue contained no hardcore photos, but with a personal ads section entitled "Cocks and Cunts" and a centrefold featuring full frontal nudity — bodypainting in

Central Park — SCREW crossed the threshold of smut for most people at a time when PLAYBOY was still air-brushing pubic hair and hardcore pornography had yet to appear on any movie screen. Much has been made of Sixties liberality, but with regards to average American mores in 1968, it might as well as been 1948.

Goldstein found a newsstand at 53rd and 3rd avenue that would take the paper. He was so grateful he told them they could keep all the money. Proceeds from the 2,000 copies they managed to sell — now with no cut to a distributor — were funnelled into the second issue.

STAIRWAY TO HEAVING a lonely vice yells

Once established, success came quickly. For, despite its lack of graphics and marketing sophistication, it was that classic product that filled a need that did exist in the market place, and it quickly found its audience.

By issue nine (April 1969), SCREW went from a bi-weekly to a weekly. It endorsed Lou Abolafia — who advocated copulation in public — for Mayor, and slammed Jackie Gleason for hosting a "decency rally" in Miami in reaction to Jim Morrison's obscenity bust. And it launched it's own obscene crossword puzzle.

In issue 13 (May 1969), Goldstein lashed out at New York City DA assistant, Kenneth Conboy. He accused him of rudely grilling his 56-year-old mother, Gertrude Goldstein, in retaliation for SCREW coverage three weeks prior that highlighted Conboy's role in closing down a controversial play. The attacks had already begun from many quarters. "Some have said we created a Frankenstein monster, and can only be devoured by our own creation," noted the editorial with uncanny prescience.

Goldstein's lust for "firsts" also drove him to print in the same issue, a two-page spread of grainy gay male photos that he crowed, constituted "the first pictorial presentation of actual homosexual love ever permitted the light of day in the United States". More shocking than the less-than-revealing photos was the poem Goldstein composed to caption them:

A MAN LOVES A MAN. Warm flesh burning into wet lips. Lovers fingers intertwining and searching beneath the yoke of body apartness. A man loves a man is the same journey as a man loves a woman and a woman loves a woman. A search and a find. A giving and a taking infused with the desire to reach out and get beyond the self. A trip into the deepest recesses of selfhood.

Despite this burst of poetic sensitivity, Goldstein would have an ambiguous relationship with the gay community. He had published a gay column from the outset, and was a sympathetico and a fellow traveller, but he refused to spare gays — or anyone — from his satiric blasts. While his

6

hammering of gay paranoia and stereotypes — by ostensibly employing them with exaggerated zeal — was in the Lenny Bruce mould, it would only win over the outré fringe of a community perennially under siege.

SCREW got an interview with John and Yoko during their bed-in for peace in Montreal, and printed it in issue 18, a real scoop that gave them credibility in the underground.

In issue 104, the encomium changed from "The First and Best In The Field It Created" to "The World's Greatest Newspaper". It might have more appropriately read, "The World's Most Frequently Busted Newspaper." Goldstein and Buckley were arrested 16 times on obscenity charges over the first couple of years, placing them at the forefront of the free speech movement and giving rise to one of 1970's most popular buttons: "Free The Screw Two."

In 1971, in issue 138, the original swirly Sixties style logo was replaced with a skinnier version of the current tubular design, with the "E" goosing the "W". What would become one of the most recognisable and "loaded" logos in publishing was designed by Milton Glaser, one of the top graphic designers of the day.

In issue 171, SCREW printed one of the very first positive reviews of DEEP THROAT, giving impetus to the momentum of the movie as well as the paper, and signalling the start of a much wider acceptance of explicit sexuality in society at large — a shift SCREW was well positioned to exploit. Times had changed radically in the span of three short years.

On February 12th, 1973, in issue 206, grainy nude photos of Jackie Onassis were printed for the first time in an American publication, lifted without permission from — or fee to — the Italian PLAYMEN magazine. The cover price was upped from 50 cents to $5, and presses worked overtime as a record 500,000 copies were sold. Lucky buyers also got a photo of Linda Lovelace being mounted by a dog in same issue — the porn star being just one of many people Goldstein would fall out with over the years.

In 1975, SCREW took advantage of new developments in free public-access television and began broadcasting SCREW MAGAZINE OF THE AIR, a show documenting the outré extremes of New York City's sex cultures. In 1976, now on a leased public-access basis (Channel J), the show changed its name to MIDNIGHT BLUE and is still running.

In the mid-Seventies, SCREW founded a west coast variant called SCREW WEST to exploit the Los Angeles and San Francisco markets. However, competition from SCREW-inspired tabloids already established in these cities — such as THE SAN FRANCISCO BALL and FINGERS (the latter being all reader-contributed and clearly the most extreme sex publication ever) — saw to the demise of SCREW WEST after 54 issues.

By this time, even the more political of the underground papers, like THE BERKELEY BARB, were staying solvent with — and being attacked by feminists for — advertising revenue from the sex industry. SCREW was also weathering attacks by feminists, but at least it didn't have to fend off charges of hypocrisy. The collective of social and political subsets upon which the counterculture and the underground press had been founded in the late Sixties, was starting to unravel. By the end of the decade, most underground papers would be out of business or heading in that direction.

SCREW had always been an anomaly in the underground, and even a bit of a contradiction within its own terms. As a paper dedicated to liberating sex from the clutches of the traditional watchdogs of public morality — who had always demanded the power to define and contextualise sex — and giving this basic human right back to the individual by shattering sexual taboos and inhibitions, SCREW could be seen as a force for personal and spiritual liberation. And yet the paper was clearly founded on the most consumerist and materialistic of premises: to serve as an adjunct to the billion-dollar-a-year sex industry which in turn — as feminists would claim — sought to usurp the power to define and contextualise sexuality for its own profit.

This last idea even found space in the first issue, in "The Diary of a Sex Addict" column by Richard Field, a page after Goldstein and Buckley had promised to become the CONSUMER REPORTS of sex.

'Sex is largely mediated by the cerebral cortex.' This statement by Albert Ellis makes possible the only revolution that can really get down to it: The Revolution of Pornographic Life. A pornography of make-the-pleasure-last-as-long-as-we-can will make obsolete the jerk-off-while-you-photograph-her pornography of the horny world. A pornography to turn you on personally will replace the vicarious 42nd Street deprivation. The dirty books will become a quaint old folk

GREAT MOMENTS IN THE LIFE OF AL GOLDSTEIN

MUNICH, 1940: Al grins after palming off exorbitant check on a bemused Führer during storm troopers' luncheon at Nazis' Braune Haus HQ.

A Goldstein gag, from *Screw* N° 899.

art, because the frustration of capitalism will be gone.

Others argued that the sexuality SCREW was selling was not the consumerist variety — even though their back pages openly touted sex as a commercial commodity. In truth, SCREW rarely made sex look attractive, and always adhered to an editorial policy that stressed the humour over the sex. PLAYBOY had built up a concept of the modern woman as an untouchably perfect, airbrushed porcelain shrine, and SCREW was now busy blasting away at the foundations with the levelling power of satire. SCREW might have served as a marketplace for goods and services, but was not involved in the biggest fraud: peddling fake values and phoney ideals.

Could SCREW be an organ of both personal and industrial liberation? If by aiding individuals to seek out and obtain the accoutrements of the lifestyles they craved, perhaps SCREW was — to use a term in nobody's vocabulary back then — empowering individuals. Nonetheless, for all of Goldstein's fire-and-brimstone belief in a kind a holy crusade, SCREW was born of contradictions, and contradictions would ever be a part of the anarchy that it epitomised. He wouldn't have had it any other way.

Goldstein's variety of obsessions were manifest by the scattershot array of short-lived magazines and papers that he pumped out over the years. While SCREW was his vehicle, his "flagship" publication, he also published X, BITCH, GAY, GADGET, and, early on, in 1972 with Buckley, MOBSTER TIMES, which was subtitled "Crime Does Pay" and had no sexual content whatsoever. "We had [mobster] Joey Gallo as the film reviewer," fondly recalled Goldstein in 1985, "we glorified crime because we thought the bad guys were the FBI and the CIA." Issue three (December 1972), entices with front cover come-ons like, "How To Choose Your Own Prison", "Are You A Criminal?", and "Electronic Execution: New Ways To Kill".

But Goldstein's strangest detour into doomed publishing ventures had to be DEATH MAGAZINE, a tabloid which ran four issues in 1977, and gave him the chance to irreverently fuck with the sacred cow of death, the way SCREW fucked with the sacred cow of sex. The public wasn't buying, but with a tabloid that in form and substance played as both parody and "real thing", Goldstein had whipped up a Dadaist masterpiece of the supermarket checkout magazine rack long before THE WEEKLY WORLD NEWS became a pet of the punk set. SCREW had been created as a antidote to the culture of scare-mongering tabloids, but now Goldstein figured that if Joe and Jane Blow wanted to wallow in death, doom and tragedy, he would be honest about it and give it to them in spades, *and* of course make a profit on it. Undoubtedly Goldstein would have been bewildered had anyone accused him of creating "art", let alone conceptualist art. It should also be noted that these ancillary publications were, for the most part, not targeted at an "underground" readership but marketed to the mainstream, and Goldstein himself lived anything but an underground lifestyle!

Although Goldstein was a solid capitalist and these publications were commercially distributed, they — and SCREW — did intersect and share similarities with the punk movement in the late-Seventies. Goldstein's aesthetic was the same: he did whatever the fuck he wanted in the cause of attacking the power structures, and confronting a complacent consumer society with a series of shocks. It's interesting to observe that in retrospect nothing the punk "revolution" gener-

9

Al Goldstein today.
Photo courtesy: *Screw.*

ated in paper form was nearly as extreme or aggressively bizarre as DEATH MAGAZINE or SCREW. In part this was because punk claimed a certain political significance, whereas Goldstein, self-proclaimed "butcherer of sacred cows", was, in print at least, an anarchist.

This welter of publications also foreshadowed the fanzine movement that, based on the DIY aesthetic, began in the mid-Eighties and promoted the idea of giving a public vent to your private obsessions. But Goldstein's direct influence on these movements was virtually nil: he was simply too way out, and the publications themselves too ahead of their time, or marketed to completely different audiences. In the case of SCREW, its pornographic content was sure to alienate many who might otherwise respond to his messages.

SCREW IN THE LAND OF THE WIZARD OF OZ trails & triumphs

SCREW would weather a flurry of obscenity busts and libel suits throughout its existence, with most of the cases being won or dropped, or the plaintiffs awarded insignificant "nominal nuisance" payments. But in 1976, the Federal government itself tried to shut down the paper.

On June 18th, 1976, Goldstein, Buckley and SCREW's parent company, Milky Way Productions, were convicted in Federal Court in Wichita, Kansas, of sending obscene materials through the mail. There were six SCREW subscribers in Wichita and, as it turned out, three of them were US postal inspectors. Goldstein, who acted as front man in the proceedings and was soon to buy out the fading Buckley, faced up to 60 years in prison.

On appeal the verdict was overturned.

The Feds retried the case in Kansas City, and this trial ended in a hung jury. The government decided not to seek a third trial and SCREW was free. Nine of the jurors had voted for acquittal, and their reward was now an expense paid trip to New York City courtesy of a grateful Al Goldstein, who shuttled them around the highlights of the sex industry — such places as Plato's Retreat and the SCREW offices, housed in an old industrial building on seedy 14th street.

The cost to Goldstein to defend SCREW had amounted to well over half a million dollars, prompting him to complain that he was shelling out of his own pocket to defend the First Amendment rights of all Americans.

In 1977, SCREW was again the target of a high-powered legal attack when the Pillsbury

Company of Minneapolis claimed the paper had violated its trademark copyrights, in a layout (in issue 459) that had depicted the Pillsbury doughboy and doughgirl — Poppin' Fresh and Poppie Fresh — in various sexual acts. Goldstein had been watching TV one night when a Pillsbury commercial came on, which led him to ponder what kind of sex lives the corporate cuties led. And, of course, he concluded that they didn't lead normal sex lives. He thought it was all pretty funny, but after Pillsbury slapped him with a 1.5 million dollar lawsuit, he probably wished he'd just changed the channel.

The suit was filed not in New York or Minneapolis, but in Atlanta, leading Goldstein to conclude that Pillsbury hoped to inconvenience him and add to his expense with the long commute, and, more ominously, to intimidate him by forcing him to travel to a part of the country where HUSTLER editor, Larry Flynt, had been gunned down by an assassin not so long before. Additionally, it was clear that Pillsbury was engaging in the standard strategy of bringing big city pornographers to trial in conservative mid-west or southern towns. (DEEP THROAT had been tried — and convicted — in Memphis.) It could be assumed that sympathy in an Atlanta jurisdiction, for a bearded New York City Jew who published a sex tabloid, would be minimal, even though this was a non-jury trial.

Judge William C. Kelly, however, ruled against Pillsbury, handing down a decision that stated that Pillsbury had failed to prove infringement and that SCREW's use of the trademark was protected under the Fair Use doctrine. The rights of artists or musicians to satirise or parody familiar works under the protection of the Fair Use doctrine, would be secured and expanded in the Nineties in a series of high-profile cases, the most publicised of which involved the rap group, 2-Live Crew. SCREW's court battle helped set the precedent for this.

The appeals process dragged on until 1983, and only then was perhaps the world's most bizarre court case brought to a conclusion. SCREW was again in the clear, and Goldstein crowned his victory with an editorial in which he savaged not only the Pillsbury company, but the entire interior of the continental United States. "Shit-eating, impotent crackers," said Goldstein of the Pillsbury minions, "...with imaginations and libidos dulled by the long hibernation in the land of the shopping mall, quadra-knit leisure suit and dinette set." "Crackers" is in fact a derogatory term for southern rednecks, not inhabitants of Minnesota, but in his contempt for the entire interior of the country, and the way in which it inconveniently stretched out flight time on his frequent visits to LA, Goldstein didn't agonise over such fine distinctions.

"As I sit in my office in New York City," concluded said editorial, "and watch Poppin' Fresh grease up his pole with Pillsbury frosting in preparation for anal entry into Poppie Fresh, I revel in the knowledge that since I have custody of these two corporate orphans, they won't ever have to live in the brain-numbing interior wastelands of America."

Such were the distractions now afforded to Goldstein as he sat in his SCREW office. The sexual revolution out of which SCREW was created was long over, and now every big city had a sex tabloid based on SCREW — there were no more "firsts".

In 1978, Goldstein had teamed with publisher Lyle Stewart to launch NATIONAL SCREW in a glossy, colour magazine format. But it quickly folded, unable to compete with other men's market glossies, particularly HUSTLER which had stolen SCREW's thunder in the low-brow sexual satire department, and had the formula down pat along with access to the models. In SCREW, you always had the feeling you were seeing "real people", not models, and some of the nudies on display in early issues sported bad teeth, freaky hair and bad skin that's rather jarring to look at today. Nonetheless, SCREW remained far more outrageous than HUSTLER, whose famous cover of a woman being poured into a meatgrinder that scandalised the country was timid stuff compared to the graphic gristle served up in SCREW every week. But SCREW was primarily distributed in adult bookshops, whereas HUSTLER sold in drugstores and supermarkets.

Flynt, like Goldstein, had made a career and a fortune by rebelling against the pretentious-

I was Al Goldstein's Humidor!

DEEP INSIDE SCREW MAGAZINE'S 30th ANNIVERSARY PARTY!

by Sophie Cossette

If Uncle Sam saw Al Goldstein charging in his direction, it's a sure thing that he would run and hide at the sight of the publisher of the notoriously dirty *Screw* magazine! This former cab driver turned smut peddler — a real molotov cocktail on two legs — currently has it in for New York City mayor, Rudolph Giuliani, who, with the Disney empire's help, has given the once infamous 42nd Street a thorough enema. Goldstein thrives so eagerly on conflict that his neuroses have assured the financial well-being of his therapists *and* their descendants. He'd take his own mistresses to court at the slightest sign of a yeast infection. Yes indeed, if Central Park serves as the lungs of

Sophie on Al Goldstein's knee in Al's office, *Screw* headquarters.

Photo © Sophie Cossette/Phil Liberbaum.

ness of PLAYBOY. Goldstein always thought Flynt's claims to "born again" status indicated brain damage, but admired his courage, persistence and refusal to back down in the face of withering attacks from right-wingers, attacks that increased in the conservative Eighties.

Goldstein wasn't softening up either and found new causes and targets in the age of Reagan. It was almost too easy. With conservative figureheads like Ed Meese and Jerry Falwell leading highly publicised attacks against the commercial sex industry, pornography became one of the hot issues of the Eighties.

Although not as (in)famous as Larry Flynt, Goldstein occasionally blipped up on the media's radar screen, usually when a writer needed some outrageous quotes from the "pro-pornography" camp. The March 18th, 1985 issue of NEWSWEEK magazine, for example, featured a reactionary piece on the subject, complete with pictures of Goldstein and incendiary quotes: "Frankly I don't think it matters whether porn is degrading to women. It's a society of many voices and I don't want any of them silenced." An accompanying photo pictures a protester holding aloft a placard that reads: "SCREW magazine says a woman's place is on her knees" — surely one of the tamest quotes ever culled from the paper.

In fact, Goldstein was being unfairly typecast — he often turned his guns on subjects that had nothing to do with sex. After the bombing of the marine barracks in Lebanon that killed hundreds of American servicemen and plunged the nation into a state of shock, a satiric photo-collage appeared in SCREW, picturing Goldstein with a giant hard-on being carried from the rubble on a stretcher above the time-honoured Marine motto, "Looking For A Few Good Men." And when Salman Rushdie was targeted by the Fatwa, Goldstein took aim at Muslim zealotry. This reportedly earned him some actual death threats and encouraged him to cool it for the first time ever.

SUPPOSE THEY GAVE A BIRTHDAY PARTY AND NOBODY CAME screw turns twenty

On May 2nd, 1988, SCREW celebrated its anniversary with the publication of issue 1000. In the editorial, Goldstein summed up the state of SCREW with succinctness if not humility.

SCREW magazine has become a lonely — but always abrasive, confrontational and unassailable — stronghold of the truth. We are a living rebuttal to the self-hatings and sexual negativisms of the right wing, of the Ronald Reagans and Edwin Meeses and Jerry Falwells of the world... we have covered the sexual world with an honesty and positivism... SCREW's existence these many years is evidence that the Constitution and freedom of dissent are alive in this great land.

His reference to SCREW being a "lonely voice" is telling. Not lonely because it was attacked and surrounded by enemies — one suspects he wishes it was attacked *more*; that in his reveries he yearned to be relevant, be taken seriously, be heard, be debated, be more than a side-show. But he had played the role of dissenter so long and so loudly that maybe now it was the only role he could play. And could SCREW, conceived as a taboo busting, cutting edge publication, survive far from that edge?

SCREW published some of the most cogent and hilarious writing anywhere, and much of the reportage was first class, but the paper never transcended its primary function as Goldstein's personal soapbox — however persistently the rumour circulated that Goldstein's inspired rants were ghost-written by underpaid staffers. And it never came within shouting distance of a quality that might be termed slick or professional. SCREW remains the ballsiest underground paper in a day and age when nobody cares about an underground paper. Any other publication of comparable longevity would have undergone numerous changes in format and editorial policy over the years — and gone out of business. SCREW didn't have to worry about staying topical or fashionable — it was never there to read the trends or adopt to them or set them, but to attack and debunk the trends and prevailing accepted wisdoms.

SCREW stays in business thanks to its status as an organ of the sex industry, but between all the dildo and lubricant ads and the unattributed, smudgy, B&W fuck photos (that for many years were pulled out at random from a big cardboard box on the 11th floor), who actually *reads* it? Does the average Joe, who just wants an idea of the Times Square sex club scene, care about Goldstein's legal battles and personal vendettas? Probably not. Does Goldstein care about that? Absolutely not.

SCREW is a victim of the success of its own divine mission: never to take itself seriously, to view nothing as sacred, and to spare no man or beast. And this is an

Gotham City, you can bet Al Goldstein is its sewer system. And girls, should you ever find yourselves face-to-face with Goldstein, rest assured that the pitiless pitbull will ensure your panties stink of his cigar by the time he's through with you!

After about three years of contributing cartoons and comics to *Screw*, I finally met the testosterone-loaded egomaniac who supplements my American dollar bank account. Finding myself in New York City for a long weekend in order to attend *Screw*'s 30th Anniversary Party, I dropped by the magazine's offices. Unluckily for me, the big boss was in and upon entering his private sanctuary, I had the gut feeling that I'd be treated like Bill Clinton's humidor. When I asked to have a photo taken with him, Goldstein offered me his knee. I had the distinct sensation of being a little mouse in the arms of Genghis Khan! He inquired if I'd prefer to be brought to orgasm orally or courtesy of his Jewish family jewels. Faced with this dilemma, I wisely opted for abstinence; not surprisingly, for the second snapshot he

Grampa Munster chatting up prostitutes at *Screw* party.

honoured me with a fat middle finger. Nevertheless, he invited my husband and I to join him two days later at Katz's, a famous Lower East Side deli where he'd be pigging out with a number of his disciples.

Three long tables were reserved for Goldstein's gang at one end of the eatery. I suspected that most of Al's journalist cronies were old enough to have covered the Lindberg child kidnapping case. Al "Grampa" Lewis of *Munsters* TV series fame was sitting by himself, swearing under his breath as if Tourette's Syndrome had taken grip. I decided that asking him to autograph my *Munsters* postcard wouldn't be such a smart idea after all. Goldstein, however, had the temerity to ask Grampa if he'd be joining him and other human barf bags in doing the Full Monty at the following evening's festivities. Grampa's response wasn't long in coming: "Fuck you, you fat fuck! You're gonna put shame on all of us with your dirty underwear!"

Monday, Sept. 14, 7:15 PM. One limousine follows another, discharging passengers in front of the Carbon club in midtown Manhattan. Enough transvestites, bimbos, weirdoes, mafiosos, gigolos, and porn biz types to give Mayor Giuliani indigestion for days on end!

"Take that! And this!" Fetish felines in action at *Screw*y celebration.

approach even more radical today than it was in 1968. Even its biggest fans and supporters have all been repelled at one time or another by its excesses. With inexhaustible energy, Goldstein has made SCREW gloriously untouchable. As Jackie Onassis replied when asked why she didn't sue the paper, "you don't want to get in a fight with a skunk" — a quote proudly reprinted in issue 1000. At a celebrity AIDS benefit in the late-Eighties, Kelvin Klein refused to be a part of a group photo that included Al Goldstein, and a scene ensued that caused Goldstein some humiliation. Not that Klein stayed for long at the top of SCREW's hate list — there were too many other candidates coming and going.

There was constant friction... and friction beget life.

SILVER SCREEN EXPOSURES
the movies

In spite of — or because of — all this, Goldstein and SCREW became fixtures in the lore of American subculture, as evidenced by appearances in a range of films.

In the beginning of Woody Allen's 1972 film, EVERYTHING YOU ALWAYS WANTED TO KNOW ABOUT SEX BUT WERE AFRAID TO ASK, Allen wanders morosely through a New York City porn shop as copies of SCREW appear conspicuously in the racks behind him.

Goldstein had roles in a number of early-Seventies porno films, such as EROTICON, but this writer has never seen these titles and can't verify whether Goldstein had performing or non-performing parts — and is happy to remain in ignorance.

Buckley got screen time in Dusan Makavevej's episodic 1971 underground classic, W.R., MYSTERIES OF THE ORGANISM, in which a woman enters the SCREW offices and makes a plaster cast of his erect member.

Goldstein was featured at length in a 1977 documentary entitled, DEATH MAGAZINE, OR HOW TO BECOME A FLOWER POT, by German filmmaker, Rosa Von Praunheim. Von Praunheim uses DEATH MAGAZINE as a springboard into an investigation of how death is dealt with in various cultures. The viewer is treated to a rotund and unhealthy looking Goldstein who, sitting on a couch with Von Praunheim, pages through a copy of DEATH MAGAZINE wherein is revealed a construction schematic for a do-it-yourself gallows. Goldstein advises any viewers contemplating suicide not to jump from a tall building because they might land on somebody else. "Are *you* afraid of death?" asks the filmmaker. "I'm scared shitless,"

Goldstein replies.

Goldstein had a cameo in Jonathan Nossitor's 1992 documentary about Quentin Crisp entitled RESIDENT ALIEN. Nossitor chats with Goldstein as they stroll down a sleazy Manhattan sidestreet.

It's interesting to note how two previously vilified and ridiculed personalities from the world of Seventies' hardcore porno — Larry Flynt and John Holmes — have been heroically, or at least sympathetically, resurrected in a pair of recent major motion pictures: THE PEOPLE VERSUS LARRY FLYNT and BOOGIE NIGHTS. On the surface of it, Goldstein's story would seem to offer up an even richer vein of drama from the same milieu, given his articulate, entertainingly bombastic persona, his pioneering status, his many court battles and his travels in various celebrity social circles. Then again, no scriptwriter on earth could reshape Goldstein into the requisite "sympathetic character", or simplify his story into the trite "product/victim of the times" morality tale, a formula that gave the Flynt biopic its mass-marketability. They could give us lite versions of Howard Stern, Larry Flynt and John Holmes, but it could never be done with Goldstein. His wilfully corrosive surface defies any Hollywood polish job.

Thus it was left to a team of underground filmmakers to give it a shot: Todd Phillips, Andrew Gurland and Alex Crawford, whose previous film, HATED: G.G. ALLIN AND THE MURDER JUNKIES, had been an acclaimed documentary of the late punk rock anti-star, G.G. Allin. After dealing with rock'n'roll's most volatile mental case, they probably figured Goldstein would be easy.

With Gurland and Phillips as hands-on producers and Crawford directing, the picture, entitled SCREWED, was completed in the summer of 1996. Phillips and Gurland wanted to focus on Goldstein — whose mercurial mood swings drove Phillips nuts as they tried to interview him — while Crawford conceived the film to be more about pornography in general. With little input in the editing process, Phillips found the finished product to be hopelessly unfocused and disowned it. It saw limited theatrical release in America, garnered mixed reviews and did less than boffo at the box office.

The puzzle of how Goldstein's potentially rich story might be brought to the screen continues to entice…

With the world's most brutally irreverent and politically incorrect paper having turned 30 in November 1998, its survival is challenged as never before. New York City is cleaning up and shocking rumours circulate that it's even safe for Yuppies to

Sodom and Gomorrah wouldn't even hold a kinky candle next to this Screwy celebration!

Ron Jeremy in all his bulky hedgehog glory pops up, accompanied by a human Barbie doll fresh out of the factory. Her boobs are so pumped up with silicone that he's going to have to hold on to her tampon string to prevent her from floating away. Ed Powers appears with a few of his Dirty Debutantes — it's all downhill from here on in, girls! Hustler magazine's Larry Flynt is perched in his gold-plated wheelchair, surrounded by his bodyguards in the middle of the street.

Later, in the VIP room of the club, Al Goldstein begins barking and orders everyone to leave: he's suffocating with all the people crowded in the room. Flynt finds himself a bona fide circus freak as camera flashbulbs constantly go off in his direction. Talk about a chance of a lifetime for me. Rarely does one have the opportunity to witness two multi-millionaire pornographers in such discomfort up close!

Up on the stage, the main event of the evening gets under way… Ron

Photo © Sophie Cossette/Phil Liberbaum.

Larry "The Hustler" Flynt says a few kind words about Goldstein.

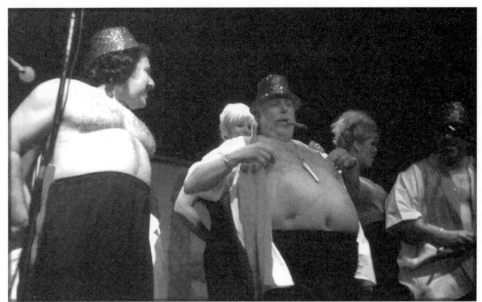

Brace yourself! *The Full Monty… Screw* style!
L–R Ron Jeremy, Al Goldstein, Ed Powers.

Jeremy and Grampa Lewis are the masters of ceremonies and their jokes ricocheting off one another are strictly of the below-the-belt variety. They introduce the first performers of the *Screw* party freak show: a duo of stand-up comics who flunked out from the Howard Stern school of humour. Their schtick culminates with the black broad in the comedian couple giving us a demonstration of female orgasm that sounds more like a fat politician defecating than anything else. The not-so-funny wise-asses are followed by four fetish nymphets going through the motions of spanking each other, with hot candle wax to boot. The Marquis de Sade on Prozac would be an accurate way of describing the banality of their choreography.

The 300lb High Priest of Sleazedom in whose honour this party is being held, Al Goldstein himself, appears on stage, his dick still hidden in his pants, I unhappily note. He introduces his vicar, Larry Flynt, who is ready to kiss walk the streets at night now. America's kinkiest and most diverse urban sex culture — which created SCREW and guaranteed its financial viability — is being zoned out of existence. And porno, thanks to Ken Starr, is freely available on the Internet and discussed exhaustively on the nightly news in circumstances so bizarre that probably even Goldstein is left speechless.

So, after 62 years of broken marriages, radical weight-loss schemes and the weekly search for something to get fired up about, does Goldstein ever think about retiring?

He won't say. But if SCREW's pulse is fading, you won't find out by feeling its wrist. 💀

NOTE *Shortly before this edition went to press, Screw launched their website:* **www.screwmag.com**

Goldstein's ass. With teary eyes, the *Hustler* head honcho appears uncomfortable paying tribute to his ol' pal Al, something he nevertheless flew from LA to New York with the express purpose of doing. Goldstein licks Flynt's butt in return and both exit stage right to make room for a beauty contest to select New York City's hottest transsexual. The audience picks the winner and to the loser, Ron Jeremy cracks: "Sorry, you lose. Now Giuliani's gonna piss on you!"

The winner elicits this comment from the Hedgehog: "You win a year of free ads in *Screw* and a week with Grampa!" Well, what he/she's saved in 800 bucks of weekly advertising will have to be invested in pesticide to survive those seven days with Grampa.

Goldstein soon reappears brandishing an over-sized drawing of Rudolph Giuliani dressed up in women's lingerie, thus revealing the holier-than-thou mayor as a closet pervert. The *Screw* publisher then tips Giuliani's head in the direction of his crotch and proceeds to get a mock blowjob by the Mayor.

The moment comes (even if Goldstein doesn't) for the handing out of the *Screw* Awards for filthy folks "who've made invaluable contributions to America's sexual underworld". I'll do the reader a big favour by not describing the speeches made by the recipients, suffice to say that they all seemed to accept their plastic statuettes in the spirit of Lenny Bruce.

Grampa returns to the spotlight, wittily yells back at some smart-ass hecklers, and introduces the crowd to a 72-year-old grandma who struts her wrinkled stuff in her birthday suit while doing a lascivious dance, which I'm sure she must have practised on a stretcher.

Which finally brings us to the moment we'd all been either eagerly anticipating or dreading, depending on one's taste (or lack of it): the grand finale of the *Screw* party freak show. Goldstein, Ron Jeremy, Ed Powers, and their cohorts whose bodies have obviously seen better days, hit the stage to music from *The Full Monty. The* most grotesque striptease in the history of humanity ensues, one that would make even an inflatable doll sick to its stomach. Standing there in front of the stage directly facing Goldstein, the horrible truth is suddenly revealed to me! The dirty old man of porn publishing has no prick! Holding a dildo to create an optical illusion in the eyes of the spectators, it hardly covers the tiny hole where his overcooked macaroni is supposed to be! Now at last the eternal mystery about Goldstein is solved. Why his incredible obsession with going down on pussy? Why his incurable fascination with cigars, handguns, and dildos? Elementary, my dear reader: Al "Eunuch" Goldstein can screw these objects in where his cock would normally be, thereby satisfying the harem girls who bolster his faltering ego in exchange for a fistful of dollars! Well, wouldn't you do the same if you shared his poor pathetic predicament?! 🐾

Article translated from French by Phil Liberbaum

Photo © Sophie Cossette/Phil Liberbaum.

Not bad for 72, huh?

Antonio Ghura as he was in the Seventies. Self-portrait.
All artwork in this article © Antonio Ghura.

antonio ghura
beyond the edge publishing co.

DAVID KEREKES

Underground comics are comics that exist outside of the mainstream. The phenomenon of the Undergrounds evolved out of a piece of legislation in 1954, which set out to redress the growing tide of crime comics and horror comics polluting the minds of American children. The introduction of this Comics Code meant that every comic book now had to carry a seal of approval in order to ensure news-stand distribution — as well as having to adhere to a sizeable set of guidelines outlining what could and couldn't be shown, a central body scrutinised each comic prior to publication. Faced with such crippling confides, many comic publishers vanished overnight; others, who tried to adapt, produced work which was anaemic and surreal to the point that kids no longer bought them, and so the comics died anyway.

A decade-or-so later, a new generation of artists started to emerge who were freely inspired by the pre-Code comics they had read as children. Their comics, however, were independently produced, came in small print runs and didn't rely on news-stand distribution. And while the social and political climate of the Sixties gave these Underground artists the 'nerve' to take on the subjects they did — sex, drugs, violence and religion — it was the Comics Code that gave them their agenda: ridicule the Code at every turn, wallow in and glorify every objection raised in that piece of straitjacket legislation.

Underground comics were an outlet for a lot of diverse ideas, but to a bunch of young, hot-blooded, heterosexual males, "absolute freedom" — as Robert Crumb defined the Undergrounds — meant for many of the artists only one thing. And it didn't take long for Sex to become the dominant force.

Like horror comics had filtered through in the Fifties, the first Undergrounds to appear in Britain consisted mainly of reprints of work by US artists (quite often, ripped-off without permission, under the proviso that it was all in the 'spirit'

Andy, about to love Katie and leave her, in a page from 'Lonely Hearts'. *Bogey* Nº 2.

of the Underground). Alternative newspapers *Oz* and *International Times* both had comicbook imprints, pitting budding British talent alongside their more famous American counterparts. As the Seventies progressed, more British titles appeared that were dedicated to home-grown artists. A series of obscenity charges brought against 'subversive' British presses in the late-Sixties and early-Seventies, however, ensured that the British Undergrounds in general feared to be as overtly sexual as the American comics.

Oz had found itself in the dock faced with Obscenity charges over their 'Schoolkids' issue, as had the publishers of *Nasty Tales* when they reprinted some Crumb art in their debut number. One other publication to land in court in 1977 was *Libertine*, a self-proclaimed 'new journal of authentic Victorian and period erotica,' whose issue No 7 was tried and found not guilty of obscenity. A one-page comic strip entitled 'Home on Leave', was singled out by the prosecution. The artist was Antonio Ghura.

Whilst researching the article 'Thrill To Stories of Graphic Lust' that appeared in the book *Critical Vision*,[1] I had tried without success to contact Antonio Ghura. The article took an historical look at two decades of sex-orientated Underground comics from both sides of the Atlantic, but the idea was to bring the criminally neglected Ghura into the

19

Front covers for *Truly Amazing Love Stories* Nº 1 and Nº 2, respectively.

picture. As far as my research showed, no interview with Ghura had ever appeared in print, and no books or articles devoted to comics — Underground or otherwise — had ever bothered to acknowledge him. And yet, Ghura was responsible for some of the funniest, sexiest, most outrageous comics ever to make it into print — that he was printing and publishing them in Britain seemed only to make them all the more outrageous. His work was rarely dampened by the self-indulgent excesses associated with many of the Underground artists, but rather it followed a traditional comic book style: concise narratives, with an old-school comic book look. Ghura seemed to care not where he tread with his comics. His work was a fetid beacon in a marketplace slowly collapsing under its own sterility.

So what went wrong?

During the weeks I spent trying to track him down — asking distributors, possible acquaintances of his, even arriving at a telephone number that was no longer in service — a rather unsettling picture of Ghura began to emerge. He seemed to be a wild man. There were stories of him physically attacking people who he believed had wronged him, and in one tale breaking into somebody's home and brandishing a knife. I already suspected that the phased, long-haired and dishevelled hippies that frequented his strips might have been caricatures of Ghura himself (particularly the one in 'Love Conquers All!', reeling in agony after some bird accidentally spills ice cold Coke on his naked balls at the Scunthorpe pop festival) — now I became certain.

It wasn't until some years after that article was published that I came into contact with Antonio.

Outside of occasional strips, spot illustrations, and ads for head shops contributed to **Home Grown**, **ZigZag** and the like, Ghura's main body of work is to be found in several comic titles which he single-handedly wrote and illustrated. The first of these was **Bogey**, published in 1975, which featured several mock advertisements, a lengthy drug strip called 'The Peyote Connection', and an incest-themed strip titled 'Fatherly Love'. The whole thing was a dry run for Ghura's next project, the comic he's possibly best known for: **Truly Amazing Love Stories**. Published in

1977, *Truly Amazing Love Stories* is a pastiche of the Romance comics so popular in Fifties America. 'Forty-four pages of crotch ticklin' tales!' the cover boasted. Indeed, the very funny hardcore strips — which have themes such as male and female homosexuality, the clap, and bestiality — combined with a dodgy Agony Aunt and fake ads for cannabis and police recruitment, made *Truly Amazing Love Stories* No 1 a success. The print run of 3,000 copies soon sold out, but it wasn't until 1983 that Ghura got around to producing the second edition. By this time, however, Ghura's main outlets for distribution were closed to him, and, left to handle the comic himself, *Truly Amazing Love Stories* No 2 did very badly. When I spoke with the artist in mid-1998, lack of distribution ensured that only 200 copies of the 3,000 print run had thus far been sold. (Which made it particularly fortuitous that I should have picked up a copy when it came out in the early-Eighties.)

If the first issue was a Bronx Cheer in the face of British censorship laws, *Truly Amazing Love Stories* No 2 succeeded in kicking them out of the ball park altogether. The format was the same — but with better quality paper stock, more striking artwork (Ghura said that he drew issue No 1 "very quickly"), and Madge Poops, the Agony Aunt, being replaced by Babs Cartfart. This time the stories were better developed, and appeared to go less for out-and-out laughs and more for vivid depictions of the sex act. Themes included a sex-change romance, incest, and used-tampon gags. More than anything else,

Working sketches for Ghura's
Headpress 18 cover painting.

the tone of the issue was influenced by a strip titled 'I Loved A Sex Fiend!' which played out a rape scene over five excruciatingly graphic pages. If that wasn't enough, the rapist was 'Paul Rutcliffe' — a dead ringer for Peter Sutcliffe, the Yorkshire Ripper.

Raw Purple and *The Laid-Back Adventures of Suzie and Jonnie*, published in 1977 and 1981 respectively, switched sex for stories of pot, LSD and hippie drug culture. The former is essentially *Truly Amazing Love Stories* in a different jacket, but *Suzie and Jonnie* is more akin to Gilbert Shelton's early *Fabulous Furry Freak Brothers* — very intricate, self-contained page-long stories that contribute to a larger picture. Artistically, it contains some of Ghura's best work.

Ghura's only other comics are the digest-sized *Hot Nads* and *Bogey* No 2. *Hot Nads*, published in 1979 and billed as the 'first & last issue', is a rather lacklustre take on Robert Crumb's *Snatch Comics*, incorporating, for the most part, TV personalities and politicians of the day in a series of outrageous sex cartoons. *Bogey* No 2, published in 1984, is wholly more satisfying with some very crisp artwork, and a reprint of the controversial 'Home On Leave' strip from *Libertine*.

21

FIRST & LAST ISSUE.

PRESENTS

ADULTS ONLY 50p

HOT NADS

I WILL CRUSH ALL SEX PEDDLIN' PARASITIC SCUM!!

NOT APPROVED BY THE COMICS CODE AUTHORITY

CANNABIS

SUBTLE PERSUASIVE DISTINCTIVE

TRULY UNEXPURGATED!

Wraparound cover to *Hot Nads* N° 1.

M y eventual meeting with Antonio came about like this: At the beginning of 1998, I got a phone call from Roger Sabin, author of the book **Comics, Comix & Graphic Novels**. Ghura had discovered that Roger's book contained a passing mention of him and, as luck would have it, had written to the author via the publisher in order to try and blag a copy. Roger was well aware that I had been trying to reach Ghura some years earlier, and contacted me, furnishing me with Ghura's London address and phone number. That day, I mailed Ghura a copy of the **Critical Vision** book containing the 'Thrill To Stories of Graphic Lust!' article. A couple of days later, I gave him a call.

Ghura seemed happy to do an interview, so I arranged to travel down to London the following week and meet with him in a pub off Tottenham Court Road. I felt I was about to untangle another thread of my teenage youth, meeting the guy who so fried my brain with the first issue of **Truly Amazing Love Stories** back in the Seventies. There was no doubt about it — I was approaching the mysterious Ghura with reserved awe!

Ghura had with him a big holdall stuffed with his comics, which he intended to tout around London's comic shops after our interview. It had been some time since he had last bothered trying to sell them, he said, but he had heard of a new place on or near Shaftesbury Avenue which might be interested. Ghura was older than I anticipated, but then my mind was locked on that image of the crazed hippie at the Scunthorpe pop festival in **Truly Amazing Love Stories** No 1, going ballistic when ice old Coke is spilled on him.

It was fortuitous that I managed to make contact when I did, because Ghura was to leave Britain for good and return to Italy at the end of the year. He was disillusioned with the opportunities for artists in Britain, having slogged at it for most of his life for virtually no return and no recognition. Comics, it transpired, were only a part of his artistic talents. He told me he hadn't drawn a comic strip for at least 10 years, and it had been twice that since he last had a strip published. Latterly, he had been doing portraitures and selling paintings to passing tourists.

Panels from 'I Killed For Jesus!' — Ghura's first comic strip in 10 years — to be published by Headpress in *Killer Komix 2*.

Ghura spoke in an accent that was Italian and cockney in equal measures. He gave to me several comics of his that I told him I was missing, some that I already had, and photocopies of the completed artwork for his never-published third issue of **Truly Amazing Love Stories**. He seemed nervous and thrilled that he was being interviewed. Certain parts of the conversation, however, triggered memories he obviously would rather have forgotten, whereupon a black cloud crept over him and his mood changed. It got so I felt bad about going down some of these avenues, but I felt I had to do it. And in these moments, fleetingly, I could see it — Scunthorpe pop festival behind those eyes; a glass of ice cold Coke in my hands.

HEADPRESS *You had a strip called 'Home on Leave' published in* Libertine, *which landed that issue in court charged with obscenity. Can you tell us a bit about that?*

ANTONIO GHURA **What happened there was I met a couple of the guys who worked for *Libertine*, Colin [Johnson] and Arabella [Melville]. They wanted an artist to draw a strip or do illustrations. I think that was the first strip I did for *Libertine*, and they got busted! Mary Whitehouse complained and they got taken to court, and lost about £10,000. Of course, the police confiscated all the magazines in the meantime. That finished them off — so, I'm to blame!**

How close were you to that? Did you have to go to court?
No. Colin and Arabella asked me to attend, but I said leave me out of it. I had my room full of *Truly Amazing Love Stories* No 1 at

the time, using them as furniture. I didn't want the Boys in Blue to find out.

Libertine *was acquitted in the end though, wasn't it?*
Yeah, but they had to pay costs. And all the books they had were kept back so they couldn't sell them.

There's a story I've heard, that the centre pages of that issue of Libertine *featured a nude pin-up of Arabella, which the prosecution intended to use in the case. But when it was called as evidence, it turned out somebody had swiped the pin-up from the court's copy! The police themselves were suspected!*
I haven't heard that one. I can't remember the centre-spread, but I haven't seen a copy of that in years. Arabella used to spread it about a bit, though! [laughs]

That trouble obviously didn't compromise your work any.
No. I carried on the same. But *Libertine* did stop taking some of my strips which they considered too *risqué*, for a while. When they were busted, it took a year-or-so before the case came to court. So in that time they were still publishing the magazine and I kept sending them strips.

Panels/detail from 'True Love', Truly Amazing Love Stories Nº 1.

Can you tell me a little about your background? Where you was born?
I was born on the 10th July, 1949 in Bari, Italy. My father brought the family over to England in 1960, after his business in Bari folded. We moved around quite a lot, and in the early Sixties we lived in Wimbledon, Stepney and Walthamstow.

Stepney at that time was a Jewish area, full of Rabbis sitting outside their shops, plucking chickens. When the wind blew, the place looked like it was snowing — white chicken feathers all over the place, pavements covered in them.

How did you get started in comics?
I left school at 16 in 1966. I was painting in oils, and selling my paintings in Hyde Park, and doing little drawings and stuff like that. Then, in about 1969 I returned to London after a two-month holiday in Italy, and I came across all these American Undergrounds in Compendium Bookshop. So I started to draw a few myself.

I couldn't stay in Italy any longer due to the fact that I had become a British citizen in order

to avoid my Military Service — I didn't want to spend 18 months learning how to get shot!

What comics had you seen prior to the Undergrounds?

I remember reading comics as a child in Italy, stuff like *Topolino* and *Il Monello*. In the UK, I read Superman and Batman, but much preferred the ghost and horror comics. At around the age of 12 or 13, I began to read *Mad* and *The Executive Comic Book*, which featured 'Goodman Beaver' by [Bill] Elder and [Harvey] Kurtzman. That really opened my eyes and took me away from all that superhero stuff.

In 1971/72, I came across a British edition of *Fritz the Cat*. It turned out to be a pirated copy of the American edition, but I didn't know that at the time. There was an ad asking for artists and cartoonists to send artwork in, which I did, and I received a reply from a guy called John Muir, who said how much he liked my art. A while later I received a phonecall inviting me to a get-together over at Phillimore Place in Kensington. That's where I met Jonathan Holland-Gems and other cartoonists.

Jonathan Holland-Gems?

Yes. He's the son of Pamela Gems, the famous playwright. He did the magazine *Student* with Richard Branson in around 1966/67. I saw him on TV one time in 1978, on *The David Essex Show*; he had formed a band called Johnny and the Gemstones. I thought to myself, where have I seen that face before? Then it twigged!

Well, they called me over and had a little dinner party, and said "OK, can you draw some stuff for this comic we're doing called *Its All Lies* [sic]."

And the first issue that Jonathan Gems published was printed by John Muir — yellow cover, you couldn't miss it!

Gems said to the assembled cartoonists that he would pay us after issue No 6. I understood this to mean that after No 6 he would pay us for all our work to date, but what he meant was that he would pay us from No 7 upwards. Issues 1 to 6 we would work for free.

Ghura today. Self-portrait.

25

But, of course, there was no issue No 7!

Still, after six months-or-so working on *Its All Lies* I said to Gems "Well, how about paying me?!" and Jonathan Gems — dead rich bloke, his dad's dead rich — wanted to pay me with *food*! No money! He opens his big fridge freezer and said "Take all the food you want!"

So you never got paid?
No. I wasn't that hungry, either.

What happened to his and Branson's Student *magazine?*
That had folded by then.[1] It disappeared before I met Jonathan Gems. Richard Branson already had a shop in Nottinghill Gate selling records, while Gems went into comics. He also helped me to get an illustration in *Creem* magazine.

But I actually didn't get to meet John Muir until a little later. I was on my way to meet a guy called Michael Feldman, in Nottinghill Gate (who was a friend of Gems, but had a slight falling out with him). On the way there, this stranger shouted "Hey!" from across the street. He seemed to know me. I had my art folder with me. He stopped me, introduced himself. I showed him my art work. He took my art work, and that was it. I never got to meet Michael Feldman that day, but I met John Muir in the street. He had a head full of hair, pink bell bottoms and wore nine inch platform shoes.

He took your art work?
Yeah, but he didn't do anything with it. He kept it for a few months, then returned it.[2] Then some months later — maybe a year — he telephoned me and said he wanted a cover for a comicbook he was producing, which he wanted to call *Beaver* but later changed to *Hot Gravy*. So I did a cover in b&w, and mailed it to him. Some months after that, I met Muir at Charing Cross station, and he gave me four or five copies of *Hot Gravy* with this really horrible colour he had added to the cover I'd drawn. Only later did I find that it was a rip off title. I was a little naïve then. Because he had stuff in there by Robert Crumb, I thought they were regular guys and that I was in the big league now! Muir was the one who put me in touch with the *Libertine* guys.

Was there an unwritten rule in the Sixties and Seventies that said you could reproduce Underground work, to a degree...?
I think Robert Crumb said you can use work from *Snatch Comics* and print it where you like. But not that other stuff... This was back in 1972/73, thereabouts, and I was still finding my way around.

Panels from 'The Second Coming!', *Bogey* Nº 2.

Where you living in London at the time?
Yes.

Isn't Michael Feldman credited as a writer on some of your earlier work?
He only ever contributed to one story. That was in *Bogey* No 1. He wrote this story where a bloke is screwing this rubber doll. That's his. He never contributed anything else… [thinks for a moment] apart from in *Bogey* No 2, where he gave me a story in 1973/74 which I later found was ripped off from a Cheech & Chong record, about the Pope wanting a woman that's deaf, dumb and blind [for sex] so that she can't say anything afterwards. I told Feldman it was copyright, but he told me it was okay. So I did it. He read the story to me over the phone — and I forgot about it until I did *Bogey* No 2. I did ask Feldman if he wanted to work with me on comics together, and we tried to get a weekly strip going in *Time Out*, but nothing came of it. Feldman said that comics don't sell, don't get involved with them. In fact, Felix Dennis told me that as well. "Forget it," he said, "there's no money in it."

Did you have any dealings with Oz *or* Cozmic Comics *at all?*
Felix Dennis phoned me up once and said he wanted my drawings to appear in 'Spike', the news page in *Oz*. Then two or three weeks later he phoned back and said forget it, *Oz* has

folded. Something about John Lennon not giving them a cheque that was supposed to be going to pay for *Oz* to be published.[3] *Oz* folded and Felix Dennis got involved in all that kung fu stuff — *Kung Fu Monthly* — and made his millions.

So, you contributed to Creem —
Only one page, the inside front cover of one issue.

— and Home Grown*?*
I did some back covers, spot illustrations, some advertisements. One ad I remember doing is Sumartra; another is Alchemy. Both head shops.

What else did you contribute to?
During that time? *ZigZag* — I did a cover for them and a cartoon strip for The Runaways, the all-girl band. I did a bunch of eight-page war comic strips for Fleetway, which was around about the same time I did *Hot Gravy*. I had no interest in the war stories at all, and just did it for the money — which was £8 a page. Fleetway wanted someone to draw Italian and British soldiers fighting, with all the usual jingo-ism they use in those comics, but I made the Italian soldiers handsome and the British soldiers all pimply and ugly! I've no idea what happened to those strips, whether they got published or not — or even what they were called. And I never got the money for them.

I did strips, with Feldman, for *Info*, the French Chamber of Commerce publication. But we made fun of the Director, portraying him as a waiter, and that was the end of it! He kicked us out!

I think I also did something for *Science Fiction Monthly*... but I can't remember! My memory's not what it was! I was taking... you know... [laughs]

How much did the drugs you were taking influence what you were drawing?
Well, you tend to draw more... *actively*. You get involved in it more. A line seems important, you know. And you draw black a lot, I find.

In Raw Purple, *some of the panels are pretty mad.*
And the spelling goes off as well!

AS THE TRIP PROGRESSES, SOUNDS, SMELLS OF EDIOUS, FRIGHTENING SCENES FILL GEORGE'S MIND.

THE MORE HE TRIED TO SUBDUE THESE THOUGHTS...

THE MORE THEY'D ASSERT THEM- -SELVES... HE FELT POWERLESS TO CONTROL THEM... THE HORROR OF THESE VISIONS BECAME UNBEARABLE...

A 'pretty mad' panel from 'Nightmare Journey', *Raw Purple*.

What was the influence behind Truly Amazing Love Stories*?*
American romance comics. They're all kissing and lovey-dovey, not the real thing. I thought I'd make it more adult; more of what it's *all about*. Take it away from the imagination and put it on paper. See how the girls like it. That was the idea: see how the girls like it!

And did they like it?
I don't know. None of them said anything! [laughs]

Truly Amazing Love Stories *No 2 is perhaps the most over-the-top comic I think I've ever seen. You've got a story with a transsexual twist, a bestiality strip and, of course, the Yorkshire Ripper strip.*
I was trying to go for everything: lesbianism, homosexuality, incest… you name it, I wanted to go for it.

Were you never worried about getting in trouble with the law with these comics?
I didn't think of it. I sold it to guys who could sell it. Some would sell it openly; most shops would sell it under the counter. Dark They Were And Golden Eyed sold *Bogey* No 1 and *Amazing Love Stories* quite openly. No problem… until they got busted once. But a week later they were selling it again. That was in St Anne's Court, the shop they opened after Berwick Street. But they didn't blame me, and kept my name out of it. That was nice of them. The police shut down the shop for a day, and they lost a day's takings, but they just told the police that some guy — who they didn't know — had dropped all these comics off. They got done twice that I know of — once in 1978 and in 1981.

The opening page of Ghura's rejected, unpublished *Truly Amazing Love Stories* Nº 3.

Tell us a little about 'I Loved A Sex Fiend!' — the Yorkshire Ripper strip.
The rape one? I wanted to be outrageous. Everybody does action comics, fighting and battling and killing each other, and pontificating about this and that, while at the same time punching each other in the face — and I thought, well, give them *that*. Most people didn't like it, and said, "Oh, you've gone too far there. What you're doing is sexist fun, and then you put this in." Looking back at it, I thought maybe I should have left it out. I didn't want to do things that'd leave a bad feeling.

You must have done that strip around about the time Peter Sutcliffe was arrested.
The reason I did that strip was because I wasn't right in the head, because of problems I had with people like Tony Bennett [of Knockabout comics distribution]. In a way that was my

29

Top Kim Fowley spots Sandy West in a disco parking lot. 'The Story of The Runaways,' a two-part series that featured in *ZigZag*. Drawn by Ghura, written by Kris Needs. **Above** Ad for a head shop.

anger coming through, you see. That affected me. I wanted to take the strip out at the very last minute, and in fact, Tony Bennett saw it and said "I don't like it. Take it out." So I left it in. Thinking back on it, I'd have liked to have left it out. 'Rape's no fun,' you know.

Yes, it's odd because you have this graphic, prurient rape strip and at the end you say 'rape's no fun at all'.
Yeah, yeah, because I felt guilty about it. It was just anger inside me that came out on the paper.

Did you ever get any kind of critical reaction at all?
No. I went to a comics convention with Hunt Emerson near Shaftesbury Avenue, one time back in 76 or 77. And somebody asked me for my autograph. But other than that, no reaction from anybody ever. I remember speaking to Hunt Emerson and saying, you're an Underground artist, why don't you do something a little outrageous? Drugs, sex, violence? When somebody gets shot, all his brains spill out. Why don't you do it, show how shocking it is, how *real and nasty* it is? "Oh I don't wanna do anything like that," he says, "I don't wanna shock my mum."

You advertised a title called Snow Queen *on the back cover of* Truly Amazing Love Stories *No 2. Did that ever make it into print?*
I was going to do it, but I dropped it because I had no reaction from *Amazing Love Stories* No 2. Knockabout said they would take 500, then they changed their minds. I couldn't sell it to Last Gasp or Kitchen Sink in America. Well, the thing with Last Gasp, I found out years later... I tried to sell *Bogey* to Last Gasp back in

1975 — no reaction whatsoever. When it got to 83/84, I found out that they and Knockabout have an understanding whereby Last Gasp won't buy British comics directly from a comic publisher, but only through Knockabout.[4] If Knockabout said "No" you were stuffed. If I'd have known that, I'd have stopped doing comics in 1976.[5]

So did you have any American distribution at all for your comics?
A little by way of Knockabout, and Planet Wheels in Scotland.

Clockwise, from top left (i) Ghura in his studio; (ii) The Vicar's Raw Balls Co. was the imprint on *Bogey* N° 1, Ghura's first comic. For *Truly Amazing Love Stories* and *Raw Purple* the imprint became Beyond The Edge Publishing Co; (iii) Jonnie forgetting his Harry Belafonte records for *Suzie and Jonnie*'s trip to Morocco; (iv) an original Ghura post-comics watercolour.

You're completely ignored in America — well, you're ignored here, too…

Could be because people think I ripped them off with *Hot Gravy*. **When Mal Burns went around saying I'd published** *Hot Gravy*…

What was that about?

In 1977 I met Mal Burns in a pub, and he asked me who had done *Hot Gravy*. **I replied, "I did!"… meaning the cover. But Burns, who was compiling his** *Comix Index*,[6] **then spread the totally false allegation that I was responsible for it all. Not so. I have not and will not rip off another Underground artist's work. Burns also distributed copies of** *Amazing Love Stories* **No 1 and** *Raw Purple* **in 1978. When it came time to pay up, he said to me, "I don't have the money, so sue me." But with gentle persuasion he paid up… eventually… after a few bounced cheques.**

How long would it take for you to do a full comic.

Ages. This one [*Truly Amazing Love Stories*** No 3] took about six months. 48 pages.**

JUST A MINUTE, SUZIE, I LEFT MY COLLECTION!

Is that typical?
Yes. Six months, thereabouts.

It's a lot of work for no return.
Yes. And I always tried to make my work look interesting and 'sophisticated', using Letratone. So it cost me a bit to do, too.

Why did you change the physical size of your comics from A4 down to A5?
For *Hot Nads*, I tried to copy Robert Crumb's *Snatch Comics*, but for *Bogey* No 2, I just ran out of cash.

I've always wondered: did you ever draw yourself as a character in your comics?
The inside front cover of *Bogey* No 2 is supposed to be me in my studio. [*See previous page.*]

How about Suzie and Jonnie*? You yourself went to Morocco in 1976.*
Some parts of that are based on my trip over there. I had a Volkswagen 1300 at the time, and on my way home the Spanish customs took it to pieces completely because they found a big handful of grass in the glove compartment. The car wasn't the same after that. But they did let me go. They took my stuff, though, and smoked it all themselves. Next day, their eyes were all red and bloodshot.

I thought that *Suzie and Jonnie* would sell. I packed a lot into it, and made it value for money, not too much sex in it. And it didn't [sell].

When did you actually stop doing comics?
I stopped doing comics with *Amazing Love Stories* No 2. Then, in 1987, I thought I'll give it another try and did *Amazing Love Stories* No 3. I had the idea of selling it to *Torrid*, a sex magazine published by Goldstar. I thought maybe they'd be interested in it. They weren't.

You mentioned earlier you are going to return to Italy.
Yes. I'm going back in September or October of this year [1998] and not coming back. I've travelled to Italy a few times, doing portraits and selling them to tourists.

I've tried painting and drawing here in England, and people just don't want to know. I've tried getting work at design companies and they go, "We'll let you know". After seeing my portfolio, they think that whatever work they give me to do, I'll start drawing sex stuff!

"Who's that old bloke?" was one comment I recently overheard at an interview, coming from the same bloke who then proceeded to interview me!

You're still working in art then?
Yes, at the moment mainly doing portraiture from photographs. I put ads in papers and people send me photographs of their 'cute' kids, you know! They come and tell you the story of how their little boy got run over and would like you to paint his picture from this photograph. And I charge them £300 for it and feel bad. But that's what I've been doing — painting. I left school at 16 and started painting. That's what I like to do. I got into comics because I used to do oil paintings and they'd smell a lot. "What can I do that doesn't smell?" I thought. Comics! That's easy — just paper and ink, that's all you need. Most of my painting is watercolours nowadays.

And, of course, in Italy, I shall be surrounded by *art*... sculpture, paintings, and good food, good football, and lovely ladies. A nice way to spend the autumn of my life.

W hen the interview was over, not for a moment did I flinch or hesitate to ask Antonio to sign the copies of the comics he had given to me.

I had time to kill before my train back to Manchester. After mooching aimlessly for an hour, I decided to go for a coffee and a sandwich at a cheap Italian place around the corner. I bumped into Antonio, lugging his big, heavy holdall, unable to find the new comic shop that was situated in or around Shaftesbury Avenue. I felt it was ridiculous that he should be having to drag his own 20-year-old comics around shops at his age and with his talent, given that in an alternative time zone he would be nothing short of a cult phenomenon. It transpired he had given up searching for the shop and was now headed for the same café as I, so we were able to chat for a while longer. He asked whether I was worried about the nature and content of *Headpress* getting me into trouble. "You know the answer to that," I replied.

For his return to Italy, Antonio had bought a small van. He was headed for no place in particular, but intended to travel around Rome, sleeping in the back of his van, before finding a place in which to settle. Prior to leaving Britain, however, during the van's MOT, Antonio managed to get a parking ticket and, unable to pay the growing fine, lost the vehicle. It didn't deter him. The next I heard from Antonio was a postcard from Rome dated late-October 1998. There was no return address, but there was the promise that he would write again soon, when things got "more settled".

EPILOGUE An old copy of **Raw Purple** was on sale in a Manchester bookshop recently with a £7.50 price tag.

Writing this, I have a CD of the British beat-psych crossover band, The Creation, playing in the background. The track 'Painter Man' slavishly grinds into life, a violin bow dragging out the opening guitar chords. All of a sudden I'm struck by the kind-of-ironic lyrics:

Tried cartoons and comic books / dirty postcards, women's books / here was where the money lay / classic art has had its day.

NOTES

1 David Kerekes & David Slater, editors, **Critical Vision: Random Essays and Tracts Concerning Sex Religion Death**; Manchester: Critical Vision, 1995.

1 Prior to **Its All Lies** (which was almost called 'Sunshine Comix'), Gems ran Capricorn Graphics, and printed posters. Gems formed Gemsanders Publications Ltd with his brother-in-law Paul Sanders. As well as comics, they printed greetings cards, some of which were illustrated by Ghura.

2 When I spoke with Ghura a couple of weeks later in order to clarify a few points, he asked me if I had Muir's address as he wanted to get some of his artwork back for his portfolio. Or, on failing that, at least get hold of the books Muir had published (as Babylon Books), some of which contained Ghura artwork, i.e., **The Complete Bootlegs Checklist & Discography**.

3 Lennon was a source for funds for several alternative newspapers. In 1974, he denoted £1,000 to keep **It** in publication. For **Oz**, in 1971, he and Yoko Ono produced the benefit single 'God Save Us/Do The Oz'.

4 If this was the case back in the Seventies and Eighties, it isn't the situation today.

5 Ghura later told me that "I did sell 100 copies of **Amazing Love Stories** No 2 and **Hot Nads** to Last Gasp. When I asked them how **Suzie and Jonnie** was selling, they refused to tell me — so fuck 'em. I refused to sell to them after that. Did myself more harm than good, but I'd had enough by then!"

Ghura had a lot more grievances to air about distributors than are transcribed here, but it gets pretty mixed-up. However, he did say there were moves between Knockabout and **Home Grown** magazine to sell the publishing rights for **Amazing Love Stories** No 1 to Last Gasp in America, while Real Free Press distributed copies of **Amazing Love Stories** No 1 and **Suzie and Jonnie** in Holland.

6 Mal Burns, **Comix Index: The Directory of Alternative British Graphic Magazines: 1966–1977**, published in 1978.

Midian Books have a limited selection of original Ghura comics for sale. Enquire: Midian Books, 69 Park Lane, Bonehill, Tamworth, Staffs., B78 3HZ
Tel/Fax: 01-827-281391
Email: j.davies@midian-books.demon.co.uk

Swallow

the bad taste

of sweet vengeance

of HUCK BOTKO

JACK SARGEANT

Not since Divine gobbled down a mouthful of dog shit for John Waters at the climax for **Pink Flamingoes**, has a filmmaker elicited such celebrated repulsion as Huck Botko in his culinary vengeance movies: **Fruitcake** (1997), **Baked Alaska** (1997), and **Cheesecake** (1998). Three films — each of which documents an assault on the bastions of both decency and family — that have been turning stomachs at numerous underground film festivals.

The first of these pieces, **Fruitcake**, depicts Botko making a fruitcake for his father. Once the cake-mix is prepared, and before the final stages, Botko takes it down to the streets of New York. Here he encourages assorted drunks, the homeless and semi-destitute street people to hawk large globs of phlegm into the mix. Huck even gets an over-zealous and semi-intoxicated Santa Claus to participate in the action: Father Christmas leers past Huck into the camera and warns, "Kurt, you're a no good son of a gun, and this is for you on Christmas Day. Enjoy. We heard an awful lot about you at the North Pole and shame, shame, shame, everybody knows your name, you son of a gun you [*phtoow! — he gobs into the mix*]." Cut to Huck travelling to his father's house, and the regular seasonal rituals, including Huck's sister who is unwilling to believe Huck has only made his father a cake for Christmas. Finally, the video depicts the inevitable eating of the cake, with Huck's father chewing in. When he offers the director a slice, Huck says "no thanks".

35

Baked Alaska follows Huck to his mother's mobile home in Yellowstone Park. Here Huck reminisces about his last happy moments with his mother making baked alaska, soon after which she walked out of the family home. In memory of this mother/son bonding moment, and their subsequent separation, Botko makes his mother a Baked Alaska. However, this Baked Alaska contains some choice ingredients: grubs, maggots, insects, dirt, and particles scraped off of the flattened carcasses of roadkill found throughout the park. Botko's mother enjoys the meal; once again he refuses to taste it.

The most recent — and most oppressive — of this series is **Cheesecake**. In this instalment, Huck begins by illustrating the victim — his sister — immediately at the film's opening, and freezing the image on her face whilst he describes his dislike of her: "This is my sister. Ever since I can remember it has been her role in the family to lead the perfect life, with a constant smile, the perkiness, the good job, the nice car, the trained dog. She has invented a life for herself without suffering, fear, or anxiety. The problem is that I am not from that world — so this year, for Christmas, I decided to give her a taste of things she might not otherwise be accustomed to." The piece then cuts to the preparation of the food, and then the trademark 'special addition', in this case blood infected by hepatitis B which is taken from the arms of two sufferers via syringes, and then injected across the top of the cheesecake, into the carefully prepared dents which form the words 'Happy Christmas'. Later in the video, Huck's sister, her family, and the well-groomed dog, munch the cheesecake. In a moment of chilling humour, sis exclaims her fondness for the red food colouring.

When questioned about his relationship to his family, Huck states: *"Well my familial bonds are not that strong, so it allows me to think about my family in a way that a lot of other people would never even imagine. I guess I saw that as a compelling point of view and worthy of a movie."*

The modes of vengeance in these films are specific, and in part are inspired by Botko's peers. *"My friend Alex Crawford in particular is very good at vengeance and he has good ideas along these lines."*

All three films mark a special vengeance against the family, with each victim targeted for a specified reason. However, these pieces go beyond the conventional notion of revenge, firstly

Huck Botko looks up.

Botko Senior contemplates his fork.

because the targets are members of the director's immediate family, one of the few institutions which is still largely held sacrosanct. Secondly, the modes in which they are attacked are specifically geared to crossing the lines between clean/dirty and acceptable/alien, about which the family most clearly educate the child. In psychoanalytical terms, the mother and father fulfil a role for the infant in which they are responsible for defining the limits to the child, with the mother specifically educating the child about the difference between clean/foul, and the areas of the body which are taboo.

It is through engagement with the mother that the child learns to be repulsed by his/her own shit, vomit, and blood, as well as learning that decay and death are symbolic of the unclean.

In Huck Botko's culinary films, all of these psycho-social taboos are transgressed; his targets are those with whom society expects him to be closest, and the way in which they are attacked joyfully extols in the unclean and the abject: spit, bile, decay, and blood are all present in Botko's pantheon of vengeance. Further, in **Cheesecake**, Botko breaks one of the greatest of contemporary taboos via the introduction of soiled/diseased blood into food. Such a gesture transgresses not just maternal law, it also shatters conventional health notions regarding blood and needles which have been repeated as a mantra since the emergence of HIV in the mid-Eighties.

All of these pieces were produced on video, in a deceptively simple style which emphasises the subversive nature of Botko's gesture. Botko speaks directly to the camera, and thus addresses the audience about the culinary task and motivation for vengeance. However, the videos are short, and are edited. The audience is thus ambiguously positioned: certainly the events that transpire in the pieces are real — i.e., it is real roadkill, real spit, real blood — but they are simultaneously 37 edited, and thus the films could be fabrication. Botko, rightly, refuses to comment.

In addition to these pieces, Botko's cinematic outpouring also includes two other documentaries: *Until There Are None* (1995), and *Julie* (1998), co-directed with Andrew Gurland. *Until There Are None* follows Bob Lewis, "one of our most unique Americans," a huntsman who has slipped the noose of society and now lives in the forests of the American Midwest, where he has vowed to kill every bald eagle as an act of vengeance against an eagle attack on his son. The film follows Lewis as he stalks the birds, and also as he relaxes, enjoying the pastimes of singing bizarre folk songs, together with carefully cutting women from porn magazines and meticulously dressing them. Shot as a documentary film by Botko whilst he was a film-student at NYU, the film is actually a carefully scripted construction. The film emerged as a *"reaction to the other films I saw being made at the time. I found that many people at NYU were restricting themselves to stories they thought were 'acceptable' or ones that wouldn't offend, or that their parents would like. As a result, the shorts I saw were generally unoriginal and un-entertaining and unchallenging. Which in my mind is exactly the opposite of what you want to do if you're making an art film. I thought a guy killing bald eagles done as a documentary would solve a lot of those problems for me."*

Until There Are None reveals Botko's power as a director — able to skilfully construct a film which mimics the textual signifiers and verisimilitude of the documentary mode. Talking of the audience reaction to the film, Botko notes *"some people thought it was real. I think most people are so savvy to film and video that they pick up the little false notes that happen when doing a fake documentary. Usually by the end of the movie, even before the credits, most people are pretty sure it's fake."* Botko also recalls how his interest in the documentary format arose: *"the style came out of the fact that it was the best way to present material. Until There Are None could have been written as a narrative I suppose, but it wouldn't have carried the material as well. As a narrative, it would have ended up going for laughs more, which I didn't want to do."*

Huck Botko's most recent piece — made as a collaboration with Andrew Gurland — is simply titled *Julie*. It opens with the premise that "Julie is a cunt. She is the reason men hate women." It consolidates the vengeance metanarrative from the food pieces, and also showcases some of Botko's cinematic techniques. The film opens with Jim, who — having spent an evening talking to a colleague, Julie, about her childhood — has found out that her stories were lies specifically designed to humiliate him. Vengeance is called for. Andrew has got a dose of VD, Portman's Disease, which he describes as being characterised by: "itching… [it's] very contagious. This is about me giving Julie the Portman's, for being a cunt I can make her cunt so uncomfortable with the itching and irritation." The film then explores the way in which vengeance can be exorcised, with the film crew involving Julie in the construction of a fake documentary about scamming free goods, in order that Julie can be seduced by Andrew and allow the film crew to be present without raising any suspicion. The fake documentary necessitates lying, and — as the audience know — Julie likes lying. The fake documentary within the construct of the actual documentary serves to emphasise Botko's relationship to the filmmaking process, and the way in which his filmmaking practice works. Cutting between the shooting of the fake documentary and the actual documentary itself, the film deftly weaves its narrative as Andrew attempts to fuck Julie and give her the Portman's.

For Botko, the collaboration with Gurland was beneficial because *"Andrew and I have known each other since NYU and we often talked about revenge ideas. So we agreed to do Julie together. It's two people with a strong interest in getting revenge (instead of one), so the material is twice as good."*

Botko is currently working on two projects: an advert for an escort agency, and preparing a cream pie for his brother. Get ready for more documentaries of visual trouble.

AN INTERVIEW WITH POPPY Z BRITE

ADRIAN HORROCKS

Brite's vision is disturbingly dark, deliciously erotic, sweetly savage and uniquely her own...

—*Dan Simmons*

Poppy Z Brite's gay serial killer novel *Exquisite Corpse* uses purple prose and florid images to recount the brutal story of two characters, based on the murderers Jeffrey Dahmer and Dennis Nilsen. Her central conceit is what would happen if those two should have ever chanced to meet.

It's the tale of English murderer Andrew Compton, who flees to New Orleans after escaping from prison. There he meets Jay, who delights in slaughtering teenage boys, and dining on their flesh. Brite allows the two psychopaths to fall in love, and the story of their brutal passion mixes graphic gore with hardcore sex to devastating effect.

From her 1992 debut novel *Lost Souls*, it was obvious that Poppy Z Brite possessed a formidable talent. A tale of vampirism that highlighted the Gothic music scene in America, *Lost Souls* swiftly became a cult classic. Her follow up, *Drawing Blood*, consolidated her reputation as a writer to watch, and concerned a cartoonist and a com-

puter hacker, marooned in a house wracked by hallucinatory visions. Brite has also published *Swamp Foetus*, a collection of short stories, and *Courtney Love: The Real Story*, an unofficial biography written with the Hole singer's tacit approval. Here, Brite talks about *Exquisite Corpse*; her interest in serial killers; her love of violent movies, and much else besides...

HEADPRESS BEFORE THE PUBLICATION OF *EXQUISITE CORPSE*, I READ THAT YOUR PUBLISHERS WERE PUTTING PRESSURE ON YOU TO CENSOR THE BOOK. DID YOU BOW TO THAT PRESSURE?

POPPY Z BRITE Well, I did have quite a bit of trouble selling the book, because of the subject matter. Both of my normal publishers — Dell in the States, and Penguin — rejected it, because of the content. They didn't even ask me to change it really. If I had changed what had offended editors, there would be no book left.

So, it bounced from publisher to publisher, and they were all saying the same thing. They were saying that "this is some of your best writing ever, but it's just too horrible" or something like that, "it's too nihilistic, and we just can't justify publishing it."

And then finally, it was picked up by Simon and Schuster in the States, and by Orion in the UK, and it turned out great. I didn't really have to change anything in the end.

WHAT MADE YOU WANT TO WRITE THE BOOK? I tend to choose my subject matter by following whatever I'm obsessed with at any given time, and after I finished my second novel *Drawing Blood*, I just for some reason — I've no idea why — I became obsessed with Jeffrey Dahmer, and I started reading everything that I could find about him. And then through him, I found out about Dennis Nilsen, and read everything that I could find about him. And then I became intrigued by the idea of a story that involved two serial killers in a love relationship.

THE VIOLENCE IN THE BOOK IS EXTREMELY GRAPHIC. HOW DO YOU FEEL WHEN YOU'RE WRITING THINGS LIKE THAT? I enjoy it. I've always enjoyed trying to find the beauty and the poetry in violence. I like to watch graphic films, I just really like the way that stuff looks. It can be incredibly disturbing, to see the horrible things that can happen to the human body, but it also can have this weird beauty to it, and I've always been interested in trying to translate that into prose. And I realise that it's not gonna work for everyone, it's still just gonna be disgusting to a lot of people, but I can't worry about that when I'm writing, I have to do what I have to do.

DO YOU THINK THAT FICTIONAL VIOLENCE CAN INFLUENCE POTENTIAL PSYCHOPATHS? I've never really bought that theory. I mean, maybe reading a specific fictional incident, or seeing a specific thing in a movie, can give a psychopath the idea to do that particular thing. But I don't believe that if they hadn't read that book, or seen that movie, that they would be a stand up, model citizen, you know? It would have found some other way to come out.

That's like Ted Bundy blaming pornography for his acts. I really don't buy it. Even if it was true, I don't think anything could really be done about it, because I don't think it's worth the price of censorship. I'm afraid that there is a trend to assign moral responsibility to fiction. That's what I was hearing from the editors about *Exquisite Corpse*, that we cannot justify publishing this. Well, excuse me, since when have we had to justify fiction? If you think it's a good work, then what other justification do you need?

HAVE YOU DONE A LOT OF RESEARCH INTO AUTOPSIES, AND INTO THE EXPLOITS OF REAL SERIAL KILLERS, TO PREPARE FOR WRITING YOUR BOOKS? I don't really have to do that much research, because I've always been fascinated with that kind of stuff. My first ambition, when I was five-years-old, was to be a coroner. I've always been fascinated with gore, and with the insides of bodies, and very curious about it. So, I had read about autopsy procedure, and I apparently knew my anatomy, and I've also always enjoyed reading True Crime books.

DID YOU MAKE ANDREW

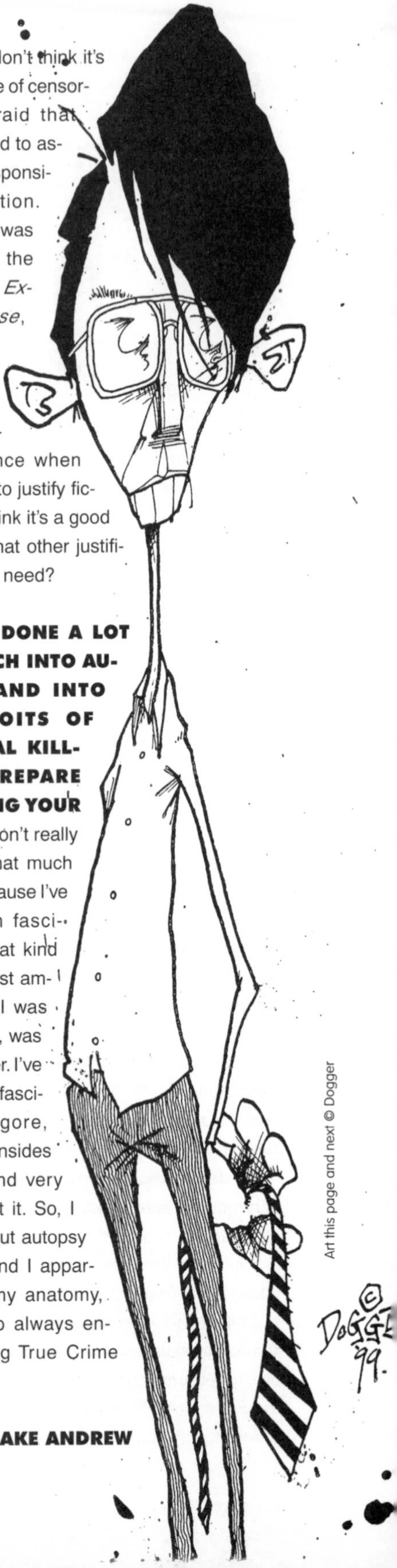

40

DOGGE 99.

AN ENGLISHMAN SIMPLY BECAUSE NILSEN WAS ENGLISH? I guess so, because I fell so in love with those two serial killers. Because their cases were so beautifully similar (except that Nilsen was not into cannibalism), I was tempted not to change a thing. I wanted to make the two of them exactly as they had been in real life. Of course, I didn't feel that I could do that, both for legal reasons, and because, when you try to translate real life directly into fiction, it doesn't usually work very well.

I was fortunate enough to be able to come to London (for the first time ever) just around the time I was working on those first few chapters. Penguin brought me over to do promotion for *Lost Souls*, so I was actually able to write about London from a perspective that I wouldn't have had otherwise. It's so difficult to write about a place you haven't been to.

I've been there twice now, I even went to Dennis Nilsen's house the first time.

DID YOU FEEL ANY VIBES? No, no. I could see through the top window, I could see the stove that he supposedly boiled the heads on. But no, I didn't feel any vibes. But I'm not very sensitive to that sort of thing, I'm afraid. My mother is psychic, and I think it skipped a generation. I'm not planning to have kids, so I guess it'll die with me.

ON THE SUBJECT OF KIDS: A HORROR OF CHILDREN AND BABIES APPEARS THROUGHOUT YOUR WORK. I have a horror of them! I've never had any sort of maternal urge, or biological clock. And I think it's just as well, because the thing is, every time I try to imagine having a kid, I get this mental image of swinging it against the wall, and smashing its little head in! So I just don't think I'd make a very good parent! I've only in recent years really learned to be comfortable around children at all.

I did a biography of Courtney Love. And her child — Frances — is a very difficult child to get to know: she hated me the first time she laid eyes on me. I've met her I think four times now, and only recently has she begun to accept me at all. Through her, I feel a little more comfortable with

children now. But it's still... I can't stand the idea of being pregnant.

IS YOUR DISLIKE OF, OR FEAR OF CHILDBIRTH... WELL PERHAPS FEAR IS TOO STRONG A WORD... It is fear. Holy fear! Fear and disgust! Not just with childbirth, but pregnancy. The whole experience seems very disgusting to me.

IS YOUR FEAR OF CHILDBIRTH A REASON WHY YOU DON'T HAVE MANY FEMALE CHARACTERS IN YOUR BOOKS? Well, that's something that I've not been happy with. I've always been fascinated with my male characters, and as a result, I think that I get inside their heads better, and they're much better drawn. But I do have an interest in writing strong female characters, I just haven't had much luck with it yet. And actually, that's one reason I decided to take on the Courtney Love project, because I knew that it would force me to develop a strong female character, even if she wasn't fictional. And so far it certainly has, because she's a great character to write about.

ARE YOU A BIG FAN OF HER MUSIC? Yeah, I am now, I really wasn't before. This is officially an unauthorised biography, but we've been friends since she tracked me down through my publisher after reading *Lost Souls*, because she really liked it.

41

IS YOUR ATTRACTION TO VIOLENT IM-AGERY A REASON WHY YOUR WORK LACKS STRONG FEMALE CHARACTERS? How do you mean?

WELL, GIRLS AREN'T SUPPOSED TO BE ATTRACTED TO HORRID THINGS, THEY'RE CONDITIONED TO PREFER CUTE THINGS. ONLY BOYS ARE ALLOWED TO LIKE NASTY THINGS. Well, I was never really brought up with that kind of conditioning, but I guess you can't really escape it in society. I was sent to pretty progressive schools, so it wasn't like girls were encouraged to just play with dolls, and boys were supposed to go out and play basketball. I was forced to play basketball, and I always hated it!

I've always felt a little more like a boy, and I spent two years telling anyone who would listen that I was a gay man who had been born in a female body. And I still sort of feel that way, but I think people are so sick of hearing me talk about it, that I've tried to shut up!

Also, I've just become a lot more confused about gender, I don't think it's as simple as that. You know, as soon as I started saying that, then I developed this intense relationship with a pre-operative male-to-female transsexual, so basically I had a girlfriend with a penis, so I dunno. Gender lines are not as easily drawn as I once thought they were.

ALL YOUR BOOKS MENTION GOTHS IN APPROVING TERMS. YOU ALSO MENTION 'RAVE' MUSIC , BUT YOU SEEM TO BE LESS IMPRESSED WITH THAT. I don't dance, and I never go out, and I don't really like Ecstasy, so there's really no way that I could be impressed with it. I think it's probably a really cool scene for people that enjoy that sort of thing, and if it had been around when I was 19, it would have been great. But now, no, it's definitely not my cup of tea.

YOU STARTED WRITING AT A VERY YOUNG AGE, SUBMITTING WORK FOR PUBLICATION FROM 12-YEARS-OLD. WHO WAS THE MAIN INFLUENCE ON YOU TO START WRITING? I guess the main influence on me to start writing was my parents, especially my mom, because she read to me. From the time that I was tiny, she read to me constantly. As a result, I learned to read from a very early age, and then I started trying to write. I was writing little stories, making up little booklets, when I was five-years-old. And I was a big fan of the writer EB White, of his children's book *Charlotte's Web*, and Stuart Little and *A Trumpet of the Swan*. And I wrote him so many fan letters that he finally wrote me a personal letter back, which unfortunately I don't have any more.

DID YOUR EARLY STORIES HAVE HORRIFIC CONTENT? Yeah, I was a morbid little kid. One of my first pieces of fiction was before I could write. It was a story that was told into a tape recorder. And it was *The Bad Mouse*. It was all about this mouse that was really bad, and he would eat people, and eat their eyes out and eat their brains, and do all this horrible stuff. It was really funny. I think I told it when I was about three-and-a-half!

GAY PARENTING FEATURES IN *EXQUISITE CORPSE*. A BRITISH RIGHT-WING POLITICIAN CALLED NORMAN TEBBIT SAID THAT IT SHOULDN'T BE ALLOWED, BECAUSE OF THE AMOUNT OF TAUNTING THE CHILD WOULD RECEIVE. Yeah well, I grew up with a mother and a father, and I was taunted at school as much as any human being could ever be, without being killed, so I think that nips that one in the bud right there. High School is hell for anyone who's different. I don't trust anyone who had a good time in High School, High School's hell for anyone who is different in any way whatsoever.

WAS THERE ANY PARTICULAR REASON WHY YOU WERE VICTIMISED IN HIGH SCHOOL? Oh, because I was weird. I can't even put my finger on what the first reason was. They can smell it if you're not like them. You can try to wear exactly the right clothes, and say the right things, and hate the right people, and they'll still know if you're not one of them. I don't know how they know, I don't know what the marker is. But the turning point for me was when I was about

15, I just decided I didn't give a damn. I wasn't going to try to fit in any more, because they'd made my life hell for the past three years. I started putting out an underground newspaper, and I started dressing like a freak, and doing whatever I wanted. And soon discovered that I was a lot happier, and had a lot more friends that way.

IN *EXQUISITE CORPSE*, WHY DOESN'T ANDREW EAT ANY HUMAN BRAINS? Oh, but eating brains is so bad for you, you get Mad Cow disease from that.

HE'S ENGLISH. IT WOULD SHOW HE'S PATRIOTIC. Mad Cow disease is the exact same disease that you can get from eating brains, human brains. It's just very bad to eat nerve tissue. But I still could have had him do it, I suppose. I'm not opposed to brain-eating in fiction! Maybe that'll be the sequel! 🐯

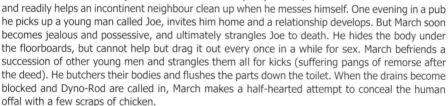

COLD LIGHT OF DAY

dir/wr: FHIONA LOUISE
Great Britain 1989; pr: Richard Driscoll; music: Paul Stuart Davies; cast: Bob Flag, Martin Byrne Quinn, Jackie Cox, Bill Merrow, Paul Jay
Screen Edge, cert 18

In spite of the opening statement that all names have been changed to protect the innocent, the advertising for this thinly veiled ad-aptation of the Dennis Nilsen case is a lot less coy. As with its original release on the obscure Tower Home Video label (the packaging for which likened Nilsen to Hannibal Lector), Screen Edge don't skirt around the film's true life source material, and even choose as the sleeve a shot of the real Nilsen.

Jorden March works in a job centre. He is outwardly respectable, and readily helps an incontinent neighbour clean up when he messes himself. One evening in a pub he picks up a young man called Joe, invites him home and a relationship develops. But March soon becomes jealous and possessive, and ultimately strangles Joe to death. He hides the body under the floorboards, but cannot help but drag it out every once in a while for sex. March befriends a succession of other young men and strangles them all for kicks (suffering pangs of remorse after the deed). He butchers their bodies and flushes the parts down the toilet. When the drains become blocked and Dyno-Rod are called in, March makes a half-hearted attempt to conceal the human offal with a few scraps of chicken.

Told via flashback during March's interrogation at the hands of the police, **Cold Light of Day** is compelling viewing from start to finish. Bob Flag is unnervingly convincing as the homosexual killer. Indeed, so sleazy is his portrayal that one half expects a pool of goo to be gathering at his feet... which might be one reason why he won't stand still for a minute, fidgeting, squirming, wanking at a keyhole. Not that Flag is a particularly good actor (he seems to have genuine trouble negotiating the stairs), but he's a better actor than most in the production. A priceless bad scene comes each time the detective interrogating March loses his rag, knocking things off the desk, bawling lines like "Did they urinate? Did they mess themselves? *Pervert*!... Did you *fuck their bodies*?!" Faced with such thunderous ineptitude, Flag can do nothing but blubber into his hands and reply meekly, "Leave me alone, will you!"

But it's a blessing that **Cold Light of Day** has such moments of unintentional levity. There is no other release for the rank, stifling air that comes with concentrating exclusively on the miserable March, his miserable mis-deeds and his miserable apartment (virtually without furniture and in which a kettle seems to be permanently whistling). The film has shots aplenty of hacked-off limbs, innards being stuffed into black bin bags, and even a head boiling on a stove. (Plus a cameo by Lol Coxhill.) The sequences in which the killer throttles his victims are pretty disgusting. No quick deaths here — each murder is played out in agonising, limb-flailing detail.

No doubt about it, in the echelons of sleazy killers in British cinema, Jorden March ranks right alongside Donald Sumpter's portrayal of the Black Panther (**The Black Panther**, 1977).

"Did you enter the body at any time?... LIAR!" **David Kerekes**

43

ATTACK
of the
tokyo sluts

ANTHONY PETKOVICH

"I so a shame."

Translation: "I'm so ashamed."

That's a line repeated quite a bit in the films from Samurai Video. The line, of course, is stated in Japanese, with English subtitles. And the individual delivering this choice morsel of dialogue is typically a lovely 18-year-old Japanese porn starlet who looks like she should be working in a travel agency, rather than standing naked in a dark, dank, near-empty basement occupied by a mattress and a disembodied male demon's voice telling her (in Japanese) to pee on the cold concrete floor... after this she's called (in Japanese) a "whore," told to throw herself on the same mattress, stick her big, fair-skinned, baby-fat-coated, fan-fucking-tastic ass up in the air, and take a stiff Tokyo torpedo right between her sashimi lips.

It's a beautiful thing.

It's the a-*mazing* universe of Samurai Video.

A mere seven months old, SV is definitely an enfant terrible in the XXX-film market. Simply put, the videos are a distinct breath of fresh air in the tired American porn industry. Yes, they're made in Japan (in Tokyo or the outskirts thereof), by Japanese technicians, and with Japanese stars and starlets. Since there's no English spoken in these videos, they have an even more intensified exotic feel. The videos are also *distributed* in America, meaning actual genital manipulation and penetration (illegal for viewing purposes in Japan) are not digitised out. You see the nasty action up close and crystal clear. And the girls are cute, 'shameful' and shame*less* as ever.

SV puts out five videos per month, so we've got a lot of catching up to do here at *Headpress*. How about five titles to start with? You got it. Also, should you have trouble finding any of these SV titles at your finer mom and pop video stores, feel free to call Samurai Video at 800-492-3700 or drop them a note at 9610 DeSoto Ave., Chatsworth, CA, 91311, USA.

Tokyo Summer Camp Girls.

TOKYO SLUTS

Starring (the sluts:) Koyuki Yanagisawa, Serena Izumi, Midori Saeki (a.k.a. Shiori Midorikawa), Yoko Sugisawa, Kazuko Asaoka; *also starring (the slobs:)* Mirai Mochizuki, Mickey Yanai (a.k.a. Helicopter Man), Rocky Ishibashi, Natsuya Togawa, Susumu Kenzaki, and Hama; *written by* Randa Mai, *produced and directed by* Masao Tanaka.

And the title says it all. *Tokyo Sluts* is an all-out winner from first frisky fuck scene to last sweaty five-way orgy. But, due to space constraints here, if I had to pick the two best sluts, they'd be that irresistible doll Midori and charismatic nympho Koyuki Yanagisawa (man, what a name! How about plain ol' Koyuki, Koyuki?) By the way, the myth about all Asians having small breasts is quickly proven as just that — a myth. And Midori amply provides the proof. Oddly enough, she almost seems embarrassed by the size of her bountiful, totally-natural chest as she slowly, coyly disrobes for the camera, trying as best she can to hide those heart-stopping hooters. Japanese porn 'stud' Mirai Mochizuki, who claims he's "slept with" 500 women as a male dancer (and how many men I wonder?), does a fine job of bringing the best/beast out of Midori. It's also nice seeing Midori's girlish bangs cascade across her face as the hump heat reaches the broiling level.

And then there's Koyuki. Ah, Koyuki. A petite girl (like most of the sluts featured in these tapes), Koyuki has small breasts, a thin waist line, and a big — yet not fat — ass. She also has long black hair (subtly streaked with red), large dark eyes, prominent slightly crooked teeth, and a wonderfully happy-go-lucky smile. And, oh yes, she boinks like there's no tomorrow. In *Tokyo Sluts* Koyuki makes it with no less than three penises, throwing body and soul into it; most notably on a plush office sofa upon which she is ruthlessly hammered to screaming submission by the thoroughly repugnant Rocky Ishibashi and Helicopter Man, who at one point tells Rocky to "stop spitting on (him)" as Rock sputters on and on — in Ron Jeremy/Don Fernando fashion — about nothing in par-

Helicopter Man on the job.
Tokyo Sluts.

ticular. Another thing that's fun about these Japanese videos is their incongruously innocent goofiness. And sometimes, as in the case of *Tokyo Sluts*, it pleasantly borders on the surreal. Koyuki, for one, gives us a fun montage in which, fully dressed, she struts from office building elevator, to stairwell, to bathroom stall, getting one messenger boy after another hot and bothered, as some weird 'underwater' elevator-synth music plays.

The singer, even more oddly, sounds like a robot reciting the news in Japanese over a radio. Definitely worth a look... and a listen.

TOKYO SUMMER CAMP GIRLS

Starring (the girls:) Natsumi Asai, Eri Nakazawa, Ayumi Kyoumo, Moe, Asami Kashiwagi and (*the "counselors":*) Helicopter Man, Chocoball, Rocky Ishibashi, Kazu Itsuki, Ken Katayama, Mr. Nakamura, Ginji Sagawa, Natsuya Togawa, and Shun. *Written by* Randa Mai. *Produced and directed by* Masao Tanaka.

Undoubtedly one of SV's best features. Simply put, it has... well... uh... EVERYTHING. Cute "summer camp girls" wearing their Japanese school uniforms, running nude (except, of course,

45

for socks and tennies) through forests, fucking and sucking younger and older Japanese dudes in saunas, hot tubs (indoors and outdoors), as well as mindlessly screwing on a one-on-one, ménage à trois, and orgy basis. Also, lots of sweet Tokyo pussies getting wet and gushy (making distinctive noises like *kishy-slooshy-plusht!-plusht!*) as guys ram four fingers in and out of those dripping snatches, and… Whoops! There's no anal. But guess what? It doesn't matter. The girls here — like the magnificently stacked Eri Nakazawa and the seductively innocent-looking Moe (pronounced Mo-ee, I think) — are so cute and sincerely *into* the sex that the lack of ass fucking is of no great consequence.

There are several other provocative things to note here, too… strictly from the pornographer's perspective. Firstly, there's a lot of kissing going on in these tapes. Definitely a nice, intimate, romantic change of pace in comparison to the wham-bam-*fuck*-you-mam angry 'n' arrogant porking seen in American porn. Secondly, there's no big ageism hang-up in these videos. That is, young Japanese girls have no problem doing it with guys old enough to be their fathers… or in the case of Helicopter Man, their grandfathers. I don't know… maybe it all has to do with the dol-lar amount listed on the girls' paycheques. But even if that's the case, the girls should be duly credited for their admirable acting prowess. We also see the inspiration here for many an American porn director (Max Hardcore, for instance). More specifically, the schoolgirl motif. The Japanese have paid cultural reverence to this uniformed icon for decades. In turn, I raise my dick in salute to such uncompromising good taste.

Last note on *TSCG*: the orgy sequence between summer camp girls Moe, Ayumi Kyouno, Asami Kashiwagi and male 'counsellors' Shun and Natsuya Togawa is simply not-to-be-missed rewind material. The five-way takes place in a private yet outdoor, stone-made hot tub with lots of slamming, and kissing, and oohing, and AHHHHing.

Absolutely the *last note* on *TSCG*: Porn starlet Moe has gotta be one of the most darling Asian girls ever to hit the international porn screen. No more than 18-years-old — with red hair done up in pig tails — Moe has thick lips, bucked teeth, a bit of an upturned nose, and is slightly cross-eyed. Wowie! Her body is lusciously slim, too, with lean yet meaty ass and small, healthy tits. Lemme tell ya', if this girl is heaven-sent, then… *beam me up, Lord!*

Tokyo Sluts.

My Tokyo Tutor.

MY TOKYO TUTOR

Starring (the tooters:) Rumi Shirasaki, Nana, Ayaka Sakurai, Maki Takahashi and (the tutees:) Helicopter Man, Chocoball, Genki Enomoto, Ryuji Maeda, Kengo Aikawa, Mirai Machizuki. Produced and directed by Masao Tanaka.

Here's another video which refreshingly breaks down the barrier between various age groups. *My Tokyo Tutor* has younger stud-ents banging their shy-yet-desperately-horny female tutors, who are mostly in their early to late thirties. One of the more creative interludes is the very first scene, wherein our macho dancin' fool Mirai Machizuki slips his sexy older teacher (Rumi Shirasaki) a Mickey. Little does he realise, however, that she's also slipped *him* a Finn. Each comically awaits the other's 'fall' when — bam! — both pass out on the floor. Mirai dreams of righteously finger fucking Rumi to mad ecstasy. "Your pussy juice is dripping all the way to your asshole," he hoarsely tells her. It's no lie. Rumi's cunt is so soppy, you can actually see Mirai's dopey reflection in it. Next,

we turn to Rumi's drug-induced sex fantasy. Naturally she dreams of getting royally slam-dunked by Mirai. And it is, indeed, a vigorous schtupping, with Rumi eventually driving herself into a fuck-till-I-sob frenzy as she wildly rides Mirai, who exercises his fashion muscles by everso symmetrically ripping holes in Rumi's blouse to see, suck, and slime her rather large breasts. Versace *lives*!

The next memorable episode is a blackmail-for-tail tale. As the lusciously-built Maki Takahashi seduces her male student (Genki Enomoto), a lurking Helicopter Man takes a Polaroid of the boffing. The next day, H.M. shows up at Maki's home demanding that she buy some of his lingerie — or else. "You want me to show this photo all over town?" he asks her, wagging the Polaroid in her cute, pouting face. "Heh! Heh! Then do to me what you're doing to the guy in this photo, hmm?" As Maki and H.M. fuck on the standard sofa, Genki walks in. Helicopter Man has him join in, too. The three have a hearty fuckfest during which H.M. gets Maki to crack a smile when he looks at her pussy and exclaims, "Wow! Hair all the way down to your asshole!"

"I so a shame," Maki eventually blurts out, naturally loving every filthy minute of her double-barrelled invasion.

Tokyo Sluts.

Perverted Older Asians.

47

PERVERTED OLDER ASIANS

Starring (the mamas:) Marisu Kamijo, Ayane Nakayama, Sanae, Kanae Yoshida, Miho Yuki, and (the papas:) Joe Oshima, Rocky Ishibashi, Helicopter Man, Kazuchika Oku, and Jiro Itsuki. Produced, directed, and photographed by Masao Tanaka.

Oddly enough, *Perverted Older Asians* doesn't really have a lot of older Asians in it. So what's up with the title? Nyahh, no matter. But of the few older women actually in *POA*, Ayane Nakayama is one of the more memorable 'mamas,' though she's probably only in her mid-thirties. A redhead with an insatiable appetite for cock

My Tokyo Tutor.

meat, Ayane (who is, supposedly, both "single" and "a jeweller") pulls down a total of four bald-headed rats in this one. We see her cleaning vegetables (cucumbers, naturally), dusting off furniture, and washing the bathtub in her Ginza District home, with each 'chore' smoothly segueing into a perverted fantasy. The best 'dream' is a three-way with Helicopter Man (labelled here as a "physical trainer") and Joe ("delivery man") Oshima. As H.M. rubs Ayane's underwear back and forth against her crotch, he asks, "Does this hurt?" "It prickles," she answers. "How is it deep?" he then asks, giving it to her doggie-style as she sucks on Joey's joint. Her subtitled response is (and I shit you not): "Gurgle... Gurgle... (???)" Questions marks *not* mine.

Aside from these comically scrambled subtitles, *Perverted Older Asians* is further interesting because it brings up, once again, the age old issue of Japanese shame. Conservative upbringings. Saving face. Honour. All that shit ties into this girlie thing of "I so a shame." It's obviously a fed line of dialogue, but the girls deliver it so realistically (with wavering whispers, pouting faces, lowered or nervously wandering eyes) that it's a major turn-on. And an appreciated bit of culture shock, too. Connecting further into this whole angel/slut motif is the way these Japanese girls react to heavy penetration. As if torn between embarrassment and ecstasy, they seem to really cry when the 'going gets rough.' Talk about being *besides* yourself. It's great. And all the girls do it, too. All of 'em. But let's go ahead and summon the devil's advocate. For the sake of argument, let's just say our Japanese porn starlets are, in fact, faking it. Fine. Then I can only say: *Ah-so! Origami! Gojira! Cibo Matto!* Excellent acting, ladies.

SAMURAI DEBUTANTES

Starring (the debs:) Miyu, Haruka, Arisa, Karen Izumi, Lina Shinjo; (the dudes:) Rin Kurogi, Chocoball, Natsuya Togawa, Helicopter Man; and (the dorks:)

Steve and the "fabulous" Ed Powers.

There are basically two great things about this Samurai feature: 1) Karen Izumi's five-stud gang bang and 2) finally seeing Helicopter Man live up to his unique name.

Izumi is a small girl with full breasts, cute floppy ears, large eyes, and a curious case of "post-coital orgasm." That is, in a large, luxurious living room, after getting happily passed around from one Japanese dude to another, DP'd, and face washed via many dollops of ninja nectar, Karen lies on the floor in the foetal position and goes into violent convulsions (while her satiated gang bangers sit around, rib each other, and chuckle at this odd, unnatural vision). Personally, I think she's having petite mal seizures. But, hey, I could be wrong. Maybe it is an orgasm. Maybe she's acting. Check it out for yourself. Strange.

Meanwhile, in a much smaller room, on the thirtieth floor of a Shinjuko high-rise hotel, Helicopter Man turns himself into a human propeller as he does adorable Arisa in the doggie position. Amazingly, H.M. spins himself around and around Arisa's delightfully upturned ass while managing to keep his erect sushi roll deep inside her donburi den. A must-see.

In conclusion, for what it's worth, my advice to Samurai is to keep this series heavily steeped in Japanese culture. In other words, keep ugly Americans like Ed Powers and 'Steve' (who looks like a reject from the island of Dr. Moreau, i.e. a relative of Mr. Powers) the hell *out* of these shows. American culture — the little that exists — only helps cheapen the special foreign universe created in these equally special titles. Great videography, creative post-production effects, fun music, delicious young Asian starlets who appreciate passionate sex, and, of course, the distant land of Japan give Samurai Video its edge over other porn companies at large. Consequently, rather than blow a good thing, Samurai should leave that particular task to their Tokyo sluts.

SAYONARA! 💀

the rubber and urine clinic of dr. monteil

Did I tell you about the German Viola Film production called The Rubber and Urine Clinic of Miss Dr. Monteil? Well, it's one of the strangest things I've ever seen. There are three videos in the series so far: Dr. Monteil #1, #2, and #3. It's a totally bizarre world made up of, well, rubber and urine. The story is too weird to tell in a few words, but here are some of the scenes... A guy — patient Nº 27 — dressed in a black rubber outfit with mask and all, strapped in a gynaecological chair, has a catheter introduced into his urine "hole" (sorry, I can't remember the name of the piece of the dick we are pissing through), and this catheter is connected into his rectum, and the rectum is again connected with a tube that is put into his mouth — and he then pisses into his own mouth, drinking the piss that has passed through his own rectum... do you follow me? Well, in the next scene, the "Rubber Nurse" (and she looks STRANGE in a very, very STRANGE skin-coloured rubber nurse outfit) SWALLOWS a tube that connects his bladder with her stomach... and he pisses DIRECTLY into her stomach, the DOMINATRIX saying: "Now, how does it feel to have the patient pissing directly into your stomach?!" If that is strange, what about the sequel? Here the patient has a URINE-NARCOTIC. He is forced to breathe through a system of air and gas from a huge flask filled with urine, the urine going *blob blob blob blob* in the flasks while he is breathing through a tube connected with the flask in some kind of rubber-anaesthetic system, pumping — *blob blob blob* — and then the nurse comes and puts two pieces of glass filled with URINE-CRYSTALS into his nose. Total URINE-NARCOTIC! And so, on to #3. What now? Well, a catheter is pushed into the patient's bladder. Then the rubber nurse puts a catheter into herself, way up into the bladder, and she connects the tubes and pisses DIRECTLY into the man's bladder — and they show it FROM THE INSIDE, that is, they show how his bladder is getting filled with her urine via a clinical ultra-sound picture... how does this sound to you? INSANE? Well, I don't know, but this is definitely the weirdest thing I've ever seen, ever. This will definitely set a mark in the history of strange German porn, I mean... really, how weird can it get? This is the first film-review I've written. **Knud Romer Jørgenson**

49

Knud lives in Denmark. He appears in Lars von Triers' new film *The Idiots* and is co-editor of the tie-in book, *Din store idiot*.

Punk & Pornography

DAVID KEREKES

BACK IN HEADPRESS 13, we ran a piece on an American fetish mag from the late-Sixties/early-Seventies called *Bondage Hippies*. It focused on the story of a hippie chick and her square flatmate, and the tussles that erupted following an altercation one day regarding chores around the apartment. The hippie chick tries to eschew philosophies of peace and understanding while her flatmate sets to tying her up and beating some sense into her. By the end of the story everyone has found their own space, courtesy of a little bondage.

In keeping with the pornographically prohibitive times, *Bondage Hippies* made no attempt to be sexually explicit. The girls in the photographs — despite their compromising situations — retained items of underwear, and the text never ventured beyond words as coarse as 'breasts' and 'bum'.

It's unlikely that the *Bondage Hippies* readership was composed of the free loving fraternity itself, but comprised instead males outside of that culture, completely removed from it. Indeed, the *Bondage Hippies* readers probably viewed the hippie culture with disdain, outwardly at least; the magazine most certainly appeared at a time when factions of American youth were rebelling against the war in Vietnam, and hippies were synonymous with the breakdown of the 'American way'.

It is interesting that Punk, the most notable youth movement to have emerged since the hippies, should also have been regarded as a damaging influence on the social order. Just as interesting is the fact that, as with *Bondage Hippies*, there too exists a 'pornography' dedicated to this particular youth phenomenon. The title of the publication in this instance is *Punk Dominatrix*.

50

Punk Dominatrix was published in 1981 by a company calling itself Holly Publications, of Hollywood, California. It bills itself as Vol 1 No 1, but I doubt subsequent editions exist. The copy under consideration would appear to be a poor quality reprint, as the murkiness of some of the photographs gives rise to the impression that they're b&w lifts of colour images. Also the text has undergone some rather clumsy censorship in parts — more of which later.

Punk Dominatrix is not that dissimilar to *Bondage Hippies* before it, with its theme of subjugation and discipline. Here we have Candi, the "queen of leather", who one day realises there is more to punk than "short hair, safety pins and dancing to the music of Devo". Motivated by a desire to dominate and discipline (age-old areas of sexuality she believes intrinsic to punk), Candi leaves her friends, and moves out of the clubs and onto the streets in search of 'action'. Haunting the Boulevard, dressed in studded leathers, sporting dark eye makeup, a hefty industrial earring (some sort of grip or clamp), and a whip in her hand, she gets a reputation for having the ability to turn any man into her sex slave. Enter Zero Jim, a cocky young soul with a Fifties quiff, leather dog collar and cosmetic zigzag down his left cheek.[1]

"You think you're ready for me?" Candi asks Zero Jim.

"Hey, baby, I've been with the worst," Zero replies. "I've been beaten, whipped, chained and forced to crawl through mud. Ain't nothing you can do to shake me."

Candi plays along with Zero Jim. The two of them go down a back alley. Zero pulls his penis out, and believes that Candi is swooning at the size of his manhood. (It's in fact tiny, girls.) But when Candi invites Zero back to her apartment, things quickly change. On her own turf, Candi asserts herself and Zero Jim, "a punk, arrogant and blinded by his own image," soon crumbles powerless.

The text and photographs in *Punk Dominatrix* compliment one another. Surprisingly, it looks as though the (unaccredited) author has had access to the images prior to his writing the story. Even more surprising is the fact that he is conscientious enough to try and keep the text and photos running a close parallel. His descriptions of the characters match the descriptions of those people we see in the photos, as they do the scenarios in which we see them finding themselves. Rather they do to a point: despite the text, none of the images show an erection, or penetration. And in parts a censorious hand has obliterated certain words,

"An entire generation is turning onto the joys of pain. Their bizarre and unusual movement is called 'punk', and it's sweeping the world with its outrageous brand of sex."

—*Punk Dominatrix*

passages and sentences. The fact that 'offensive' aspects of the text have been whitened out, leaving gaping holes, further fuels the notion that the copy of *Punk Dominatrix* under review is a page-for-page lift. Quite possibly a special import for the British market.[2]

In her apartment, Candi thrashes Zero Jim with her whip, whereupon Zero feels "a sudden loss of power, a sudden reeling sensation within himself". Most every picture shows Zero Jim with his Levis wrapped around his ankles, and his face frozen in a ridiculous expression of abject horror. Candi, topless, snarls as she subjects Zero to a barrage of physical torment.

"There will be no mercy until you satisfy me!" she yells, tugging hard on the rope that Zero fashionably wears around his neck. Here's what she puts him through…

TORMENT #1 **Candi sits astride Zero, the spike of her high heel boot digging deep into the soft flesh of his buttocks. There are a lot of shots of Zero's ass cheeks and hairy crevice.**

TORMENT #2 **Candi pulls Zero across her thighs, rips open his zipper and jams the butt end of her whip into his groin, crushing his penis.**
"Please! Stop it! I'll do anything, anything!!!" Zero cries.
Candi only laughs. "You little prick! You arrogant stupid fool! You think that just because you are a punk in leather that you know it all! You are stupid, and you will pay for that stupidity!"

TORMENT #3 **The spike of Candi's heel is driven between Zero's buttocks, causing him to emit 'a shrill wail'. Further and further into him it goes.**

TORMENT #4 **With what looks like a car aerial, Candi threatens Zero Jim's genitals. And here comes the first instance of censored text:**

Candi teaches Zero a lesson.

place on the sensitive flesh. **She knew how to play the potentially** ally **metal and take her victim to the limits of his own pain endurance.**
Suddenly, Candi withdrew the

'Potentially lethal' perhaps? 'Potentially damaging'? Not so apparent is the word missing from the sentence that follows:

pain endurance.
Suddenly, Candi withdrew the prod. She lay on the
mattress and spread her thighs.

TORMENT #5 Words aplenty go missing in a situation that has Zero Jim being menaced with a pair of pliers. Indeed, the text completely obliterates all reference to the tool. If not for the accompanying pictures, which clearly show Zero's limp member hanging between a pair of pliers in Candi's hand, it would be entertaining to try and figure what insidious apparatus lay at the heart of this particular torment:

onto his flanks, straddling him.
She held a pair of in her **hands and showed them to Zero Jim.**
"No! Please no!" Zero Jim

TORMENT #6 The final and most severe punishment is left 'til last, but whole paragraphs are gone and not even the pictures give anything away. The only suggestion as to what the source of anguish here might be, comes with the line:

left! Nothing!"
The nightmare of pain began as Zero Jim felt the heat between his thighs.
That heat grew more intense with

The tale ends with Zero Jim a broken man (a common sight on the punk streets, apparently), no longer walking upright but "chained and on all fours next to his master, the punk dominatrix Candi".

In order to fill the remaining pages of *Punk Dominatrix*, we get a solo picture spread of Candi and "Punk and Pain", a supposed 'factual' article on the 'meaning' of punk and its parallels with other cultures. Here you will be enlightened to the fact that the punk dress sense indicates "a churning, violent reaction against motherhood". Want to hear why punks lean towards S&M? It's because "many of the young people now involved within the [punk] movement carry a deep sense of guilt over what they are doing".

It wouldn't be fair to dismiss the article outright though. It does make for an entertaining read and strives admirably to convince the reader that all 'punksters' are closet sadomasochists.

NOTES

1 As far as representations of punk fashions go, *Punk Dominatrix* isn't that bad. It's quite sober and relatively free from the zany makeup and crazy-colour nonsense usually associated with 'punk rockers'. Compare and contrast with *Leather Punks*, an S&M mag from the Swedish Erotica stable which features face paint aplenty.

2 It's a copy all right. On close inspection, just above and below the staples on the centre pages can be seen a reproduction of the *original* staple holes. I don't usually examine pages of smut mags in such detail, but my interest was piqued after the centre spread in *Punk Dominatrix* fell free, and I was left to ponder whether this rather common facet of loose centre pages in pornography was down to natural wear and tear, or by design (courtesy of some masturbation-crazed previous owner, eager to scatter as many dirty pictures around the house as possible).

... the punks are not as oriented to traditional methods of expression, and therefore seek to create their own system. In essence, many of the punks turn themselves into 'slaves', whether that state be within the industrial society or within the world of sex. They shave their heads, don the metal bracelets of sexual slavery, and literally chain themselves into a state of bondage. Since they are rebels, they cannot accept the formal ministrations of a dominatrix. The leather mistress is from another world, a world which they have left.

The photos that accompany the piece reveal a variety of models going through their best 'punk poses'. Naturally, a number of these are a little embarrassing. Take the middle-aged gal in studded leathers, for instance, wearing a buckle on her belt inscribed 'EVIL'.

Which reminds me, if you do see your mother this weekend, be sure to tell her "SATAN!"

Make you beautiful, Baby!

ANTON BLACK

Is Soho the sleaze centre of Britain? If you're a gullible tourist whose bulging wallet and swelling crotch is matched by your happiness in getting burned then yes, it is. For those of us living on Planet Real though, the most bare flesh you're liable to find in W1 will be on the rippling torsos of the muscled gayboys posing along Old Compton Street. Granted, the sleaze emporia littered amidst Soho's poncey bistros and piss-smelling alleyways were more plentiful before the clampdown of the Sixties and Seventies, but the place has always been known as a media centre first and foremost. The high-rent office blocks housing respected film companies far outnumber the jizz-sodden wank booths. Wardour Street, Dean Street, Soho Square — they teem not with XXX-cinemas but with trendy modernist offices housing stroppy receptionists and vacuously-smiling PR girls… all with their clothes *on*. These gals disrobe for career-aiding shags with pot-bellied executives, not for the gratification of rain-coated scum with bad breath.

Lights! Camera! Cocaine! Courtesy of Scottish junkies and chinless fops, the British film industry grows in strength daily, and starry-eyed dreamers resolve to make it big in the 'flicks'. The glamour, the glory… the unutterable fucking boredom. Whether or not work on an actual film set is tough, it remains only about a quarter of the graft needed to get the finished film onto the big screen. For every movie made, there is a ton of desk work required to secure a release, persuade exhibitors to show it, conjure up publicity, and so on. For the people whose job it is to do this, the product may as well be baked beans as films; the tedium factor remains the same. An office is an office is an office. Yet the bureaucratic side of film still draws people in, people who believe that *any* film-related work must be *exciting* work.

You are a pallid film obsessive who should get out more. You spend three years in Kent doing an interesting (but vocationally useless) degree in film theory. Believing in your small-town way that London is the cure to your small-town ennui, you move into a fleabag flat in Charlton, the arsehole of nowhere. You send CVs to all the movie companies in the British Film Institute handbook. You begin voluntary work with the Pandemonium avant-garde film festival at the ICA, but soon after are offered a paid job with Iron Lung, a Soho arthouse distribution outlet whose stuff you like. You go for the money. You tell your housemate — also a film geek — about the ICA job going spare, so he takes it. He meets lots of cool people, is given copious amounts of cocaine, sets up a shag between Michael Brynntrup and Bruce La Bruce and then gets a well-paid number with the London Film Festival. You get to work for Iron Lung Film Company Limited.

Or you do if you're me. Fool that I am.

Okay, I wasn't that naïve. I knew that holding the lowly position of General Assistant ('receptionist' to you and me) wasn't likely to lead straight to Hollywood, but it was film work and I loved films so it couldn't be bad, right? No two ways about it, it had its advantages. Free cinema admission anywhere in London was groovy, and there was this one Monday morning I staggered downstairs for a consciousness-gathering caffeine buzz to find a tall stranger idling about the kitchen. "You're Paul Auster, aren't you?" I said. It isn't every day you find your favourite novelist in the basement.

The press shows weren't bad either. Once the journo pricks had finished trading "I stood next to Dustin at Cannes" stories and fucked off to see the film, myself and the press officer would get pissed on the complimentary Becks and have a gas. Ah, but Yin and Yang and all that — the bad always outweighs the good.

The management set-up at Iron Lung was what you might describe as quirky. Actually, it's what you night describe as a fucking nightmare. The boss was Josef Marx, a 50-year-old German. The MD was Elaine Marx, his English wife. They were separated. The second-in-command, the general manager, was Matthew Bull. Elaine left Josef to live with Matthew. They are still together. This created a little *tension* in the workplace.

Josef hated both Elaine and Matthew, and pretty much everyone else who worked for him. He was a belligerent alcoholic and looked like a grumpy Einstein. He was also one of the nastiest people I've ever met, and I quickly discovered why Iron Lung had the highest staff turnover rate of any film company in the area: Every day bar none, by about 2.00 PM, Josef would have consumed two bottles of malt whiskey and be ranting at whoever was near enough. Job satisfaction becomes as distant an ideal as a Norman Rockwell family when your boss calls you a "useless fucking cunt" every afternoon. Occassionally he'd get all chummy and avuncular, which, if anything was even scarier. Sometimes, mercifully, he'd just pass out at his desk.

Adversity breeds bonding and, united against Josef, my Iron Lung colleagues were mostly pretty cool. Elaine herself, however, despite being the focus for most of Josef's ranting, was a leather-skinned harpy *cunt*. While Josef was a lonely, bitter old bastard who revelled in causing misery, Elaine was too stupid to realise that she was upsetting anybody.

But upset people she did.

56

She was all sweetness if on the 'phone to David Aukin or David Puttnam, but dare to buy her the wrong brand of decaf coffee and she whined at you incessantly for the next half an hour. I have yet to come across anyone with more misplaced self-importance than Elaine. This wrinkled reptile acted like the Queen or Ivana Trump, regularly getting people's backs up, mercilessly belittling her assistant (who was excellent at her job, by the way) and sending her PA crying from the room. Unaware of her own cuntishness, she would then wonder how on earth she had elicited such a reaction.

Senility was another characteristic of Elaine. She once passed the video assistant in the corridor, then rang me to ask who that person was. The company only had 14 staff, yet she couldn't recognise someone who had been in her employment for a year-and-a-half.

Then she could be a pathetic bitch, bawling like a baby when a high-up member of the BFI died (someone she had frequently badmouthed in the past) or being genuinely mystified when one staff member handed in their notice.

"What happened to loyalty?" she bleated.

Josef, astute for all his other loathsome qualities, yelled at her, "You stupid cow, they *hate* us!"

Josef and Elaine deserved to die slowly and painfully, but at least they didn't go unnoticed. Not so Matthew. Matthew was a pathetic cumstain of a man. Life with Elaine had reduced him to miasma. On the rare occasions that he ventured to speak — a slow nervous mumble — it was necessary to ask him to repeat himself. The owner of a West London cinema once told me that booking films from him, with his oohs and aahs and barely audible grunts, was like doing business with a constipated man trying to pass a painful stool. He wasn't so much Elaine's boyfriend as her scapegoat, often putting up with humiliating verbal barrages from her in front of the staff. This invertebrate had been Elaine's lover for nearly as long as he'd been her employee — close on 20 years — but I can't for the life of me imagine him ever being able to get even a close approximation of a hard-on, for her or for anyone else. I'm told that he was actually a very good-looking bloke when he was young. To be fair, I *can* imagine it — peeling off the wrinkles, receding hair and layers of fat the years had gifted him with — but I'm still looking for someone with a copy of the student film he allegedly starred in at Oxford, butt-naked except for a pair of cowboy boots.

Oddly, Elaine and Matthew have been reported wandering around leafy Chiswick, hand in hand like a pair of teenagers. It seems that they are, inexplicably, still in love. I just thank Satan that they never spawned. The world isn't ready.

Arseholes though they are, the evil triumvirate have put out some fine films. However, I can't help thinking that becoming a film distributor is what you do when you really want to be a film director but don't have the talent or courage. The Lion, the Witch and the Wardrobe (the nickname given to Josef, Elaine and Matthew by the film critic of a national broadsheet) didn't have a creative bone in their repugnant bodies. My mistake — Josef co-wrote and directed a film in the late-Eighties, the BFI-financed *Unhappiness*.

Have you ever seen a BFI film? Yes? Good, you know what to expect.

The British Film Institute serves little function. It makes dreary films for dreary audiences (it does have a fine archive and library, but that's us Brits for you — our government-funded film production isn't worth a fart in a windstorm, but when it comes to anal retentivity we've got it pegged). It makes films like *Unhappiness*. Before I'm accused of bias, let me state that I saw the film before I started at Iron Lung. *Unhappiness* — or "Total Fucking Misery" as I like to call it — is a political thriller devoid of thrills. Josef makes Joel Schumacher look like an auteur.

So, then, how did it ever get financed?

Hmm, that's a toughie. The fact that Josef runs a respected and valued company couldn't have had anything to do with it, could it? The fact that the stuff he releases is seen as important to the diversity of UK film culture, couldn't have influenced the BFI's decision to give him around £1M of taxpayers money? If Joe Unknown had sent the same script to the BFI headquarters would they have funded it just as enthusiastically? Of course they would. And maybe Myra Hindley will represent England in the next Eurovision Song Contest. (It could only be more entertaining than *Unhappiness*.)

Of all Iron Lung's releases to date, Josef's film remains their biggest loss-maker. Inexplicably, I know two people who actually like the film. One is a boring fuckwad and the other writes for *Samhain*. Draw your own conclusions.

Given that he'd kept a small arthouse business afloat for 20 years— no mean feat it must be said — Josef seemed to have little business acumen. The company continued to run despite him rather than because of him. His response to one film's flopping was to fax the producer and say, "We've lost money on this. We're not going to honour our contract or pay you your basic fee. Okay?" Funny enough it wasn't okay, and Josef narrowly avoided a lawsuit. Another time, the head of a different distro outfit passed away. Upon hearing the news, sensitive Josef rang up the distraught, inconsolable widow and offered to buy her dead husband's share of the company.

Still, I'm hardly the first pleb to have had a shitbag for a boss. My most important duty may have been emptying the bins at night, but I emptied those suckers with a smile on my face. After all, like Barbara Windsor says, mustn't grumble… We're all turning brain dead, the world's going to hell in a handbasket, but *mustn't grumble!* No, I didn't grumble. I gave lip where I could, got sacked once for my troubles, then reinstated the next day (one of Josef's hobbies was temporarily sacking his staff; he once fired the lot in the morning, then realising the difficulty of running a firm with a workforce of 14 reduced to two — and not wanting to empty his own bin — recalled them all an hour later). I generally did what I could to pay the rent and still retain some vestige of self respect.

But then I had a *real* shitty weekend.

I should have seen it coming when I sliced open my tongue on a yoghurt carton on Saturday morning. Then when the tattoo appointment I had in Camden got screwed up I should have gone back home to bed. But no. I was on a promise with this girl I knew. When the cock-teasing vixen got off with my best mate later that night, I decided to call it a day… but got mugged (again) in Brixton, 100 yards from my flat. Well, I was a real happy boy that Monday. I was on my best behaviour. I suppressed the urge to garrotte the hippie student swaying along to his sound-dribbling Walkman on the overcrowded Victoria Line, despite being crushed against him from Brixton to Oxford Circus. I ignored the ignorant Sloaney media shitbags talking on their fucking cellphones in Soho Square. And when Josef started berating me at noon for a mistake I hadn't made, I tried to be reasonable.

I started: "Well, I thought—"

To which Josef butted with the witty managerial retort: "DON'T THINK! I DON'T PAY YOU TO THINK! WHEN YOU START THINKING WE ARE IN TROUBLE!"

What can I say? I'm normally a happy person. I stroke cats, ring my mum on Mother's Day and cross to the other side of the street if I'm walking behind a lone woman late at night. But Hell — I just lost it. I yelled back, "YEAH? WELL, FUCK YOU AND ALL, PAL!"

He stormed over.

"We need to have a discussion, you and I." He drew me to one side and said, "You're dismissed. Give me your keys."

"Well Josef," I said, "that wasn't so much a discussion, more a monologue. Discussion implies a two-way process."

He didn't seem that impressed with my repartee. He just took my keys with nary a backward glance. This time I stayed sacked. And now I'm stuck in my dismal home-town, writing unpaid articles for dodgy magazines. It's grim, and I have to pay to go to the flicks. But the only bin I empty now is my own. And Josef, if you're reading this, I hope you die soon. By the way, I pissed in your whisky and jizzed in your salad dressing. 🐽

Many of the names in this article have been changed.

"AND THEN MY SHOE FELL OFF"

40 Years of Blue Peter

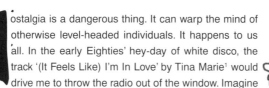

PHIL TONGE

Nostalgia is a dangerous thing. It can warp the mind of otherwise level-headed individuals. It happens to us all. In the early Eighties' hey-day of white disco, the track '(It Feels Like) I'm In Love' by Tina Marie[1] would drive me to throw the radio out of the window. Imagine my horror then, many years later, of being in some run-down nightclub and, upon hearing the aforementioned track, go "Hey, I remember this!" and tap my feet and singalong. Oh yes.

It's 1998 and kiddies' 'Television Magazine' *Blue Peter* celebrates its 40th anniversary. There are newspaper articles, there are TV interviews with old presenters, and there is even a themed evening of programmes on BBC2.

And it's all based on bullshit.

Let's look at what spawned this article: I was happily watching the *Blue Peter* theme-night on BBC2, as television history is something I find interesting (along with the desire to bathe in the smothering comfort of childhood memory). One of the mini-documentaries was titled *Blue Peter Confidential*. It promised to dish all the dirt on the show's production over the years. "Oh, goody," I thought, pouring the cocoa and opening the Gypsy Creams, "I know of a few scandals. It'll be nice to hear their side."

What the viewers got was PROPAGANDA and WHITEWASH. Ex-editor of *Blue Peter*, Biddy Baxter,[2] still wields a lot of power at the Beeb and has a lot of her protégés in key positions, all still loyal Biddittes. This probably accounts for the cover-up.

So here is the truth. From the top…

Blue Peter was the brainchild of BBC producer John Hunter Blair, who thought it would be fun for kids to have a jolly little show where the male presenter would demonstrate train sets and the female presenter would look at knitting. Mmmm, nice. The programme debuted in October 1958. Biddy Baxter, editor, along with producer Edward Barnes, would guide the programme through its glory years, 1962–1988.[3]

"Glory for what?" you may well ask. OK, for those of you who were too young, too foreign, or too lucky to have missed the show in its prime, here's a typical — yet satirical — line-up…

THE SCENE

Any living room in Britain on a pissing-down-with-rain Wednesday afternoon. The kids are home from Secondary School, and are waiting for mum (who has just clocked-off from her shift at the

CAKWATCH

BLUE PETER

TWELFTH BOOK

Lucozade factory) to get the fish fingers out of the freezer compartment. The eldest brat switches on the recently acquired GEC 24" colour set from Radio Rentals. The five-ton cathode ray tube starts to whine and warm up...

TV announcer: "*mmmurpfrrl*/there will be more adventures with *Boss Cat*[4] next week at the same time. Now on BBC1, it's time for *Blue Peter*."

The drum roll kicks into the *BP* theme tune — the wretched 'Barnacle Bill'. This theme tune has been abused over the years with many 'Producers' (i.e., 'Fuckwits') thinking that the way to make the show appear 'new' is to bugger up the theme to make it 'sound new'. It started with Mike Oldfield putting a synth on it. Nowadays it sounds like a bag of spanners falling down the stairs.[5]

On screen, John and Pete are cycling into Studio One of Television Centre in a giant novelty fibreglass Fireman's helmet. Shep the dog is circling the machine with the skill of a born Equity member. They come to a halt near Val, who is pinning a psychotic Siamese cat to some psychedelic, yet functional, seating unit.

With a cheeriness derived from three hours of solid rehearsal, industrial strength Benzedrine and a flagon of Merrydown, all shout: *"HELLO!!"*

John (pally Yorkshireman hiding sour, misanthropic tendencies): "Later in the programme we'll be showing you some film of our *Blue Peter* summer exh... exhibee... existeness... trip to Amsterdam, where me and Pete looked at some interesting museums. Also, I'll be cooking some cheese and tomato flan!"

Pete (flagrantly dressed Lancashire fop with his sense of irony surgically removed): "Yes, I'll be in the garden with Percy Thrower, looking at the location for our new *Blue Peter* Italian Sunken Garden and helping to prune our roses. Plus, there'll be a film report of my visit with Prince Edward to train 'Filth' the *Blue Peter* Anaconda for the Blind... [*Looks vacant for a second*] Val!"

Val: "Mmmm, yes. We'll also be checking the totaliser for our *Blue Peter* Rusty Razors and Used Johnnies for the Starving Sambos of Kenya Appeal, and also I'll be showing you how to make an ideal gift for Mother's Day... a crack pipe!"

All: "Hmmm. Yes."

Close-up on John: "But first of all, you're probably wondering what this is..." Two terrified, sweating firemen are viciously prodded into shot by a PA.

And so on.

That was, and still is, the basic format for the show. Maybe there would be a film on an historical figure included — although, according to *Blue Peter*, the only figures in history have been Florence Nightingale, Horatio Nelson, Marie Antoinette (who, hey, fancy that, is always presented as someone rather gorgeous who shouldn't have had their block chopped off), Greyfriars Bobby — the moronic jock dog — and last and least Joey Deacon.[6]

Or to jazz up that week's output, one of the mental presenters would endanger life and limb by being thrown out of a plane at 15,000 feet, or strapped upside down from Nelson's Column while playing 'Tangerine' on nose-flute and spoons. Noakes was always doing that one.

To give it that colonial street appeal, maybe a Bristol-based Oil Drum Band would be dragged into the studio. This, of course, was the only time any ethnic group could get on *BP* proper — as time-filling wallpaper. Apart from that, until 1990, when Diane-Louise Jordan joined up, the only black face on *BP* would be four-stone underweight and clutching a begging bowl.

Where was I? Scandal, that was it…

THE PRESENTERS

- CHRISTOPHER TRACE (1958–67) Rather dead these days. First male presenter in 1958. Ex-army officer and actor (Charlton Heston's stand-in on *Ben Hur*). Kicked off the show for screwing teenage quim during *Blue Peter* expedition to Norway. Ended up working in a factory and dying.

- LEILA WILLIAMS (1958–62) Miss Great Britain 1957. Booted off the show by producer who thought she should write her own material. Now has socially useful occupation selling booze and fags in a pub.

- VALERIE SINGLETON (1962–71) Lesbian icon. Best evil rumour: Shacked up with Joan Armatrading.

- JOHN NOAKES (1965–79) Actor turned presenter, accused of transvestism when revealed he was wearing wife's knickers while showing his bruised arse to nation's children after going down Cresta Run on his cheeks. Sour, miserable sod who hated television and the people who worked in it (that explains *15* years on *BP*, then). Best evil rumour: The bloke in the RAF team bobsleigh on the Cresta Run, took a dislike to the mardy Noakes and, rather than John falling out, the RAF geezer elbowed him out at the last bend.

- PETER PURVES (1967–79) Another actor (he was a companion in *Doctor Who*) turned patroniser. Clicked with Noakes to become the *BP* Pisshead Crew and would, allegedly, often turn up to run-throughs red-eyed and crippled by hangovers. Now runs his own magazine called *Peter Purves' Mad About Dogs*. True.

- LESLEY JUDD (1971–79) Ex-dancer and nutter. Kept falling in love with studio crew and then vanishing to the countryside with them. Feigned illness to avoid appearing on television. Eventually stayed in the countryside. Still mental. Attacked on film by randy ape.

- SIMON GROOM (1978–86) Farmer's son, DJ, Elvis fan, Grebo, Anarchist. The wild man of *Blue Peter*. Famous for being the first presenter to answer back at Biddy Baxter. The king of the double-entendre ("Mmmm. What a beautiful pair of knockers"), and the first presenter to turn up in shit-covered jeans and an Iron Maiden T-shirt. Top man! Famously, during the *BP* expedition to Japan, he got pissed in Tokyo, stole an inflatable waiter from outside a restaurant and was instantly nicked by the Nipponese Sweeney. After much crawling to the authorities, he was let out without charge, leaving the BBC damage control bloke with sleepless nights trying to crush the story — which, in the end, never got out of Tokyo. Importantly, Groom was the first western reporter into Cambodia after the defeat of the dangerously unfunny Pol Pot and his Khmer Rouge. Ironic that the children of Britain gave their every effort into Bring and Buy Sales to aid the starving and abused people of Cambodia/Kampuchea, while at the same time the British government (bless 'em) were training and equipping the Khmer Rouge. Best evil rumour: Did over the *Blue Peter* Ital-

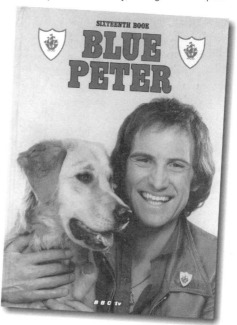

61

NOTES

1 Don't even ask.

2 Imagine a gauleiter in a Laura Ashley frock. Used as bogeyman figure to frighten BBC staff, e.g., "If you don't have that voiceover dubbed by 3:30, Biddy Baxter will get you." Biddy is currently working on BBC Director-General John Birt's 'Team'.

3 Barnes left *Blue Peter* in 1970 to become Deputy Head of BBC Children's Programmes. After giving the world *John Craven's Newsround*, he became Head of BBC Children's Programmes from 1978–86. Since then, he's returned to the trenches as producer and director.

4 Modern Mysteries Revealed: The BBC always referred to the Yank cartoon show *Top Cat* as *Boss Cat*. Even to the extent of changing the title with their own, rather slap-dash, caption slide that read 'Boss Cat'. Why? Well, on the market at the time was a brand of cat food with the name 'top cat' [sic], and the prats in hats at the Beeb thought that having a popular cartoon cat in a show called *Top Cat* would encourage five-year-olds to pester their parents for cat food of the same name. Logically, by calling the show *Boss Cat*, the connection would be eliminated. What a shame, then, after all the effort of changing the title and getting the presenter to announce repeatedly that "*Boss Cat* is on", the theme tune to the show had the words "TOP CAT!!" shouted out at the beginning of every other bar, and the fact that every character in the show refered to the lead as "Top Cat", or even better "T.C." What a waste of time and money. And yes, *Top Cat* was a rip-off of *Bilko*.

5 Any producer worth his salt knows that any long-running television (or radio) programme relies on its theme tune becoming a signature tune. It makes the viewer/ listener at ease, and settles them in for what's in store.

6 The Joey Deacon incident is something that brings hushed voices even today in the halls of the BBC. Why not try running up to the *BP* production office and shouting "And then my show fell off!" Tell me of their reaction. If you have no idea what I'm talking about — neither did Joey.

7 Just a final note — please don't mention *Magpie*.

Further Reading

Blue Peter: The Inside Story, Biddy Baxter & Edward Barnes, 1989, RingPress.

The Golden Age of Children's Television, Geoff Tibbals, 1991, Titan Books.

ian Sunken Garden (BPISG) with a gang of Young Farmers as revenge on Percy Thrower, whom he loathed.

🐞 CHRISTOPHER WENNER (1979–80) Unbelievably upper-class bloke. Son of a diplomat and failed actor. Fan of the 'Method' and so would embarrass crew and directors by walking around on-camera going "Hey! Ummm, er, ummm, Ah! Hey!" in a vain effort to 'find' his voice. Booted off the show with as much dignity as possible. Has since eaten all the pies and is war correspondent.

🐞 TINA HEATH (1979–80) Non-entity. Got pregnant.

🐞 SARAH GREENE (1980–84) Woman who dressed in the dark. Married irritating 'personality' Mike Smith after interesting getting-off-with-someone-when-they-are-supposed-to-be-working incident during the 1981 London Marathon.

🐞 PETER DUNCAN (1980–84, 1986) Git with the punchable face. Got his own spin-off show *Duncan Dares*, which was a rip-off of the lower key *Go with Noakes*. Appeared in naff British sex film while still a struggling actor. Big deal. Best evil rumour: Smashed up the BPISG on the second occasion.

🐞 MICHAEL SUNDIN (1984–86) The worst *BP* presenter ever. A stuntman/acrobat and short-arse hampered by his voice. Originally a Geordie, Sundin had some elocution lessons, which he gave up halfway through. The resulting voice veered from Tyneside to mid-Atlantic and back again, resulting in the effect 'Pissed'. Given the big elbow — caught on a trampoline in just his underpants with a male stripper in a gay club. Not a bad night's work when you consider no one could understand a word he said… well, apart from Joey Deacon. Dead from the big 'A'… yes, an enormous Aardvark sat on him. Sorry. Conspicuous by his absence from the *BP* Night documentaries. Best evil rumour: Managed to gain extra access to ***'s [*No bloody way!— Legal dept.*] mansion for a film report by giving *** [*No!*] a blow *** [*Again, No!*].

🐞 JANET ELLIS (1984–87] Sex Goddess for the Anarcho-Punk generation. Has own fanzine devoted to her. Allegedly booted off the show because of unmarried status while preggers. Not true. First piece of TV fame as student totty wearing Nazi helmet in bed with John Thaw in an episode of *The Sweeney*. Best evil —yet strangely alluring — rumour: Has two tattoos in private areas. No, I don't mean the potting shed.

And that's it, really. Oh, except for the fact that *BP* only took up using autocue, not as a mark of progress (as the documentary stated), but rather the fact that dizzy northerner Yvette Fielding couldn't learn her lines, even when threatened with her marching orders. Since then it's been a cavalcade of shiny haired, sparkly toothed cretins who wouldn't even fart out of turn... until...

 RICHARD BACON (1997–98) Hurrah! Hours before receiving an award marking *Blue Peter's* 40th Anniversary, young Richard from Mansfield, Nottinghamshire, was spotted by loveable tabloid hacks. He was chugging vodka and snorting cocaine for *eight hours*! I admire his stamina.

Enough of this. I must have my say, for the last time, in plain English: *Blue Peter* is the most unholy, patronising, middle-class, worker-baiting, piece of offal on the face of television. I don't care if John Noakes was like a big brother to you — it was CAK!

And the fucking thing is still on television. 🐆

Cakwatch Supplemental
a public information film update

Hello readers. Following on from my **Cakwatch on Public Information Films** [HEADPRESS 16], I bring you **Public Information**. (By the way, thanks to everyone who's been writing in on Cakwatch subjects!)

There is much good news for David Greenall (who reviewed the MPI Video release of CHARLEY SAYS). Network Video have bought up the rights and re-released CHARLEY SAYS (video #7951095). Network have also re-mastered and expanded the previous version, so there's a good six minutes of extra mayhem.

Released simultaneously is CHARLEY LIVE!, the live action compilation (#7951109). LIVE! is a value-for-money burn-up from Fancy a Jar? Forget the Car **to Mr Kerekes' fave** Chided-Leaky-Cistern-Family **and back again.**

Be warned — The Spirit of Dark Water **is also on the tape, so always hold mummy's hand.**

I hope there's a volume three of CHARLEY in the works, 'cos as much as I enjoyed the How To Vote, The 1971 Census **and the** We're Going Decimal, So Fuck You **films, I did miss** Driver Fatigue. **And** Your Rat Bag of a Wife Will Perish on the Hard Shoulder. **And** Mullard and Williams are Gnomes.

The tapes are in the shops now. If you can't find them, contact: Network Video/Sound and Media Ltd, Unit 3, Well's Place, New Battlebridge Lane, Redhill, Surrey, RH1 3DR.

The other good news for us TV pervert-researcher-warrior-poet types is that thanks to Tony 'Auntie Stalin' Blair's Nanny State, the PIF is back!

Certain governmental departments have been allocated cash to patronise us openly again. Huzzah! Witness the Get Ready for the Euro **ad featuring the really punchable boss. That is a PIF. The** Action 2000/Millenium Bug **ads, they're PIFs. The DoEE** Reading is Gear **ad, it is a PIF. See the repeating of the** Zippy Mouth **electoral roll ads, they're PIFs! Plus, better news for those in the Central TV region — in the dead of night slot, the 2 AM to 4 AM yawn-fest where no advertising agency fears to stalk, they run PIFs. Captured examples so far include: (i) A mid-Eighties** Rowan Atkinson Blood Donor **effort, (ii) The classic animated** Touched By The Hand Of God On A Junction Box **clip, featuring updated narration, and, most promising of all, (iii) Two suspiciously contemporary films on** Travel Insurance/Scooter Horror **and** Don't Give Fire a Chance. 'Don't...' **brilliantly contains the old patronising device of putting up the slogan and** *then* **having the chiding, heavy reverb voiceover tell you what it says. It also features a sweaty bald bloke who looks like the geezer out of** *Schramm*.

Could it be true, my beloved readers? Have Blairite Nanny Boys resurrected the old-fashioned style PIF? Will the Spirit be able to jack in the mini-cabbing? Will we finally see those Princess Di/Necro-Clunk Click **ads? Keep 'em peeled, brothers and sisters.**

If you see anything suspicious, tell us. Crossplies and radials.

Phil Tonge

PIF Thanks for the Cakwatch on Public Information Films in *Headpress 16*. It stirred up many nostalgic memories of my childhood TV viewing, especially 'The Spirit of Dark Water', which I have a fairly vivid recollection of, and yes indeed, it completely shit-scared my delicate, little, three-year-old person. I've never been able to foget the fucking thing, 22 years on. I'm sure it will still haunt me when I'm an old geezer.

Just one thing, though, I could have sworn that the 'spirit' actually said "I'll be ba-a-a-a-ack" and it kind of echoed out. I could be wrong.

From the same time, I can remember a TV show called *Sandokan*, for which I still recall the theme tune. Recently there has been a cartoon of it, which was shit. Anyone else remember the live-action one?

Jamie Stringer,
Nottingham

PIF The PIF that always stuck in my mind was a mid-Seventies affair that, with the wisdom of passing years, I now realise was telling us that putting rugs on polished wooden floors was a really bad idea — as you're liable to slip and break your fucking legs — but in my five or six year old mind, I was witnessing a tale of appalling sadism and bloodlust. Picture the scene: a bloke with a broken leg is coming out of hospital.

Back home, his dear old mum tidies the house, ready for his arrival, giving the floor a right good polishing. Then she lays down the dreaded rug... cue ominous voiceover: "She might just as well have put down a man-trap," accompanied by a shot of the rug fading into a shot of a huge, vicious-looking man-trap that could take the leg off a rhino, then back to the rug again.

Two things bothered my young mind. Firstly, the point of the metaphorical man-trap having gone straight over my infant head, I was convinced that this cruel, sadistic bitch was deliberately laying a trap for her poor injured son. Secondly, I couldn't figure why the rug was still lying perfectly flat on the floor, considering it was now covering a big, fucking man-trap.

The punch-line was a shot of the bloke leaving hospital with *two* broken legs… though, to me, this second plaster cast was obviously hiding a raw, bloody stump following the encounter with the demon mother's implement of torture.

That fucking film used to scare the crap out of me. So much so, that I'd have to leave the room whenever it came on. Mind you, in all my 27 years on this earth, I can honestly say that I have never once put a rug on a highly polished wooden floor.

Mark Mason,
Stockport

AF After reading, and thoroughly enjoying, the many articles and memories of this notorious film (I had never seen it, but had heard of many 'key' scenes, more of which later), I was 'fortunate' enough to acquire a rather good quality copy of this video from the local porn merchant, and would like to share a breakdown of the parts which go together to form the whole that is 'Animal Farm'.

The first film is called *Animal Orgy* and starts with two women in a field, naked, enjoying each other's company. The scene cuts to another two women forcing themselves on a dog — who for the remainder of the film(s) I shall call Lassie. The dog has clearly had enough of the attention being given to him and tries to make a break for it, but is forcibly held down by the two women. The usual women/dog antics follow. We then return to the first two women who have found themselves a Shetland pony to play with.

The second film is *Animal Bizarre* and this is one of the infamous 'key' scenes. It opens with the sight of a fully grown horse standing in what looks like someone's house. The horse seems quite calm. A woman arrives and immediately gets going on the horse's considerable length. After licking and forcing the cock between her legs, she then covers it with a large condom (!) and gives a few gentle tugs.

64

What follows made me sick for the rest of the day: She empties the copious contents over herself, leaving us with the lingering image of her covered from head to waist in ejaculate. By the look on her face I think she quite enjoyed herself.

The next scene, still part of the same film, features the above woman with a pig in the same room. At first it is quite hard to ascertain the type of animal outstretched on the couch, but once the trotters and corkscrew penis come into view there is no mistake.

On the same — but now soiled — couch, the same woman brings in two of her friends: one a woman and one a dog; not Lassie but a black Labrador. You can probably guess what follows.

Animal Passion is the next film, opening with a picturesque farmyard scene. A woman walks into camera shot — she is far from picturesque! She is immediately pounced on by a very randy dog and literally knocked to the ground, all the time being observed by a shifty looking man from the farmhouse. The observer then rescues the woman from the amorous attentions of the dog, and takes her into a pig sty. They both strip. The woman gives the man a blow-job, and the man licks the pig's ass, in readiness for what's to follow. He ejaculates onto the pig's back, grabs a stool, forces his cock into the pig and the sound of squealing fills the air. The woman leaves and enters another barn where her dog is waiting for her. They resume

their coupling until the dog loses interest. But wait! What is that lurking behind the wall of the barn? The woman strips and then her new friend — another pig — comes into full view. The pig dwarves her, this pig is huge. The woman has a piss onto the straw floor and then the pig mounts her from behind. She then lies on her back until, finally, the pig finishes her off 'doggy' — or should that be 'piggy' — style.

The title *Dog Fuckers* should need no explanation. This film features a red-haired woman, who I am reliably informed was a regular in the numerous Color Climax films of the Seventies. She doesn't exactly fuck Lassie but she does give his red-head some attention.

The action then focuses on a couple shagging in a field. They are interrupted by Lassie and a young blonde woman, and then all attention is turned to the dog. Following this, the couple resume their shagging, and Lassie starts licking them both. The man ejaculates onto the woman's thighs and lucky old Lassie has the privilege of licking the man's cock clean — a nauseating image.

Horse Lover follows. By this time the repetitiveness is getting rather boring. This segment is slightly enlivened by the fact that the two women are having trouble controlling the horse. Once the steed is held firm, one of the women attempts to force its cock up her. Finding that he's just too big to fit, he turns his attentions

to the other horse that has just entered the farmyard. The two women look on, with some disappointment, as the horse mates with his own kind.

Horse Power. Shetland Pony and Lassie again, although not together — what sick person would enjoy a horse/dog session!

Snake Fuckers is another infamous scene. Two fairly attractive women purchase some eels, cook some and one of them stuffs the remainder up her vagina and arse simultaneously. It is difficult to see if the eels are alive or dead, as their movements are caused by the thrusting hands of the second female as she pleases her fellow chef. The eels are then eaten and the women turn their attentions to the male guest. *Snake Fuckers* is probably made by the same people as the aforementioned films. How do we know this? Look at the walls of the dining room — they are covered in horse pictures. [*?—Ed.*]

Finally, it's *Chicken Lover.* I won't go into too much detail, suffice to say it includes a postman, a chicken and much stomach churning.

That's 'Animal Farm', or at least my complete version. All films seem to be from the Color Climax stable (excuse the pun). Whilst watching this, I tried to understand what possesses people to film and perform these sort of activities? After a couple of minutes, I concluded that there are some sick fuckers in this world.

Nick Marsh,
Flintshire

EXPLORING THE LIMITS OF FREE EXPRESSION
An interview with Barry Hoffman, editor-in-chief of
GAUNTLET magazine

BILL BABOURIS

POLITICAL CORRECTNESS SUFFERS A SETBACK

GAUNTLET
Exploring the Limits of Free Expression
Murder by the Book

HIT MAN

The Controversy over *Hit Man*

Banning Beetle Bailey

ANDREI CODRESCU ON ROMANIA'S MADE-FOR-TELEVISION REVOLUTION

Gauntlet N° 13. "There are some ardent supporters of the First Amendment who feel *that* book goes too far."

Barry Hoffman's bi-annual *Gauntlet* is one of the most important publications in the alternative press field, a strong and consistent voice against those who threaten our inalienable right to free expression. Covering the whole spectrum of beliefs and ideologies, its pages often host a varied assortment of people, from racists to anarchists and from pornographers to ultra-conservative Christians. But don't mistake *Gauntlet* for a Speaker's Corner for the extreme, a forum where one can preach one's favourite kind of hatred. Being an anti-censorship magazine means that it deals with cases of (or attempts at) suppression, and offers all involved parties a chance to tell their side of the story. Moreover, it always publishes the suppressed material in question, thereby, if not cancelling the censors' work out, at least giving the reader a chance to see what the whole fuss has been about and to form an objective opinion.

Bold and controversial, *Gauntlet* is chronicling the on-going fight against censorship and educating the public in both the direct and indirect methods used to suppress free expression. Its founder and editor-in-chief, Barry Hoffman, spoke to *Headpress*.

HEADPRESS For how long have you been publishing *Gauntlet* and what was the goal you set out to achieve by publishing such a magazine?
BARRY HOFFMAN I set out publishing *Gauntlet* after I'd been censored at the school I taught at. I'd written a play dealing with teen runaways, and had it line-edited by my principal. And around that same time, a parent contacted the school unhappy with some short stories my students were reading (oddly enough "The Wishgiver" by Henry

Slesar). I had to submit my entire reading list to the principal, even though it was just *one* parent out of 33 who was offended. It made me aware just how special interest groups wield such power, at the expense of the majority. As I was interested in publishing a magazine (*Gauntlet* is not a 'zine: while it's not a glossy, it has circulation nation-wide, in Canada and the UK, though I'd like to get even greater exposure), censorship seemed like the perfect vehicle for me. What I wanted to do was what the dailies and weeklies didn't (*couldn't*, actually) and publish censored material along with debates/commentary about the censored art or writings. With Robert Mapplethorpe, for example, there was an awful lot written, but the photos in the papers were always of a non-controversial nature or cropped. We printed the photos that caused the problems for him, in their entirety.

Gauntlet Nº 8.
"Scientology didn't come after us."

other than what is illegal (kiddie porn — photos taken without the permission of the children and their parents — is a crime). I personally will defend the right of hate groups to spread their teachings, but I won't publish material that espouses hate and violence towards anyone. Rappers have the right to preach violence and violence towards women. That doesn't mean I have to publish what they write. However, in the case of 2-Live Crew[2], the situation was more complex. We ran a number of stories in issue 2, because they were being prosecuted for their material. I may not personally agree with the content of their songs, but I will defend their right to record and publish them.

Personally and as editor of *Gauntlet*, I deal in issues. We talked about the "outing" of gays by certain publications. However, in an article I ran on the subject, the writer who supported outing listed names of supposedly gay celebrities. I wouldn't print the names, as I could see he was trying to use *Gauntlet* for his agenda — to out celebrities who hadn't wanted to make their personal sexual orientation public. I think privacy is just as important as the right for journalists to dig and write a story. So, both personally and as an editor, we're not a forum to smear or spread innuendoes. And, I can't see giving those who feel the Holocaust didn't occur a forum for their views. Again, I defend their right to espouse their views, but that doesn't mean I have to run articles debating whether the Holocaust occurred or not. That's editorial prerogative, not censorship — a difference too many people are now aware of, or choose to ignore.

Other than that, I see no limits to free expression.

After 15 issues, do you think that this goal has been realised?

I think so. We've covered any number of issues and *always* have been able to publish the suppressed/censored material in question. Sometimes it's been difficult getting dissenting opinions (a number of those opposed to pornography didn't want to appear in our first porn issue [No 5], because they didn't want to be in the same publications as purveyors or porn), but that's their loss. While we oppose all forms of censorship, there are some issues that fall into a grey area (the *Hitman*[1] book from Paladin Press, for instance). There are some ardent supporters of the First Amendment who feel *that* book goes too far. My goal is to provide enough information and arguments on both sides of the issue, so the reader can make an informed decision.

Your magazine is entitled: "Gauntlet — Exploring the Limits of Free Expression." Do you think there are any such limits? Where do you draw the line a) as a person and b) as *Gauntlet*'s editor?

Personally, I don't think there are *any* limits,

All of your issues feature controversial material. Have there ever been any attempts to censor *Gauntlet* itself and if so by whom? (This refers to either direct censorship or indirect, i.e. boycotting by distributors or bookshops, cease-and-desist letters, etc.) How did you counter them?

Oddly enough, those times I've been warned by friends to expect those "cease and desist" letters, there has been surprisingly little censorship of *Gauntlet* itself. We ran a series of articles on

Scientology, and I did fear the possibility of a nuisance suit that could have put us out of business. But our facts were checked, double and triple checked and Scientology didn't come after us.

Two of our issues were detained at the Canadian Border (Issues 1 and 3), according to a distributor who is now out of business, but upon appeal they were let into the country. Prisons have been a problem at times. Unlike *Penthouse* and *Playboy*, who have lawyers on retainer for just such a situation, I can't afford to legally challenge a prison that won't allow *Gauntlet* in. Issue 2 contained an article written *by* a serial killer.[3] I tried to get the issue (then later, just the article) to him to check for accuracy and each time I was denied. I wrote letter after letter, and tried to get the American Civil Liberties Union interested, but to no avail.

There was, I believe, indirect suppression of issue 9, due to its cover — the one with Matuschka[4] on the cover with her one breast exposed. That issue had more returns than any other. I know of one store that returned its copies upon receipt from their distributor. But, other than that one store, it's difficult to prove how many others caved in. As we also featured an article on Harlan Ellison, it was an issue that should have sold reasonably well. With the percentage of returns I experienced on that issue, I have to conclude that a large number of stores refused to go with the cover. In the US it may have been the first time that a magazine showed a naked breast on its cover (a picture of the same artist *did* appear in the New York Times magazine, but that is an insert in the Sunday paper. It's not something that is on the news-stand or on a bookshelf for all to see). I guess the US (or at least stores who set policy) aren't ready for such a cover yet. Look at the cover, though, and what's more distasteful than the breast is the Hitler moustache. This was not a cover to titillate. It was an artistic expression from a well-respected artist.

What about self-censorship? Have you ever left any articles/photos/artwork out because you thought they were "too strong" or would cause you trouble?

I've never censored any artists/photos or artwork. Issue 15 has some art that makes me personally uncomfortable — not the art, but the concept — but it's art and I wouldn't censor it (for example, Charles Gatewood's blooding photos — we wanted to look at the underground of S/M and, boy, did we find it. People intentionally slicing and dicing themselves personally doesn't do anything for me, but I found the pictures interesting). The *only* time I didn't run a cover was also issue

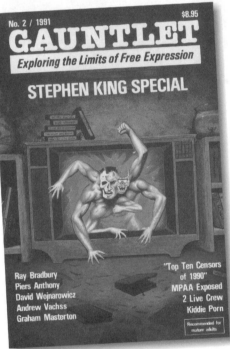

Gauntlet N° 2. "Prisons have been a problem at times."

15. Justice Howard had this wonderful sacrilegious photo, which is run as a full-page interior, with a caption under it, saying I'd considered it for the cover, but with Justice's assent, decided not to put it on the cover. Why? I knew many stores would pull the issue. And, I had to decide what was more important, having the issue available to be read or making a statement with the cover. As I'd been burned once with the Matuschka cover (a lot of excellent material was never read by people who *should* have been given the chance), I felt getting the issue out was more important than going with a sensational cover. If I was *Penthouse*, *Playboy*, or any mainstream magazine that sold in the millions, I could get away with such a cover, and even get a ton of free publicity. But censors can be subtle (they're not

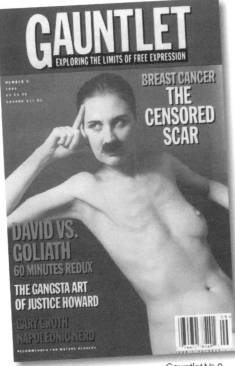

GAUNTLET
EXPLORING THE LIMITS OF FREE EXPRESSION

NUMBER 9
1995
US $9.95
CANADA $11.95

BREAST CANCER
THE CENSORED SCAR

DAVID VS.
GOLIATH
60 MINUTES REDUX

THE GANGSTA ART
OF JUSTICE HOWARD

GARY GROTH
NAPOLEONIC NERD

RECOMMENDED FOR MATURE READERS

Gauntlet N° 9.
"Indirect suppression."

Yes, I do. I made a concerted effort to separate my two jobs — that of a teacher and that of editor/publisher of a magazine that had material many parents would find objectionable. The fiction I write is for adults, and while I don't hide the fact that I write such books, I don't bring the books into my school. I think some of the worst censorship deals with television, due to the almighty advertising dollar. Having seen what happens when a controversial show is aired (advertising is often pulled), you get a lot of producers who won't even propose a controversial show (even an episode), knowing it will be rejected out of hand. So, you have people censoring themselves because they decide it's not worth putting the effort in when the show will be rejected anyway.

I'm sure you have often featured opinions in *Gauntlet* you don't agree with. Why do you feel it is important to provide a forum of expression to a censored child-pornographer or racist?

I won't use *Gauntlet* as a forum to express hate. I won't publish racist dogma in *Gauntlet*. On the other hand, we did publish the story of a black lawyer who faced severe repercussions to his practice for defending the KKK's right to free expression. I think there are two separate issues here. One is publishing stories that deal with suppression of groups like the Klan. The other is publishing racist material itself. I'll defend the Klan, much as I abhor what they have to say, but I won't publish their writings. As for child pornography, well, it's illegal, so while I'll publish debates on the merits of publishing child pornography, I won't publish something that's illegal. On the other hand, in issue 16 we'll be discussing the work of David Hamilton, among others, *and* publishing his work. That's not child pornography. To date, the courts have agreed it's art, so we'll publish what some believe to be child pornography, simply because it's not. To me child pornography is when there is no consent, or when parents or others take pictures of their children in sexually provocative positions solely to make a buck. And, obviously, when there is force involved, that's not art. On this issue, I feel the courts in this country have — at least up to now — been pretty liberal

all fools), and we wouldn't have received increased coverage due to the cover. And, we did run the photo as an interior illo — the only one we gave full-page coverage. As for what goes *in* the magazine, there are no taboos. I've gotten flak for running some of Justice Howard's sexually explicit, but wonderful, photos in the same issue as the story and photos dealing with mastectomies. Some feel that women's rights groups didn't want to touch the issue — even though we were the first to run a detailed fully illustrated piece dealing with the art of breast cancer survivors — because the photos by Justice Howard were in the same issue. I've argued with any number of people who felt we were losing sales by not running a "clean" issue. Had not the Justice Howard photos appeared, the feeling is, breast cancer survivor groups would have bought large quantities of the magazine. They may be right, but when I put an issue together, I'm not thinking who I might offend. If people are so intolerant they can't see beauty in art where there is nudity, it's their loss.

Do you think we censor ourselves in our everyday lives?

69

and have allowed artistic photos of naked children to be published. Those illos, we'll publish. 🐾

Subscriptions and back issues of *Gauntlet* are available from: Gauntlet, Dept. A97, 309 Powell Rd., Springfield, PA 19064, USA. Foreign postage is $7 per issue (all copies shipped via air) and $12 to Japan and Australia.

You can visit the *Gauntlet* website at: *www.gauntletpress.com* and read, among other interesting things, a full contents table for each issue published and the opening chapter of Hoffman's controversial novel, *Hungry Eyes*, a Bram Stoker Award nominee.

Barry Hoffman can be contacted via e-mail at the following address: *Gauntlet66@aol.com*

Barry Hoffman.
Photo courtesy Barry Hoffman.

NOTES

1 The controversy surrounding *Hitman* has to do with the murder of Janice Saunders, Mildred Horn and her crippled child by Edward Perry on March 3, 1993. During the trial it was revealed that Perry (now on death row) had purchased Rex Feral's *Hitman: A Technical Manual for Independent Contractors* prior to the murder, and the close correlation between his acts and the recommendations in the book was used as evidence against him. The publishers, Paladin Press, were taken to court by the victims' families (*Gauntlet*, issue 13).

2 Rappers 2-Live Crew saw their *As Nasty As They Want to Be* album getting banned in certain states because of its "explicit lyrics" (haven't you heard it all before?). For more on the case, see Penelope Ann Spheeris' documentary, *Banned in the USA — Featuring 2-Live Crew* (*Gauntlet*, issue 2).

3 Alleged murderer of 33 women, Gerald Schaefer (now deceased) wrote an article entitled "Let's Rethink the Son of Sam Laws". The Son of Sam laws were voted on and put into effect to prevent convicted criminals earning money by means such as selling the rights to books or filmscripts they had written about their crimes (*Gauntlet*, issue 2).

4 Controversial photographer Matuschka was nominated for the 1994 Pulitzer prize for her self-portrait photograph which depicted her mastectomy scar. Her photos of women who have undergone mastectomy have subsequently been banned from several publications and galleries (*Gauntlet*, issue 9).

LED ZEPPELIN

VIA

THE MC5, JOHNNY WINTER,
BIKERS vs POLICE

&

SQUIRMING FEMALES

OCTOBER 25, 1969

at

NARRAGANSETT'S
FIRST TRIBAL ROCK FESTIVAL
BOSTON GARDEN,
BOSTON, MASSACHUSETTS

TOM BRINKMANN

there was no place to see professional, big name rock acts in Concord, New Hampshire in 1969, so at the time my only experience had been with Jr. High and YMCA dances at which friends' bands usually played. Being 14 and just beginning to start many years of experimenting with and abusing marijuana and alcohol, I thought myself quite the little hippie, not to mention radical. Only a couple of months into "Woodstock Nation", as it were, my interests ran towards hippies, Yippies, Black Panthers & White, Abbie, Jerry, and The Chicago 8. Of course, living at home with Mom and Dad in middle class suburban (or subrural) N.H., I was removed from the reality of the "movement". My favourite bands at the time were the MC5 and The Stooges, to name but two.

Man had landed on the Moon, people had been slaughtered in the Hollywood hills mysteriously and Woodstock Nation had been born in Rock 'n' Roll, acid, marijuana, sunshine and mud. I was one year away from my first of many LSD trips. A new band from England could be heard on certain airwaves singing about good times and bad, and communications breaking down. I was vaguely interested.

It was 1969 all across the USA, another year for me and you, another year with nothin' to do except to go to Boston Garden one fine October night with a friend to see and experience my first rock concert. It had been dubbed "Narragansett's (after the Indian tribe and the brewer of beer) First Tribal Rock Festival". I was finally going to see the legendary MC5,

1510 HILL ST. ANN ARBOR 48104

(313) 769-2017   (313) 761-3223

FUN...GAMES...SEND $2.00 and receive from the MC5 Social and
Athletic Club pictures, biographies, posters, bi-monthly in
detail band happenings, and letters from the band. We're
working for communication without the money ruse, but for now
we have to buy the pictures, etc. If you have requested it,
White Panther information is on the way to you from Genie,
Corresponding Secretary of the Panthers.

Love to you,
Darlene, for the MC5

Copy of only surviving piece of correspondence
I have left from MC5 and WPP, circa '69 or '70.
(Buttons and stacks of propaganda I traded and
sold to a collector in NYC in late-Seventies.)

brothers and sisters! Oh yeah, and Johnny Winter and Led Zeppelin too.

Being the age I was, my friend and I were driven the 70 miles south to Boston by my parents, who had also bought the tickets, and dropped us off at the Garden (while they went to visit some friends of their's outside of Bean Town until it was time to gather us up again).

My friend and I had no drugs for this momentous occasion (sigh, weep, weep etc). We got fairly good seats only a couple rows up from the main floor and right in the middle with the stage straight ahead. I was studiously wearing my White Panther Party buttons, one of which was a "Free John Sinclair" button and all of which I had received from the WPP by writing to the address on the inside cover of the MC5's LP *Kick Out the Jams*. The out-in-the-open smoking of pot, which was going on all around us, made our little 14-year-old heads spin. Nobody of course passed any our way though, possibly because we looked too young.

I had come to see the MC5, who were the first of the kick-off bands, second being Mr. Winter whom I also liked, then of course the main attraction for most, Led Zeppelin, whose first album was the only one that had been released at the time. As we were waiting for the show to start we couldn't help but notice the group of bikers in the last couple rows of floor seats directly in front of us, all wearing their colours. Memory doesn't serve me as to what club it was, but it was not the Hell's Angels as stated in the *Boston Herald Tribune* a day or so later (see clipping below).

The MC5 finally came out and kicked out the jams with a loud and fast sound that got you moving. Rob Tyner, with characteristically permed Afro, was bouncing all over the stage to the boogie beat! My friend had brought a small Brownie Instamatic-type camera along, and was taking some photos (which I never saw and don't even know if any ever came out). We were both MC5 fans, but me more so than him. I got their first album after hearing it at another friend's house. The copy I had heard belonged to my friend's older brother, and it had the infamous "motherfucker" line uncensored. By the time I bought my copy, the line had been changed to "brothers and sisters". I also heard you could steam off the inside fold-out sleeve where the original liner notes had been pasted over and censored — which I promptly did. Lo and Behold! It was true and it worked! Not only did I become a member of The White Panther Party (at 14), but also subscribed to the *Ann Arbor Argus* which was the local underground paper from Michigan and mouth organ for the WPP and MC5.

During the MC5's set they "passed the hat" so to speak, for the John Sinclair Legal Defence Fund and the WPP in general, while playing their "Pledge Song" that can be heard on the *Power Trip* CD. They also played songs from their up-coming LP *Back In the USA*. I was a happy camper! They could have played Johnny's and Led Zep's sets as well and it would still have been fine by me.

Between sets we went to the concession stand for drinks or whatever and while milling around with my WPP buttons proudly on display, some kid, maybe a year or two older than me, came up and asked me accusingly where I had gotten the buttons!?! Like I wasn't supposed to have them without his approval. I simply explained that I had written to the address on the inside of the album jacket — not unlike many others I'm sure. He did an "Oh yeah, forgot about that possibility"-type thing and wandered off.

Back in our seats, Johnny Winter eventually made his entrance and proceeded to amaze one and all by bending some incredible strings — Rock'n'Roll hoochie koo! Sometime in the middle of his set, cops showed up for a friendly chat with the bikers sitting in front of us. The bikers didn't find their chat too friendly because a fight broke out between the two. Before we knew it, it had turned into a brawl for everybody concerned. House lights were turned on, but Johnny's guitar kept a-wailing through it all without missing a note, which was a good thing, because it helped keep the situation from getting completely out of control. People were throwing things, a couple rows of seats had been over-turned, and we thought the whole thing was going to end up where we were sitting — too close for comfort. One biker, who had a leg in a cast and was on wooden crutches, used a crutch to bash a cop over the head! After maybe five minutes of chaos and violence, the cops eventually won through, thanks to reinforcements, and the offending parties were arrested and led off in handcuffs to assorted cheers and booing (more booing than cheers). Things settled down. There were some pools of blood on the floor which were promptly covered with sawdust. Johnny finished up to much deserved applause, and we collectively awaited Led Zeppelin.

When Led Zep finally took the stage, everybody was on their feet. Kicking it off with "Good Times Bad Times" and "Communication Breakdown" I was easily converted from "vaguely interested" to Zep fan. Robert Plant with his trademark hip-hugging, ball-busting bell bottoms singing the ever lovin' blues; Jimmy Page wearing a white suit acoustically rendering "White Summer/Black Mountain Side" centre stage, got everybody appropriately cosmic. Strangely enough, the low point of the concert for me was Bonham's "Moby Dick" which was overly long, being a good 20 minutes at least. I say "strangely enough" because I was also a drummer at the time. Nevertheless, I thought "enough already" after the first 10 or so minutes! They did a mixture of tunes from the first two albums, the second being as yet unheard by

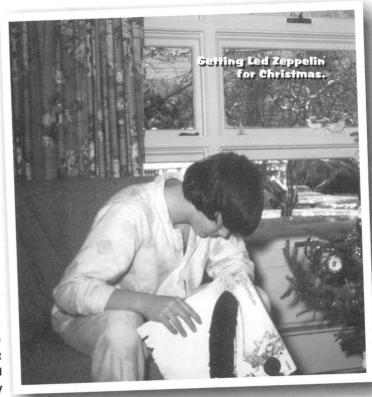

Getting Led Zeppelin for Christmas.

the audience — it was being sold at the concert that night but was not yet in the stores. My friend bought one that night. I held off until a week or two later when it came out in the stores, and then also received the first Zep album for Christmas that year (see photo).

As Zeppelin were wrapping it up (probably with "How Many More Times/The Hunter"), my friend dropped his camera onto the main floor and we went down to get it, also getting closer to the exit so as to avoid the crush. Many had the same idea and we had the good fortune to find ourselves standing behind a group of young ladies who were not much older than us, beside themselves with almost masturbatory excitement, squirming to the tunes and cooing in delight! This being a most memorable and educational moment of the Led Zeppelin concert to my 14-year-old mind and hormones (not surprisingly a virgin at that stage of the game). We left when it was over, found Mom and Dad, and went home with our memories... and our Rock'n'Roll concert-going veils torn asunder! All this and no "Stairway To Heaven"! I never saw Zeppelin again, unfortunately.

● ●

HOUSES OF THE HOMOS? As to whether Robert Plant religiously let Jimmy Page screw his whisky-soaked British butthole after which Plant licked his own poo-poo off Jimbo's hot dog so as to thoroughly coat his throat and thus confidently hit all those 'god-like' high notes... as to whether dead drummer John "Bonzo" Bonham's mania with racing cars was, in fact, connected to a deep-rooted childhood obsession with fondling the heads and shafts of stick shifts... as to whether fat-fuck-of-a-manager Peter Grant exploded his heart whilst desperately trying to locate his willie beneath his beached-whale's belly so that he could sodomise *just one more* Pakistani midget... as to whether Robert, Jimmy, and Bonzo all had the hots for the Swan Song archangel because of that same mascot's oh-so-"gay"-in-a-Romanesque-sense physique... as to whether Page wanted to meet William Burroughs to tell him how much he "weely, weely" enjoyed all the naughty bits on anal mucous and ass washing in *Naked Lunch*... as to whether the Zep logo was derived from an airship-like turd which Bonzo slurped out of his male nurse brother-in-law's kah-kah cave whilst felching his own jizz from the same queen's backside... as to whether the supposed bulge in Robert Plant's pants was really a double-headed, two-foot-long dildo starting from his crotch area and ending deep inside his black custard pie hole... as to whether Bonzo died when Peter Grant sat and farted on his face, thus making the drunken drummer gasp, puke, and drown on his own regurgitated chunks... and, all in all, as to whether or not Led Zeppelin are latent homosexuals, i.e. faggots, queers, cowboys, dolls, turd burglars, butt boys, circle jerk-offs, and the rest... well, who friggin' knows, mates? Guess we'll just have to wait and see it on the *Jerry Springer Show*, eh? **Anthony Petkovich**

LED ZEPPELIN

VS

IRON BUTTERFLY

G.J.BASSETT

Why even bother comparing two old hippie rock bands? Well, since Headpress was looking for pieces about Zep, I sensed there was something to be learned here. First off, both bands (Led Zeppelin and Iron Butterfly) had lousy names. Both bands' signature songs ('Stairway To Heaven', 'In-A-Gadda-Da-Vida') are part of our collective consciousness. Question is, why are these songs so famous?… or infamous, as ultimately seen in the case of Iron Butterfly (IB). Let me tell you, if I was locked in a room and forced to listen to one of those songs over and over again — say for two days — I pray it would be 'Gadda'. At least with that one you could trance out and maybe hardly *hear* it at some point. Not so with 'Heaven'. Why? Because Zep tries being 'complex,' tries building a musical (mystical?) 'bridge' or something with lyrics which after a while, would drive you insane they're so pretentiously indecipherable. And if the words didn't, Plant's vocals surely would. That voice is simply dreadful. I challenge anyone to come up with worse. Strangely enough, that awful voice inspired a million bean boys to imitate and form Zep-like bands. And somebody should be held responsible. At the other end of the spectrum, the vocalist for Iron Butterfly hardly had a *great* voice, but it's tolerable, sort of like a lesser-known Tom Jones. He stays within his range and it grows on you, whereas Plant's becomes more aggravating with each listen.

But let's go back a piece…

The first time I heard Zep I was beginning to experiment with LSD. They were touted as the next big thing, so I took another tab, lit up, and put the record on the turntable. Even back then I remember thinking, "There's something *wrong* with this guy's vocals." Page I knew was from the Yardbirds, an exceptional rock and roll band. But even the music of Zep sounded wrong somehow. And when it *did* sound okay, in came that most annoying of vocals to ruin it. Why did he *always* have to be singing? Then there was the guitar. More notes than are ever needed in rock and roll; some nice riffs here and there, but then Page would simply go over-board. And, again, this spawned an endless amount of pimple-faced lads to get electric guitars and learn to overplay them. Even to-day, just walk into any music store and there's some moron sitting there 'trying out a guitar', playing

75

IN-A-GADDA-DA-VIDA
From 12" L.P. "Iron Butterfly-In-A-Gadda-Da-Vida"
(S)AL-33,002
(D. Ingle)

ATLANTIC

AK-2498
MX28097
(6606)
(2.52)

COPYRIGHT
CONTROL

IRON BUTTERFLY
Produced by Jim Hilton
A Green & Stone Production
for York/Pala

Growin' Up!

CRAWDADDY

Exclusive Contributions by

JOHN LENNON, ERICA JONG, MUHAMMAD ALI

Studs Terkel, Souther, Hillman AND Furay, Steve Garvey,
Loudon Wainwright III, I.F. Stone, Rodney Dangerfield
and many, many more!

Led Zeppelin,
Jimmy Page & Rock Magic
by William Burroughs

Page and Burroughs, *Crawdaddy* June 75.
Courtesy: Tom Brinkmann

endless 'Page-like' notes to the point you want to spray guitar polish in his eyes and strangle him with a cord. They should have taken all of Page's strings away from him except for the low E. Plant simply should have had his vocal cords removed and made do with a voice box hooked up to a synthesiser. But listen to the guitar in IB. Psychedelic yet simple. He (Erik Brann) gets down occasionally Blue Cheer-style but doesn't get carried away with himself. He just plays the tune. But in the spirit of fairness, I decided to shop and compare.

For 'research' I purchased the first Zep and the first (?) IB... did they do more albums? Turns out they did; Gadda was actually their second LP, but nobody had ever heard the first one, so I didn't consider it relevant. Now, if I ruled the world, bands would actually only be *allowed* to do one album, one tour, and *no* reunions... ever! True, we would miss out on a couple of great albums (**The Stones'** Satanic Majesty's Request **and The Bee Gee's** Saturday Night Fever **come to mind) but think of all the boring repetitive ones we'd never be subjected to! It's interesting (I guess) that neither group's signature song is a first effort. Also that both songs deal with spiritual issues (Heaven and the Garden of Eden*).**

First, I played side one of Led Zeppelin. Oh brother, that voice is even more irritating than I remember it. And every time the music starts to sound okay, in comes that strangled ostrich squawk to ruin it. Page, as if sensing the horror of it all, overplays to mangle it even more. I forced myself to listen to the whole side and just couldn't wait to play side one of IB. Now, on side one of In-A-Gadda-Da-Vida (album title same as signature song) what immediately comes over the speakers is a richer, far more interesting sound... mind bending yet with an edge. Most people I talked to didn't even know IB had written songs other than 'Gadda'. The first tune on side one is 'Most Anything You Want'. It has a groovy feeling to it, embellished by a druggie, fuzzed-out guitar that's short and sweet. A rinky dink organ plays alongside adding an almost subliminal insanity. The background vocals give it a real upbeat feel. Next is 'Flowers and Beads', which continues with the whole groovy thing, but, let's face it, that was a big part of the band's vibe. This tune, however, has a pop-nostalgia thing going for it, a feeling of perhaps a first summer love. But what's most unique about the song is the group's first hints of actually being a lounge act. 'My Mirage' — a personal favourite — gets heavy, even moves into an eerie funk mood. The words and pacing sound like the singer might lose it at any second as he sings about drawing a mirage on a wall. It drifts off, remote, then comes back to the cool funk, quite unlike the pompous, practised blues rock of Zep. IB's lead vocalist (Doug Ingle) croons on about 'beautiful people' coming over to his house and seeing the mirage which he's going to paint on his wall. And I guess he's talking *to* the mirage! There's even a hint of a Tiny Tim-like falsetto. Wacky and great.

* Editor's note: This may be worth pointing out, as it wasn't very apparent to me until very recently, but 'In-A-Gadda-Da-Vidda' is actually 'In The Garden Of Eden' in baby-talk.

'Termination' is up next, and at first it seems a throwaway, but everybody does at least one bad song, right? And on repeated listening, 'Termination' works okay with the rest of the album, even gets trippy with hippie chimes (or something) at the end. And the song actually makes me chuckle, something Zep could never do. 'Are You Happy?' solidly ends side one with some fun, laid-back vocals incon-

Led Zep's Physical Graffiti **album and an entire run of** Headpress. **These are "a few of my favourite things", says regular reader André Huckvale.**

gruously accompanied by raunchy (but not bombastic) lead guitar.

Onwards — side two of Zep. 'Good Times Bad Times' is pretty *good*, in spite of everything, but by the same token any band does at least *one* good song. And just when I'm liking the tune — man, oh, man — in comes that high, annoying voice once again sabotaging everything else. Plant sings normal at the beginning. Check it out. I don't know, maybe it's not even him singing. Maybe it's Marlon Brando. Whatever. The rest of Zep 1/side two is sorry, poseur blues rock crappola. Just listen to the end of 'Shake Me'. Plant's voice and Page's guitar are a flat-out abomination. And it continues, the mirroring between the guitar and voice reaching new levels of tediousness. They obviously thought they'd discovered some 'wonderful' thing — and they just kept doing it!… even when it obviously doesn't work for them anymore.

Okay, it was now time for the big 'Gadda'. My whole theory would be proven or discounted on listening to the song that is perhaps the Sixties' 'Louie Louie' (except for the glaring difference that it was *never* covered). From the first note it's obvious to me that this thing is too big to even decipher, you know who and what it is because the *presence* is so strong. A cool organ starts it off with a dreamy riff, quickly leading into the ultimate trance number (to this day, some listeners are still trapped in those trances). It reminds me of the Get Smart **episode where KAOS was trying to hypnotise youth with a psychedelic rock group. This was it!** Later in 'Gadda' (the song is 17 minutes 5 seconds long) the singer stops completely and everyone takes turns tripping out, conjuring up an acid-laced sex orgy. The dreaded drum solo turns out to be more of a trip beat thing. It's tight, almost slammin'! Has anyone sampled this?— it could be down with the beat for you hoochie mammas! Near the end, the sound gets spooky like a haunted house. This group sounded like it had fun. Then there's the acid freakout and it ends. No posing… and *no* harmonica! The group was a weird cross between acid head and lounge act. Perhaps they were a lounge act that had discovered LSD? In the long run, IB are much more tolerable than Zep. One night at the local pizza parlour I was munching away and half listening to the 'rock classics' from the radio and there it was!… 'Heaven'. I listened and I listened, and I'm here to tell you that 'Gadda' blows it right out of the fucking Thames.

For further research I went to the book section of my local record store. Of course, there are *no* books on IB and way too many on Zep. I began to feel queasy thumbing through those glossy vanity affairs. At one point I picked up a small Zep bio filled with quotes from the band. In it I read that one of the members says the reason Zep "does it" is because of the rush they get from playing to large audiences. Another member admits to never listening to any other "heavy" groups… just Zep; he prefers more "mellow music." Wait a minute, these are quotes from the band that inspired a drooling, religious–like following? There's just nothing there. Dead and empty as a radioactive arena. I considered renting the Zep film but decided I'd already subjected myself to more than enough torture.

'Gadda' became so big it was later considered a joke, but most modern-day groups could learn a lesson or two here. Punk, if anything, was a reaction against groups like Zep, and any of the trendy 'alternative' bands that have pointed to them as an influence should be re-evaluated immediately. It was somewhat interesting that Page was into old Aleister Crowley, so perhaps Plant's nauseating voice was the result of some occult ritual gone amok.

A few years ago I was walking downtown and passing the Virgin Megastore, when I looked up in horror to see a giant blow-up of the reunion of Plant and Page. The hair, the clothes… they looked exactly the same! Except for puffy, wrinkled faces.

One good thing, however, did come out of Zep. Recently a friend gave me a tape entitled *Elevator Rock* and on it was a killer Muzak version of 'Heaven'; no vocals and no overplayed guitar. Brilliant!

> **Got any Led Zeppelin theories of your own? Seen them in concert? We want to know! Write to MOBY DICK at Headpress, 40 Rossall Ave, Radcliffe, Manchester, M26 1JD, UK**

SUBSCRIBE

WANTED
More Readers Like

Rondo Hatton

Some BACK ISSUES are still available

No 1 @ £10.00*
No 9–11 @ £3.50
No 12 @ £3.75
No 13, 15–17 @ £4.95

P&P per copy: UK £0.55
Europe £1.50
*Very limited—may be some damage to cover

the forefront of transgressive publishing *says* SPEAK

A subscription to **HEADPRESS** costs just £16 inclusive of p&p (Europe add £2/elsewhere add £4), which gets you the next two 144 page editions. Not only is that a saving on the cover price, but it also entitles you to further cost-saving benefits — take a look at page 89 for details. So, what are you waiting for?

Payable: 'Headpress.' Headpress, 40 Rossall Ave., Radcliffe, Manchester, M26 1JD, UK

All lined up for *Beat Girl*: Oliver Reed (**far left**), Gillian Hills (**second from right**), and Adam Faith (**right**).

THE MONOCHROME SEX

TWO SENSUAL BLACK AND WHITE ACTRESSES

MARTIN JONES

We all do it. Quite a few people might like to think they don't, out of some bizarre sense of decency. They'd be wrong. Everyone leches. Like a politically-correct student who under the influence of alcohol gradually loses his moral veneer, lecherousness rears its salivating head at the oddest of times. On the sly or full-blown eyes-a-poppin', it comes naturally. This is where cinema is a 'viking'.

The motion picture is the lazy procurer of physical attraction. If you admire a certain actor, it's usually because of an exemplary example of their work, or the fact that you fancy them; rather, you find a character they play attractive, because film stars in reality are generally not very interesting people: dullness gets mistaken for charisma, outspoken views for intelligence. Mainstream film magazines, when not trying to live vicarious hard lives through the writing, constantly disappoint the cinema-going public by allowing actors to speak their minds. Example: how many punters felt a surge of lust and — yes — even love for Sandra Bullock after watching her cute frame and cynicism-melting features act their way through *Demolition Man* and *Speed*, only to have this unreciprocated attention blown away by reading any interview with the actress, where she'd spew out her winsome, family-circle, ordinary-doll philosophy? Film audiences take on a dilemma similar to Lord Henry Wotton observing Dorian Gray: enjoying the artistic creation but unaware that the real thing is rotting away behind closed doors. Or babbling away; not for nothing does Jeff Goldblum, in *The Tall Guy*, define insanity as "anyone who is female, and has appeared on the stage".

79

Anjanette Comer as funeral cosmetician Aimée Thanatogenos, in *The Loved One*.

The players in black and white films no longer encounter this problem. Their lives are patchworks of hearsay, padded memoirs, testimonials from bitter relatives and spouses and, occasionally, a single memorable role: Joan Greenwood in *The Man in the White Suit*, Agnes Moorehead in *The Magnificent Ambersons* and hell, even Anne Heywood in *Floods of Fear*. Their co-stars (Alec Guinness, Joseph Cotten and Howard Keel respectively) are more well-known, but these actresses retain a lasting sensuality that has no need for a publicist's persuasive words. Sometimes unwilling to reveal more than an ankle (though Heywood does look fetching in a wet T-shirt), the slightest gesture of these black and white beauties speaks volumes more than Sharon Stone flashing her pussy.

In the times when producers were quick enough to exploit any subject in an instant, bad or just plain dull films were brightened up considerably by the appearance of a striking actress. This is the case with *The Loved One* and *Beat Girl*. Both are pretty much dog-eggs, unable to withstand repeated viewings, but are redeemed somewhat by sexy monochrome casting.

The Loved One, a 1965 American film based on Evelyn Waugh's novel of Brits and funeral parlours in post-war Los Angeles, seems to have lost something on its travels to the big screen. Actually, it's lost a lot. The promotional poster promises a *Here We Go Round the Mulberry Bush*-style farce, so the subtle, acidic fun of Waugh's book doesn't exactly translate well in the screenplay, where chunks of what seem to be rejected *Dr Strangelove* scenes are thrown about carelessly (the co-scripter was Terry Southern). What is unmistakable in both book and film, however, is the heroine of *The Loved One*: funeral cosmetician Aimée Thanatogenos. Arriving at her place of work — Whispering Glades — to make arrangements for the burial of his uncle, Dennis Barlow instantly sets her apart from the other employees:

> Her hair was dark and straight, her brows wide, her skin transparent and untarnished by the sun. Her lips were artificially tinctured, no doubt, but not coated like her sisters' and clogged in all their delicate pores with crimson grease; they seemed to promise instead an unmeasured range of sensual converse. Her full face was oval, her profile pure and classical and light. Her eyes greenish and remote, with a rich glint of lunacy.[1]

Her first appearance in the film is no less arresting. Played by Anjanette Comer, Waugh's description of Aimée comes vividly to life: a svelte creature beneath a white medical dress, her black hair piled up, pool-like eyes and a wide smile, effortlessly fitting the bill. Aimée is too much of a prize to ever be tarnished by Dennis Barlow's semi-decent affections; she has dedicated herself to her craft, and conceals a longing for Senior Mortician Mr Joyboy. The contrasts of Aimée's innocent view of the world — she watches, it seems, from behind the lilies — and her job are the main attractions for the viewer. Barlow may attempt to corrupt her, but he's no George Sanders: Aimée's morbid posture remains intact right up to the moment, appropriately enough, when she takes her own life.

This is a valid point regarding the attractiveness of Aimée/Anjanette: she appeals to the dodgy goth in us all. With those alluring monochrome features, Aimée is somewhere between Lily Munster and Morticia Addams, standing out in such a mediocre film like an erection at a funeral. As with lecherousness, closet gothicism is a lot more widespread than most would admit. Aimée glides her slight frame quietly through three-quarters of the film, and the patient audience is duly rewarded towards the end when she literally lets her hair down. Barlow visits Aimée at home — her house perched on the edge of a crumbling valley, filled with funeral baubles — to find her undergoing a strain of happiness, her fine black locks flowing around her pale visage. Her fragile naïveté, you realise to your anti-goth shame, the reason you find her so captivating. The gothic references are an appropriate full-stop when writing an appreciation of Aimée Thanatogenos. Venture any further and you topple into a Poppy Z Brite novel. Either that or — without wanting to dip into that whole necrophiliac bag of worms — female morticians are just plain sexy.

Aimée Thanatogenos

was born in literature and lived a life on screen. Jennifer Linden in *Beat Girl* (1960), as played by Gillian Hills, was born from some misguided youth culture only to land in a film that had its finger on the nub of British youth in the same way *Dracula AD 1972* did.[2] Jennifer resents her rich daddy remarrying, hangs out in the 'Off-Beat Café' with a bunch of prematurely aged teenagers, and has Mephistophelian dealings with a strip joint owner. Predictably, everything is tied up neatly in a moral ending. Although containing some items of cinematic interest,[3] *Beat Girl* would no doubt be categorised by some as 'so-bad-it's-good'. Fools. It's the kind of teen flick that sends one off in search of a stable domestic life.

And, like *The Loved One*, the only reason for repeated viewings is the female lead. Here it is Hills' portrayal of Jennifer, a blonde-maned delight of precocious teenage sexuality. With pouting lips, feline eyes and a succession of tight tops covering pointy breasts, the price Hills has to pay for her outstanding beauty and self-interest is to live in a world where alcohol is viewed as 'square', acoustic guitars are strummed without persecution and playing jazz records loudly is a sign of rebellion. All of which presumably is the late-1950s equivalent of smoking crack and nodding off to drum'n'bass. What Jennifer really needs is a good roll in the hay, but unfortunately her desire is a moody beatnik prick who unwisely thinks sex is 'square'.

The first time we see Jennifer she is descending a staircase, the title BEAT GIRL superimposed beneath her foxy black and white features. Dancing to shite jazz, her eyes roll back in their sockets as if she is under the influence of her first orgasm (at times her movements resemble one of Gerry Anderson's string puppets). Eventually, Jennifer's ultimate act of rebellion is an impromptu striptease at her father's house, though here the viewer is tricked: as a 'mature' teenager warbles a number called 'It's Legal' ("just think of the things we can do without even breaking the law"), a faceless body-double teasingly sheds her clothes. Hills was no doubt standing behind the cameras, concerned parents protecting the shrine that is her untouched adolescent form.

For all Jennifer's alluring qualities, *Beat Girl* builds up to a fake climax. Earlier, 'Exotic Strip Dancer' Pascaline performs a bump-and-grind more suited to a primitive Mondo movie than this tame teen pic, playing with a length of cloth as if it were a huge phallus. Saucy. As with Anjanette Comer in *The Loved One*, Gillian Hills' most revealing moment comes at the end of the film, when she rushes for the welcoming arms of her father, her hair down and unkempt after witnessing a murder, the one thing — apart from extensive sexual activity — that can break her precociousness.[4]

I've not seen Anjanette Comer in anything else apart from *The Loved One*. She must be in her fifties by now. Gillian Hills, it seems, followed a similar career path as that other embodiment of teenage lust, Linda Hayden; acting in art or horror films such as Georges Franju's *The Sin of Father Mouret* (1970) and Hammer's *Demons of the Mind* (1971), though I've seen neither. Actors suffer the fairly unique embarrasment of having their past mapped out and catalogued in moving pictures, which in turn can be subjected to a rigorous selection process. Comer and Hills, immaculate and sexy in black and white, may just as well have starred in one film each and no others. Both remain untouchable objects of celluloid lechery.

In James Ellroy's novel *White Jazz*, the protagonist Dave Klein, recalling his past, tells how he has shunned every TV show and movie featuring his ex-lover, a now-famous actress, preferring instead to remember her through photos taken on the last day they spent together in 1959. A courageous move, to keep that beauty firmly in monochrome, perfection remembered. But then there's still Kim Novak, Elsa Lanchester, Gene Tierney...

NOTES

1 Page 46 of the 1965 Penguin paperback.

2 Unsurprisingly, *Beat Girl*'s alternative title was *Wild For Kicks*. Let's face it, no film can ever fully represent the young because there are a lot of stubborn non-conforming nonconformists out there. You bastards.

3 This ain't *Sight and Sound* but, briefly, they are: John Barry's first film score, Adam Faith's 'acting' début, and great turns by Christopher Lee as the villainous strip club owner ("Well, somebody down there likes me") and Oliver Reed as a drunken (and so 'square') teenager. Also, the pretty explicit exotic dance led to *Beat Girl* being banned for some time, I believe.

4 I defy anyone with even a slight attraction towards Jennifer/ Gillian to watch *Beat Girl* and not think "she needs a good seeing to" within five minutes. There, just done it again. Whoever coined the phrase 'pause for thought' saved many a dirty-minded individual from social exile.

beautiful lettuce pages

write Headpress, 40 Rossall Avenue, Radcliffe, Manchester, M26 1JD, Great Britain
email david.headpress@zen.co.uk

One of the pubs near to me has strippers on the occasional Sunday afternoon, and I try to go to see them whenever I can come up with a convincing enough excuse for my wife. I was lucky enough to get to see a show this weekend and, having read the interview with the Dragon Ladies in HEADPRESS 17, I decided to try and make a mental note of what kind of music the strippers used in their act. First of all, only one of the two girls scheduled to appear actually turned up. The landlord announced prior to the show that the other girl wouldn't be appearing on account of her being in a car accident (at which point someone shouted out, "Are her tits OK?") and that her partner would have to do all three of the spots herself. Which she did. She came out first to a C&W song about a hat (she was wearing a cowboy hat and had a cap-gun which she fired off near her crotch). This was followed by the track 'Female of the Species' by Space. Unfortunately, the only other song I can remember her dancing to is the famous AOR track,

'I Wanna Know What Love Is' by Foreigner. I remember this because when the first few bars started, someone in the audience shouted excitedly "It's Foreigner!" I forgot to make any further musical notes after this (more pressing things on my mind, perhaps?).

Earl Jones (not my real name), Lancashire

The highlights of HEADPRESS 17 for me were the interview with Maxon Crumb, and the cultural insights and implications of the Pammy and Tommy video (which I have only seen stills from). The CRUMB movie in my opinion is a classic. I've been a fan of R's comix since I bought his HEADCOMIX when just a young lad. Also, I had the opportunity and privilege of hearing Robert and Harvey Kurtzman give a talk on underground comix in 1976 in NYC, after which the Cheapsuit Serenaders played. The brothers Crumb seem to have grown up in an almost hermetically sealed fantasy life as children, drawing these incredibly involved comics and stories, all

struggling with sexual angst of one kind or another. Whether you agree with him or not, Maxon has some interesting insights into the world around him. Charles, so talented at such an early age, seems to have degenerated into some form of graphic mental illness — *cacoethes scribendi* — filling notebooks with minute scribbling.

Tom Brinkmann, New York

Some rabid Crumb nut has probably already mentioned this, but there really was a BIG YUM YUM BOOK. [*Editor's note: In the Maxon Crumb interview, I questioned the existence of a Robert Crumb comic by the title of BIG YUM YUM BOOK to which Maxon referred.*] Crumb published it in the mid-Seventies. It had a reprint a few years ago, and it gets a couple of mentions in the new Fantagraphics Crumb letters collection. I've seen the reprint around (a pricey softcover), but I've never picked it up.

Anthony Thorne, Australia

Re: Jayne County. I remember the book MAN ENOUGH TO BE A WOMAN [*Culture Guide, HEADPRESS 17*] receiving some mention in the UK's glossy music mags when it was released, but I don't think it really set the world on fire. Were it not for the snip op., I doubt that he/she would be remembered at all. However, I do have a song by him/her called 'Eddie And Sheena' off some indie scene compilation from the late-Seventies. It's actually really good, a

83

punk Romeo and Juliet about Eddie the Teddy Boy and Sheena his punk girlfriend. It starts (and continues for most of its length) with a cheesy standard rock'n'roll guitar riff, as we learn of the respective ostracisms of Eddie and Sheena from their peer groups. Then the music cuts to virtually nothing and we discover:

Eddie and Sheena are married now, their friends can't understand / All the love and happiness they've gotten / Eddie is a daddy now, Sheena is a mum / And they named their little brat [music cuts out totally] [in a rockabilly drool] Eeeelvissss... [punk sneer] Rotten! [manic punk guitar] / Eddie is a teddy boy, Sheena is a punk...

Good stuff, to be sure. It's a novelty punk disc that Stewart Home doesn't mention in CRANKED UP REALLY HIGH, but then neither does he mention Jilted John or Splodgenessabounds, which seems like a big oversight.

Anton Black, Rugby

84 **W**hen Jack Sargeant isn't writing his diaries from America, what's he doing? Harass-

ing unsuspecting, semi-naked young ladies in the back of cars with pictures of his travels, that's what! If you don't believe me, take a look at this [*above*] I cut out of MENSWORLD...

Joseph L., Brighton

Here's a bizarre urban myth I heard when I was back at school, and so far I've yet to meet anyone else who has heard it (not that I recount the tale to everyone I meet). The era for the story is unknown. Picture the scene: The lonely Outback in Australia (though it could easily be America or Africa). Small communities of farmers with very little in the way of entertainment decide to go cow-fucking. Nothing new here, except they fuck the cows up the nose! This, the legend has it, was partly down to the moisture, but mainly because of the suction. Now, before you all go rushing out in search of the nearest heifer, there is a bizarre twist to the tale. Some men were found dead. How? Well, the lung power in the cows was so great that they were able to suck the men's innards out through the penis! Okay, it sounds insane, but hell, I had to share!

Kris, Mid Glam.

Surprise! Here comes an little letter to you, and it comes from Sweden, and a Swedish prison! Brinkeberg prison, which is an security prison, and it's located about 5 Swedish kilometres outside the city of Vänersborg. This letter has gone rather a

long way to reach you, so I hope that you will receive it safely! But, sometimes, those sadistic pigs that are working here stops and reads our outgoing mail, and for no reason at all, they can decide that the letter shall not be allowed to leave this prison. And then, those scumbags, tear the letter to pieces, and throws it in the trash-can, without letting us prisoners know anything about it! Shit! Let's hope that those retards can't understand English so good, otherwise I will be in big trouble!! Let me introduce myself: My name is Ulf Bågenhammar, and I am prisoner Nr: 98/487, into this completely fucked-up hellhole of a prison. I have been here for a very long time now, and I don't yet know when I shall be released from this place. But if I'm lucky, it will be next year, and if I'm not lucky, well, I don't wanna talk about it. Life is a bitch here but we prisoners stick together, in every way, and we are fighting daily harassments, and provocations from those sadistic pigs that are working here. But even if they can lock up our bodys, they can never lock up our souls, minds and thoughts. Never! And that's a fucking fact!

Ulf Bågenhammar, Vänersborg, Sweden

By the way, any more pictures of Chris M.'s wife???

Barney, London

Chris M.'s wife appeared in the letters pages of HEADPRESS 17, *wearing a silver UFO catsuit.*

She Ain't Heavy, She's Just Rubber

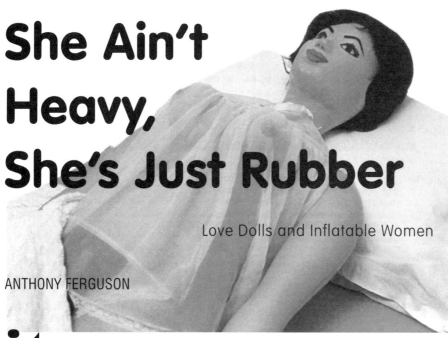

Love Dolls and Inflatable Women

ANTHONY FERGUSON

it was as a curious 11-year-old, nosing through my dad's personal belongings while the rest of the family were out, that I first encountered the saddo's ultimate plaything, that synthetic representation of the sexually available female known as the inflatable woman. There she was, on a full-page spread in some long forgotten 1970s jazz mag: Frieda the love machine, replete with filmy lingerie panties, and the pulsating pussy and pubic hair options.

Did you ever notice they never show you a picture of the actual product in those sleazy ads? Yeah, well there's a good reason. When I was a kiddie I was quite turned on by the concept of having a real life-like woman to commit sordid and depraved acts on. In my pre-juvenile imagination, I always thought the love doll would have the same texture, feel, and weight of a real life woman. That's kinda creepy when you think about it, thankfully I didn't grow up to be a necrophile.

Jump forward 10 years to my university days, and my roommates club together and actually buy me one of the things for my birthday. I was quite chuffed actually, the inflatables cost about $50 by that time, and that was some commitment just to play an undergraduate joke.

I was now the proud owner of my very own vinyl girlfriend — "Miss Elizabeth" we named her, after a popular valet in the World Wrestling Federation. All fake blonde hair and three working orifices (cue: crap gag about the busy executive love doll with three working offices). I must admit I was disappointed with the shoddiness of the actual product. A bloke would have to be really fucking lonely or a bit sick to shag one of these things, and I can assure you that it remained unused by the entire household for the two years of its existence, until the fateful day it went down (cue: that other crap love doll gag) with a puncture after some of us gave it a particularly heavy beating.

These days I reside in Canberra, not only the capital but also the sex capital of Australia. The only

85

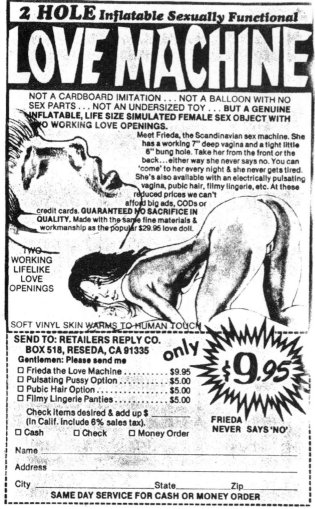

The ad that started it all, says Anthony.

State outside of the Northern Territory where X-rated videos, and certain other related paraphernalia, are freely available. Being interested in pornography and paraphilia in general — from a purely academic perspective, of course — I have taken the opportunity to examine the development of the love doll phenomenon. Do men really fuck these pathetic plastic balloons? I can only conclude that they must, judging by the number and variety of products available these days, as well as the cost.

In contemporary Australia, you can, for a mere $50–$100, purchase the vinyl girlfriend of your choice — white, Asian, or Afro-American. You can have a 'mature woman' inflatable if you're a granny-plucker, or a little 'teeny doll' if you like 'em young. You can buy a transsexual dolly if that's the way you swing, hell you can even have a pregnant blow-up doll if you're so inclined.

This, to me, suggests that the market for inflatables has not subsided over the years. So what's the attraction? Well I have a little theory I'd like to share with you.

Throughout the history of Western society, man has demonstrated a constant desire to conceptualise woman as a sexual ideal. This commodification of the female body is illustrated in areas like fashion and advertising in today's world, and also in women's magazines — particularly those aimed at young women — and, of course, in pornography. While I'm not suggesting that this is all part of some giant conspiracy to objectify every woman as a male fuck fantasy, I am suggesting that there are certain attitudes prevalent in our society which dominate and continually reproduce themselves through our discourse and literature.

It was in examining issues like fashion, advertising, and pornography that I began to consider notions of the ultimate subordinated female — one who is utterly voiceless, powerless, and continually available for masculine consumption. The two types of female which fit this idealised image are the prostitute and the inflatable woman. However, as even a prostitute is able to partake of the exchange of meanings, feelings, desires and needs (i.e., she can tell you to fuck off if she wants), I am left to hypothesise that the inflatable woman is the ultimate representation of subordinated female sexuality.

What I mean by this is that the love doll signifies an idealised vision of female sexuality, receptive and available, subordinate to masculine desire, totally silent and therefore devoid of any threat. Think of this concept in terms of Freud's notion of the vagina dentata — man's fear of castration by woman. Then take it a step further and consider the love doll not as what it consists of in a material sense — a manufactured piece of plastic in human form with specific orifices — but rather as what it signifies: woman in her most powerless, voiceless, commodified form.

Above An ad taken from *Police Detective* dated June 1971. What is that guy trying to say?!

Check out the type of advertising in wank mags which normally accompanies this type of product. Look at the language used to market the love doll — "sexually functional", "genuine", "realistic", "female sex object", "companion", "working love openings", "sex machine", "never says no", "never gets tired" — language which draws upon the myths of man's conception of the perfect woman. The love doll never has a headache, nor a period, it never gets pregnant, keeps its mouth shut, and doesn't nag you to take out the garbage. Then consider the visual images used to market the inflatable woman in your average skin mag or even on the box of the product itself. Notice that there's never a photograph or a drawing of the actual product? No, that's because if you saw what you were getting you wouldn't buy it. You'd walk out of the shop and check yourself in for some therapy instead. Alternatively, what you get visually is either a photograph of a model or a porn star the doll is supposedly modelled on, or in some cases an artist's impression of what the manufacturer would like the customer to think they are buying. I'll give you a clue, it looks nothing like the ridiculous blow-up balloon you're about to fork out the readies for.

Now let's have a look at the positioning of the doll in the artist's rendition. Perhaps it shows the product on its hands and knees, begging to be taken from behind. Ever tried to get an inflatable into the doggie position? Ever tried to get one to kneel down and gobble you? It can't be done. (Gee, maybe they're more lifelike than I thought!) The real inflatable product is of course only designed to perform in one set position, and to try and bend it any other way means that (*a*) you have to forcibly hold it down in that position, and (*b*) it looks bloody ridiculous.

Let me shed a bit of light on the situation. Your love dolly cannot put her legs behind her ears, she can't put her arms around you, she can't dig her nails into your back — she doesn't even have any goddamn nails — she won't whisper sweet nothings in your ear (unless you buy a soundtrack or something, and then you really are fucking sad), and she certainly isn't warm.

However, I digress. The actual set pose of the manufactured inflatable doll, with its supine position, and its open arms, legs and mouth, can be compared to the positioning of women in other forms of popular cultural reproduction, such as cinema and advertising.

87

LINDA LOVELIPS Code A103

Think of ads for chocolate bars and cars in particular. Once again, I draw a parallel between the positioning of the love doll and man's idealised vision of a woman's ultimate function. The love doll, with its open legs and completely silent yet sexually functioning mouth, is symbolically presented in a similar manner to real women in certain media images, in that both types are implicitly shown to be receptive and totally subordinate.

Take this thought a step further and you can also draw a parallel to the idea of women as objects of masculine consumption. Consider the sexual connotations associated with female make-up and dress: eye shadow and nail polish, suspender belts and stockings, high-heeled shoes, dark and aggressive colours. The symbols are many and various, but they all serve to sexually stereotype women as men would like them to be — carefully packaged products for our consumption. What could be better in that case, than to be able to pack a woman away into a cardboard box once we've satiated our needs.

So what I am saying in essence is that the promotion of sex aids such as the inflatable woman serve ultimately to perpetuate the masculine desire to reduce women to their most basic function, and thus ultimately replenish the myths which surround female (and indeed male) sexuality.

That's my theory. It has to be ideology at work. It can't *seriously* be that loads of blokes enjoy shagging bits of inflated plastic — can it?

COME INTO MY EVER-LOVING ARMS! LIFE SIZE INFLATABLE DOLL

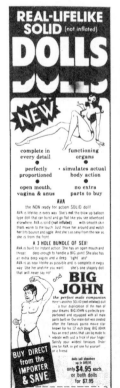

BUY BOOKS

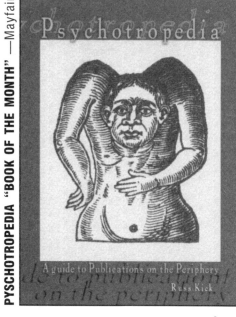

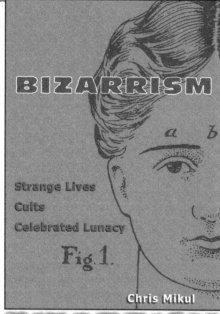

Psychotropedia

Russ Kick
576pp • £15.95 • ISBN 1900486032 • Illus.

BIZARRISM

Chris Mikul
160pp • £11.95 • ISBN 1900486067 • Illus.

Psychotropedia is the follow-up to Russ Kick's acclaimed book *Outposts*. A massive survey of publications that exist outside the mainstream, *Psychotropedia* provides detailed reviews (and ordering information) for a breath-taking cross-section of books, zines, catalogues, and other media...

Learn about the skills no one wants you to have: beating lie detectors, hacking cellular phones, and giving yourself oral sex... Get the inside stories on the Oklahoma City Bombing, sex work, cockfights, the Men in Black, breast implants, body modification, marijuana, Mother Teresa, Heaven's Gate, offshore money havens, suicide, free energy, juror nullification, bestiality, secrets of famous magicians, and suppressed treatments for cancer and AIDS... Discover the work of taboo-shattering artists and writers, like Andres Serrano, Annie Sprinkle, David Hamilton, Joel-Peter Witkin, Negativland, Diamanda Galas, Mike Diana, David Britton, and Elissa Wald... Unearth the scary facts about vaccines and fluoride.

Psychotropedia covers these and hundreds of other touchy and unorthodox topics.

"I am going because I would have no peace if I stayed."

So said Donald Crowhurst, 36-year-old owner of a small electronics firm in Somerset, as he set sail on an intended single-handed, non-stop, round-the-world boat voyage in a boat he himself had made. In the middle of the Sargasso Sea, his boat falling to pieces, he had an idea...

When Chris Mikul first heard the curious tale of Donald Crowhurst in the early 1980s, it inspired him to begin collating information and writing about other strange lives, eccentrics, and "beacons of shining if erratic brilliance in a world of sensible conformity". This book is the end result, a series of fascinating essays which chronicle a diverse spectrum of real people whose lives have been governed by inner voices, sexual aversions, bovver, interplanetary heroics, and UFO magazines.

From lesbian vampires and death cults, through to lobster boys and the anonymous pamphleteer of **DRUGS VIRUS GERMS**, *Bizarrism* has them all.

a death in the family

personal reminiscences of H.E.Sawyer

The first burial re-
corded in Christchurch
cemetery in the county
of Dorset was held in 1859. Or
so the senior gravedigger tells
me. The last, two days ago, was
my uncle Ken. The gravedigger
points out the plot, and returns
to prepare for a new incumbent,
who, at that point in time, is already lying cold on a slab some-
where local. I couldn't be more specific as to their actual whereabouts, which slab in which parlour,
because the thing with Christchurch that strikes me, is that there seems to be more undertakers
per capita, than anywhere else I can recall.

Christchurch is not the sort of place I'd wish to spend my autumnal years. There's too many
old people, and there's too many small white boats. But my uncle liked the place, and swotted up
on the local history to take his place with the natives. Early retirement saw him 'officially' join the
club and blend right in.

Now he's lying for eternity six foot under the mud and a frail line of floral tributes at my feet.
The earth, I note, is not soft and crumpled as is usual with a fresh grave. It's tight and compact. The
gravediggers have hammered the mud flat with the backs of their spades. They seem to be saying,
"When we bury you in Christchurch cemetery, you stay down. It's the Dorset way." The flowers look
pathetic, and I have to confess I don't know which 'tribute' is mine. None of them look anything like
the one I picked from the florist's brochure.

I was unable to attend in person, or rather I chose not to, in the knowledge that my father
would be there. While I believe we could have restricted our hostility to fatal glances within the
chapel, the possibility of open warfare either side of an open trench cut deep enough for one more
body, would have been more than tempting Fate. So I stayed away and sent flowers instead. The
desire, the delicious taste of malice, to address them to my father, 'in hope, expectation and eager
anticipation', knowing full well that he would read the card, was similar to my longing to fuck a
friend's wife, but in both cases I resisted. (Although I continue to fantasise about my friend's wife.)

Twenty-five quid on ritual and appeasement, and the sorry bunch is left with the rest to wither
and die. The sound of the wind whipping cellophane is all too familiar and depressing. The mourn-
ers are long gone. Only the flowers remain; "the last thing you give to someone," except
remembrances. But my uncle worked as a groundsman for county councils, and part of his work
involved planting out those elevated flower beds that formed pictures, such as those celebrating

the Queen's Silver Jubilee, or commemorating some anniversary of the Women's Institute. So in many ways, flowers were appropriate, even though the linear design, mirroring his permanent prone state, head to toe, was rather simplistic. Certainly by his standards.

I pause to reflect briefly. The truth of the matter is that we didn't see each other much. He was my mother's brother and had no children of his own. When I was growing up he used to give me pocket money when he saw me. Usually this was when he visited his mother for a cuppa after work. He'd sit on newspaper laid on the sofa, still wearing his overalls, and grin inanely with a sunny disposition, born out of a nervous breakdown, inherited from his days of National Service. Occasionally his mother would chastise him for buying her poor quality pork chops.

Other than blood, we had little in common. Different generations, outlooks, agendas. Isn't that the way with families? Would you have chosen the people you're related to? My uncle's father — my grandfather — was a bus driver, well respected and liked by his colleagues. He was dead before I was old enough to know him. Ken's mother — my grandmother — was a five foot two, hump backed Man O'War. She was the lucky twin that made it to adulthood. I know nothing of the one that died aged three, except for the influence she imposed on her sibling after her premature departure.

My grandmother, a true Cockney, the surviving twin (*did she feel guilty it wasn't her?*), seemed determined to ensure her own two children made it in the world at all costs. This passion manifested itself in an irrational hatred of anyone who thought they might be good enough to marry either of her children. On reflection, looking at my uncle's wife, and indeed my own father, she was spot on. The term "poor white trash" was unheard of back then, but I can easily imagine the tough old sparrow's diagnosis: that her son and daughter had both married "scum". When her daughter succumbed to tuberculosis aged 34, granny toughened up, from diamond hard to double diamond hard. And most of her facets were gnarled. The word 'cantankerous' springs to mind.

It's this that makes my grandmother 'interesting'. A staunch Socialist of the old school, she adored Tony Benn and at the end of the televised Labour Party conference, would be singing 'Red Flag Flying' with the rest of them.

Her pent-up aggression, fuelled by inefficient home help and regular trips to the chiropodist, spilled out big time on a Saturday. She started the weekly countdown to **Dallas** at 4 PM on the dot, because that's when Kent Walton would say, "Welcome grapple fans", and whisk us off to the Leas Cliff Hall in Folkestone, or somewhere in Croydon. Three televised bouts before the football results. And top of the bill would be something she could really get her teeth into: Rollerball Rocco, Mick McManus (*"he's spiteful, that McManus — That's it! Pull his ears! Pull his ears! Go on!"*) and Jackie Pallo (*"looks like a girl! Get your hair cut!"*). She was on the brink of sitting ringside herself, I swear, but it would only have resulted in a bloodbath, and the two doddery St John's Ambulance volunteers would never have coped. Granny would have won, not by the required falls, submission, or knockout, but by an accusing finger, hard as a knitting needle, followed up with *"a piece of my mind!"*

She applauded Big Daddy's belly splashes on some hapless, spread-eagled wrestler, already flat on the canvas, and although Daddy would always be there to 'right wrongs' in the ring, granny was a shrewd spectator. She knew that there wasn't anything special about dumping 33 stone of flab from a height onto some winded middle-aged geezer in a costume. Kendo Nagasaki and Jim Breaks might have been nasty and vicious, but they were both excellent technicians at their chosen craft. It just pleased her to see someone suffer. The pair of us sat there in the sitting room of her maisonette, week after week, glued to the hired black and white; granny mimicking every toehold and half nelson, me trying to convince her that Jim Breaks was *playing* a villain, and that he didn't walk down the street forcing innocent members of the public into two falls, two submissions or a knockout on a daily basis. But granny was happy ensconced in front of the wrestling like thousands of her generation. It was what they won the War for after all, and her face lit up every week when one of her 'nice lads' — Steve Gray, Dynamite Kid, Bert Royal — got a result, which was most weeks more often than not. 'Fixing' for granny, referred to the tea.

The wrestling on a Saturday afternoon. It's how I'll chose to remember her. That, the best home-made meat pies I've ever tasted, and the inheritance she left me. And the fact that I stole £12 from her when I was old enough to know better. (OK, so I repaid it. Is that 'theft' or a 'surreptitious loan'?) And the vivid image of watching her die, a frail figure in a dingy hospital ward with high walls, under dull artificial light; flecks of spittle on the inside of her respirator, mirroring the dashing rain on the grey windows that looked out onto the world below. I cried, cried again, cried some more, and when I was exhausted, fled the hospital for the sanctuary of Crow Lane cemetery, to get soaked to the skin and contemplate mortality amongst the headstones, with only the Romford gas holders for company. That's the thing about dealing with bereavement at an early age. You think you understand, hence you've got it licked. How foolish of me. How naïve. It was 1981. Fifteen years into my future, I would understand the true meaning of Grief. But back then it all seemed plain and simple. Granny had gone and I was alone.

And now I'm standing over the grave of her dead, kind, dopey son, miles away. I look around. I'm still alone.

*a*unt Pauline's bungalow rests a stone's throw from the perimeter wall of the cemetery. She's always been a large woman, and so now she is a large widow, and won't have far to go when her time comes. She reclines on a couch with feet up like a Roman, although there the analogy abruptly ends. Two fatherless mongrels bark incessantly, and her 'companion', Jean, sits stuffed in an old armchair in front of the sofa, like a pilot waiting for clearance. Neither of them are going anywhere, other than Heaven. It would've been a great splash for the **News of the World**. A childless couple, married 30 years, living with two moth-eaten dogs

and a 'third party', who seemed to be there for no good reason, other than to assist in the relentless bullying of my uncle. *"Turn that sport off! No one wants to watch that!"*

Jean sits there, rarely making eye contact. I resist the temptation to ask her if she 'hasn't got a home to go to?' Her function now is to replace the deceased gofer, and confirm everything auntie Pauline says. She's very good at both. She shuffles off to the kitchen and returns with tea and cake. In her absence, I notice there's a hole cut in the cushion of her chair, pretty much where her anus must rest. The extracted foam is shaped for a receptacle of some description. I notice this, but decide not to mention it. It would be impolite. Auntie's talking. And furthermore, I don't think I really want to know.

"I said to Clive — that's our minister, at our church — I want a service of Witness!"

It's a statement vehemently punctuated by a stiff finger and hard piggy eyes in my direction. I flinch. Her voice cuts through the stale air. I badly want to light up a Marlboro and try to purify it. A film of *yuk!* clings to everything. (I haven't taken my coat off. The good thing about PU is that you can wipe it down.)

"I may look like I'm holding on, but inside I'm a heartbeat from tears, aren't I Jean?"

Jean murmurs in agreement, eyes still fixed to a patch of discoloured carpet. I deliberately, defiantly, hold eye contact with Buddha, inwardly smiling at the irony of this comparison. If auntie Pauline were a mind reader, I'd be tortured in eternal Hell-fire for my thoughts of blasphemy. The cinema screen inside my forehead projects the words 'Our Lord', in big red neon. It fizzes and crackles in the dark, and I cast my mind back to Tokyo for a nano second.

"But he's with Our Lord now. I know he is!"

The third sprig of blood red cherries drop into place to complete the line. There's the sound of change pouring into the win tray. It wasn't much of a gamble to be fair. There are no family photographs in evidence in the sitting room, or elsewhere in the property. The pictures are split between 'Our Lord', and the actor Richard Chamberlain, he of **The Thorn Birds** fame. We're talking Cathy Bates in **Misery** here, make no mistake. 'Our Lord' comes out best numerically in the pictorial stakes, although Richard *is* in prime position on top of the tele, and his photos *are* signed. He also walks on water in the video department. Everything he's ever done is there. Except, I'll wager, the film including the nude wrestling scene with Oliver Reed. I don't point this out. In retrospect, this is

93

a wise move, because I later learn that Alan Bates, *not* Richard Chamberlain, wrestled with Reed in front of the fire in **Women in Love**. Still, I console myself that Chamberlain drank alcohol like water in **The Towering Inferno**, and kicked weaker men (the 'Man from Uncle' included) off the Boson's Chair in his futile attempt to escape the fire in the sky.

"I know he's walking with Our Lord in heaven!"

The reiteration of the point merely reinforces the doubt. She even asked Clive what would happen if Ken wasn't Christian? I have to ask why they didn't ask Ken while he were alive? They did, but my uncle was always evasive. "Very evasive" adds Jean accusingly. It's not her husband's faith that's on trial here. She can afford to be sceptical. My aunt has to be adamant for both of them. Pauline was Born Again when she met my uncle, and even when they were courting, she, to her credit, tried to persuade him to find someone else, on the grounds that she was devout, un-touched, and (I suspect), had no intention of having it any other way. But Ken was in love with her. They went to see Billy Graham at one of the early conventions, and when Billy reached out for 'that one last person in the audience who wishes to give himself to God', it was my uncle Ken who stood up to be counted.

Having the story related to me now, I'm struck not by Billy Graham's staged theatricals, but by the decisive action of a meek and gentle man seizing the opportunity to catch his bride-to-be. He never went to church after they were wed, and my aunt got terribly upset when he repeatedly took the Lord's name in vain, but I look back on his moment of tactical brilliance and lateral thinking, and can only applaud. The centrepiece of their wedding cake, a hideous lattice chapel with spire that I've hated since the first time I saw it, sits in the glass cabinet along with the other nick-nacks comprising auntie Pauline's 'best things'. The lattice chapel is a testament to 30 years of marriage. I long to resurrect my uncle for the sole purpose of asking him if he really faked his conversion, and if he regrets it. Does he know that when his widow expires, she's going on top of him, not side by side? (Christ knows where Jean is going! I don't ask, I don't want to know. Perhaps she'll slide into that hole cut in her cushion?) But Pauline's mortal remains will lie with Ken's and that's a given. Rather him than me of course. I happen to agree with granny.

"When Clive asked about children I told him I wasn't frightened of having children, I was terrified. I always was terrified, wasn't I Jean?"

Appropriate murmur. I think back to an earlier diatribe concerning flying to Australia. On that occasion, the Lord had spoken to Pauline (she was in the bathroom at the time), telling her that He was with her, and that she would go, "to the land of your dreams." And so it came to pass, and she flew (in a plane!), and duly visited the sets of **Neighbours**, **Home & Away** (twice), and vari-ous locations used for **The Thorn Birds**. I don't think the Lord encouraged her to visit these places, which one might reasonably associate with worshipping craven images, but it's evident that The Lord works in mysterious ways. He gets a fly-o-phobic on a long haul to Oz, but isn't too hot on reassurance with childbirth. I guess it depends what you ask for. Granny always said that Pauline didn't want kids be-cause it would "ruin her figure". Granny viewed her daughter-in-law's excuse re: childbirth with utter contempt, and with-out putting too fine a point on it, auntie had the figure of a ruined abbey anyway. But I don't point any of this out either.

I'm on the back foot, ready and waiting. Pauline is going for soul conversion. She's winding herself up, lean-ing on her elbow, the well-rehearsed words

tumbling out of her mouth. She tells me how there are no seas in Heaven, just a river running through lush pasture, where the same tree produces 22 varieties of fruit. I sit incredulous with wonder. I wonder — where has all this *bollocks* has come from? Who *on earth* made this up?! I wonder how faith got so twisted and elaborate and customised, and whose purpose does this serve? Leave the Bible as it is (I like the incest in the Old Testament, and that the God that dwells within its pages has unlimited wrath when it comes to retribution). If Christ came back he'd be crucified by those whose particular brand of Christianity he didn't subscribe to. The dog at auntie's feet looks at me with sympathy, then resignation, and endeavours to get some shut-eye. I'm a dog lover. If I had a gun and a permit, I'd do the decent thing and put it down.

"Because it doesn't matter how good you are as a person, I used to say this to Ken, didn't I Jean? — [grunt] *— you can be the best person in the world, but if you don't let The Lord into your life, if you don't except Him, you won't be with Him in Heaven. You'll go to the other place. And when you are judged, and you will be, you cannot say, 'I did not know,' because I am telling you now. And The Lord may only call you once or twice, and if you don't say, 'Yes Lord, I give my life to you,' then that's it!"*

I'm doomed. My lurid past, unhealthy interests and nasty habits flicker before me. Best to let them down gently.

"So if you were best person in the world, but you didn't believe, you'd still go to Hell? That doesn't sound like a very kind God to me. Anyway — I think he's passed me by."

Auntie looks upset over the rim of my stone cold tea cup.

"Well then I'm very sorry, but you won't be with me, and Jean, and your uncle Ken in Heaven."

Family. I look out the window, past my shallow reflection, at the cul-de-sac. Bands are playing, Brian Lara's middle stump cartwheels away, ticker-tape rains down from a cloudless sky. I'm shagging Nici Stirling senseless; Debi Diamond, spread panting on the bonnet of my gleaming Ferrari, waits her turn. To cap it all, Noel Edmonds lies in a twisted broken heap under the wheels. Bliss.

genre fandom and underground film culture in Britain

"... at the end of the day anybody who wants to watch anything from TEXAS CHAIN SAW MASSACRE through to FACES OF DEATH can get hold of a copy just like that, you know. It's not a problem getting hold of a film..."

— A Fan

SHAUN KIMBER

Over the course of the past three years I have been conducting research into underground film culture in Britain. The following article about the dynamics of genre fandom and the underground genre scene is based upon the preliminary and ongoing analysis of 30 interviews and numerous correspondences with editors of underground film magazines and fans of genre film. Within the context of my research, genre film has been taken to refer to horror, thriller, science fiction, action movies and any other sub-genres that rely heavily on violence within their narrative structure, i.e. Stalk-and-Slash or Teens-in-Peril movies. The samples of editors and fans who helped me during my research were recruited using several strategies including: writing directly to editors, personal contacts, handing out flyers at major fan events and advertising in various genre related publications including *Headpress* (No 16).

The first thing to mention about genre fandom is that genre fans are not recognisable as a single homogeneous group. Rather, people who are attracted to the genre come in lots of shapes and sizes. Therefore, in many ways genre fandom represents a microcosm of wider society, except in one important way: most, though not all, genre fans seem to be men. What's more, genre fandom is not a fixed phenomena, rather it is fluid, and changes with fans becoming more or less involved depending on their particular circumstances. For example, most of the fans and editors interviewed during the course of the research spoke of the way in which genre fandom develops, from being interested in gore and obsessed with issues surrounding film cuts and censorship in the early stages, to becoming more laid-back about issues of censorship in the later stages. Moreover, several fans suggested that, as their interest in the genre develops, they become less concerned with the obvious blood and guts of genre (though they would not consider themselves above such pleasures) in favour of analysing the different sub-textual, inter-textual and thematic levels upon which genre films can operate. Genre fandom in Britain was also seen as being distinctive in so much as it was fundamentally different from genre fandom Stateside or in Europe. This is primarily because of Britain's particular history of strict regulatory measures against the viewing of sex and violence. The most notable recent examples of this are the Video Recordings Act (1984), the 1994 Amendment to the Criminal Justice Bill and current

96

government intervention by the Home Secretary Jack Straw to prevent the continued liberalisation of the R18 certificate by the British Board of Film Classification (BBFC).

Genre fandom in Britain is multi-layered and stratified by cross-cutting cleavages. One major cleavage revolves around the 1984 Video Recordings Act (VRA), in that there tends to be a clear distinction between fans who became interested in the genre before the Act's implementation, and those whose interest developed after its inception. Pre-VRA fans tend to be in their late-20s, or older, and got into genre film in the halcyon pre-cert days of Betamax video, 'straight-to-video' releases and the video shop boom of the early Eighties. Post-VRA fans tend to be in their mid-20s, or younger, and got into the genre during, or after, the Eighties' moral panic over so called 'video nasties' such as *Cannibal Holocaust* (1979), *The Driller Killer* (1979), *The Last House on the Left* (1972), *Night of the Demon* (1980) and *I Spit on Your Grave* (1979). As a result post-VRA fans were generally deprived of the relatively censorship-free days enjoyed by pre-VRA fans.

In terms of structure and organisation, genre fandom in Britain appears to operate on two broad levels: an *individual* level and a *communal* level. These two levels are distinctive, but not mutually exclusive, in so much as fans move between these two levels depending on what kind of fan activity they are engaged in at that time. Individual fandom is the level that most people work within on a day-to-day basis, and includes activities such as watching genre films, reading articles in 'zines or scouring car boots and markets looking for the most complete pre-cert tapes. Communal activity takes place on two sub-levels which are again particular but interrelated: the 'underground' and the 'scene'. The underground tends to operate on a symbolic level, in so much as fans do not have to physically meet up in order to participate in underground activities. As a result, the underground tends to operate as networks of like-minded individuals who make contact, for example, through the classified sections of genre magazines such as *The Dark Side* or *Samhain*, or at fan events, and who trade tapes, lists and correspondences. The underground can, and often does, link individuals that are dispersed throughout the UK, and acts as a bridge between individual fandom and the fan activity that takes place in the scene.

The genre scene in Britain has expanded greatly over the past few years into a niche market constituted by numerous cottage industries, including: publishing houses (Critical Vision, FAB Press, Midnight Media and Media Publications), distribution and mail-order companies (Dark Carnival, Headpress Mail Order, Midnight Media and Media Publications), video companies (One-Shot Productions, Redemption, Salvation, Satanica and Screen Edge), laser-disc companies (Elite) and independent book shops (Cinema Store, Mega-City Comics and Forbidden Planet), all supporting genre fans nation-wide. The scene appears to be structured around two

major components. The first is genre events, including film fairs, such as 'Movie Mart', and film festivals, such as 'Eurofest', which encourage fans to congregate in various locales to watch films, buy films, trade tapes, socialise and make contacts. The second is the production and distribution of genre products including CDs, T-shirts, videos, books and magazines. In terms of genre publications, these tend to range from A5/A4 fanzines such as *Attack of the Scissor People*, *Bomba Movies*, *Fandamania*, *Third Eye* and *Jugular*, which have print runs of a few hundred, through to semi-professional pro-zines, books and journals such as *Delirium*, *Diabolik*, *Eyeball*, *Flesh and Blood*, *Giallo Pages*, *Is it…Uncut?* and *Necronomicon*, which have print runs of a few thousand. According to a recent survey conducted by *Media Scene*, the most popular British genre publications are *The Dark Side*, *Flesh and Blood*, *Delirium* and *Is it…Uncut?* (not to be confused with the high street magazine of a similar name). The publishing part of the genre scene has seen a rapid professionalisation in recent years, due to the wider availability and the relative cheapness of desk top publishing (DTP) technology. The result of which has been that the 'old skool' fanzine — with its fan-ish enthusiasm, accessibility, tongue-in-cheek sarcasm and arguably politicised edge — has for the most part been replaced by pro-zines, books and journals with more intellectualised and thematic approaches to the genre. Thematic approaches to the genre include the re-reading of genre films in terms of gender, race and sexuality. Such readings are often influenced by semiotic and psychoanalytical perspectives. Yet, despite the technological advances within genre publishing, the publication schedules of underground and small press publications still tend to be erratic, with the exception of the more regular *Samhain*, *The Dark Side* and *Shivers*.

It is worth noting that most genre fans operate on the individual and/or underground levels of fandom and that far fewer fans participate in the genre scene. This is principally because making an initial contact with the scene is difficult, owing to its relatively small size and the fact that unless you know what you are looking for you probably won't find it — and you only tend to know what to look for once you're involved. This is similar to the situation where some 'old dear' is selling copies of James Bryan's *Don't Go In the Woods* (1980) for £3 on her stall at the local Greenpeace festival, because she doesn't know the difference between that and the slightly damaged copy of John Hughes' *Weird Science* (1985) next to it.

A theme which has emerged from my research is the way in which the cleavage between pre- and post-VRA fandom outlined earlier has impacted on the recent development and proliferation of the genre scene. This can be seen in the fact that the main players within the scene — for example, magazine editors and the people who run mail-order, distribution and publishing houses — all tend to be pre-VRA fans. The main ramification of this, it can be argued, is that the pre-VRA fans who own and control the mode and means of textual production and distribution within the genre, get to promote their own interests through their magazines and businesses, which in turn sets the tone of the entire scene. This may account in part for why Italian and British exploitation cinema have been so popular in many of the British pro-zines in recent years, and why issues relating to censorship have been sidelined. This is in spite of the fact that the very impositions created by film censorship are the reasons for the strength of the underground and genre scene in the first place.

It is also interesting to note that when it comes to outlining the relationship between the underground/genre scene and mainstream culture, opinion can be divided into two broad camps. The first and more optimistic view is that the recent boom in the genre has lead to a 'bottom up' influence upon the mainstream, which in turn has generated a shift in mainstream publishing and broadcasting that now allows for more genre-related pieces to be covered. In addition, these pieces are increasingly being written by genre-literate journalists, such as Mark Kermode on Radio 1 and Kim Newman in *Empire* and *Sight and Sound*. A more pessimistic view is that the genre scene could only ever have a very limited influence upon the mainstream because the vast majority of people in mainstream British culture are not interested in the genre. What's more, because genre publications have such limited print runs and distribution within the mainstream, they could never compete with more mainstream publications which only ever pay lip service to the genre anyway. Another version of this perspective is that people involved with the genre are wary of any interest paid to them by the mainstream, and as such are not interested in having any impact on the 'wider taste' culture. This is primarily because of a belief that much of the genre scene only exists as long as it doesn't impinge too much on the mainstream, and that once the press or police become aware of the scene they will try to discredit or stop it. There is also a belief that if the mainstream gets too tight a hold on the genre it may become diluted and loose its edge.

In conclusion, despite the fact that all of the ideas contained within this article were developed from the accounts of people involved within the genre scene, the process of analysis and description which takes place in such a composition inevitably 'constructs' the people and social groups it sets out to describe. In other words, fans, and underground cultures don't just exist out there waiting to be characterised and documented by people like me (who arguably have too much time on their hands), rather, the act of describing genre fandom and the genre scene in Britain can have the effect of framing it in a way that is not necessarily acceptable to those who participate within it. Therefore, if anyone feels that they want to contest any points made in this article, or, anyone wants to add their story to the others already contained within my research, they should write or e-mail their comments to me — Shaun Kimber — at: The Department of Sociological Studies, University of Sheffield, Sheffield, S10 2TU << sop95sk@sheffield.ac.uk >> 💀

99

...soon ... miss it not...

we were about halfway to Camden when the drugs began to take hold. We were blitzed on a righteous Feminax & pethedine combo and were all experiencing the most cozmik labour pains. There we were: Ninny, a cool east ender with an IQ in single figures but with an appetite for drugs unknown to any but the most terminal of cancer patients; Nonny, a cool deconstructed football hooligan with big hair that made Johnny Suede look like a bonehead and the best collection of press-clippings on Magma offshoot groups ever, plus an appetite for drugs that made Timothy Leary look like a blue baby refusing his mama's tittie; Nanny, a cool ultra-swingin' drug-takin' shiv-wieldin' tosspot from south of the river who never washed his genitals but knew the matrix number of every Italian prog-rock triple concept album; and me — Wheezer — the motherfucking coolest cocksucker on the planet, the guy who could name every Norwegian punk rock flexi-disc B-side ever recorded, who had committed to memory every write-up on Belgian private pressings included in a catalogue of super-impossible rarities, and who had explored the intestines of more uggas than you could shake your bedraggled jamoke at...

The next thing we knew we were grooving to the mega-hot sounds of a previously uncirculated tape of an unreleased LP by some Lewisham pub-rock prog wizards, needles hanging out of our armpits like piles off a constipated faggot's dirtbox, lurching around the flat of a speed-addled midget we'd never met until we took out our syringes on the tube and started shooting up on the northern line. Man, we were so unbelievably cool it's astonishing only three out of four of us died of terminal diseases in our mid-twenties! So there we were, passing these needles around to all the cats on the tube — the whole fucking carriage was shooting up, man! There was vomit everywhere, speed freaks shitting their pants, fags blowing everyone and administering heroin enemas to the sons of Tory MPs, lezbos bumping pussies with power-dressed city bitches, Arnold the midget whanging his donger in the ear of some gin-sozzled shrivel-tittied old gazoot... Yeah, unbelievable!

But first let's catch up on some history. It was some time in the mid-'70s or mid-'80s — I forget which, man, because I was so cool back then, blasting my brains out with home-grown belladonna every minute of the live-long day, living with a politically correct Venezuelan bulldyke in some motherfucking squat in Islington, hanging around fag bars selling scag and used needles, that I sort of lost track of a decade or two... But she was twenty stone, with a full beard and a surgically appended eighteen inch retractable dork, and would tie me to the kitchen table and force me to watch her ream runaway hippie chicks she'd seduced in Sapphic love bistros... One time I saw her actually engulf some sweet little thing's entire head in the fleshy folds of her unwashed cascading ass cheeks. But every time I'd open my mouth to beg for even a pump in the poop chute of one of her victims she'd bawl me out for being a macho motherfucker and belt me upside the noggin with a two foot double-ended dildo. Bitch! I figured it was time to mainline some kava-kava root and find some crazy dudes game for serious poon research. I re-wired her electric strap-on to explode once the pud was buzzing, ripped off her stash of powdered Yohimbe bark and fled the gaff...

I was puking over my two tone pointy-toed boots (so sharp they could kick off a cockroach's gonads) when I was approached by Doris, a Serbian wannabe transsexual raising the money to finish the op by draining spuzz from used condoms and selling it to sperm banks. Pretty soon we were shacked up, and she introduced me to Ninny, Nonny and Nanny, the cream of Stoke Newington's anti-literati go-go boys — guys so cool they wore their mirror shades back-to-front so they could admire their own pinpoint pupils. Ninny had been a poetry-obsessed, goatee-sporting suckarse wussy when Nonny and Nanny first encountered him at an all-night pill-popping Barry White bootleg tape exchange session, but one taste of desiccated horse-cock distillate and his mind was blown for good. Nonny was an escaped suburban pooftah who affected an eyepatch and cutlass, occasionally hacking off the schlongs of jerk-off artists in public pissoirs when he'd inhaled too much feckweed. He was a nice guy. Nanny was a scam artist whose cons included selling a ton of ripped off methedrine to the Ethiopians claiming it was powdered milk, and whose acts committed after the consumption of a gallon of scrumpy in a murky Soho ponce pad earned him the name of 'Shit-eating cocksucker', which moniker he could never quite understand... Still, he was just a regular Joe...

So Doris sets us up together, man, and that first night we crushed and ate an entire jimson weed and went catatonic for a week. When we came to we conversed only in metallic scraping sounds for a month and existed on a diet of petrol fumes and 24 hour Japanese 7" AA-side remixes of '60s Brazilian soul classics. Man, we were so far gone compared to the other unhip trippers that we were into a whole 'nother sidereal time/space continuum thing, never mind the turgid confines of this solar system's squares, destined to limp around the dancefloor to some 12" Bart and the Pygmies disco-mix.

When we could walk again we hit the dives, man. Ninny would do this kind of Peruvian soft-shoe shuffle, bouncing off the heads of pimply shtupping students in his silver platform boots and 28" parallels like some Venusian angel on rhino tranquilliser. Nonny would be smooth-talking the babes, seducing them with that old tried and trusted 'previously unreleased pre-Boney M Obby Farrell home cassette demos' routine that worked like chip fat on a well-ploughed beastie's rosebud. Nanny would be stoked to the upper, weaving around the heads, ranting fucking poetry, man, begging for a hand-job and another hit of Thunderbird. And me, man, I'd be there, man, so full of pills I fucking rattled, looking for some three-way action or even a straight raincoat job with a couple of tittie/clittie types.

One time I was conned by these bozos I thought were a she/she show into tagging along for the ride, but when we got back to their fuck pad they turned out to be two incestuous hillbilly jessies called Dirk and Dwork. Dwork had a dork so huge he could bend it round and irrigate Dirk's colon while the latter ploughed through him! They eventually met a fate worse than heterosexuality when Dwork decided to ram it to the mains supply during one exciting moment, thus achieving the ultimate high. Anyway, where was I? I got so side-tracked by my fabulousness that I almost lifted bodily off this bring-down bummer earth and flailed around in the heavens! Okay. The next low-life to orbit our shining planet was a washed-up glam-rock bed-wetter called Stinky 'Piss-Pants' Adler, an old nemesis of mine from days of yore. He had an enormous nappy habit to keep up (swathed head to foot in sodden diapers from dawn to dusk as he was) so we agreed to cut a combination comeback/farewell CD laser disc 12" jungle techno mix of his old anthem 'Dig My Diaper Soil, Motherfucking Cocksucking Anthony Wilson (You Twat) (Version)', to be released on Jubilee Day with all copies being sent directly to Norman Tebbitt in the hope of a bit of free publicity. Unfortunately the gag backfired and Stinky became a cabinet minister. But we all learn from our mistakes, and it wasn't long before Ninny decided to try his hand at suicide, having been diagnosed with an incurable case of horse crabs that dated back to his days of animal husbandry (which he unfortunately took a tad too literally). He was so successful that we're still finding parts of him on Radcliffe golf course to this day. He somehow managed to stuff an explosive golfball under his foreskin and go berserk over the course screaming 'I look pretty good!' until the inevitable explosion blew his zit-encrusted torso into atoms. We never liked him anyway.

Nanny was the next to go. He was flying high after snorting blue unction for the duration of a 48 hour Finnish rectal depilation festival and attempted to circumcise himself with a rusty pair of anus hair clippers. True to form, his parting shot was a distaff rendition of that classic

LIFE SUCKS DIE Nº 3

$5 (+$2 outside US) 48pp; Life Sucks Die, PO Box 14801, Minneapolis, MN 55414, USA; www.lifesucksdie.com

This is, without doubt, the most moronic magazine to cross the portals of Pantziarka mansions in years. *Life Sucks Die* purports to be an underground hip hop magazine, though I find it hard to believe that this is really representative of US hip hop culture in general. Here you can read incisive rants such as 'You want anarchy? Okay, I'm going to burn your parents house down then, smarty pants, how's that for anarchy?', which eventually reaches the inevitable (and tedious) conclusion 'Yeah, Karl Marks-A-Lot, tell me when your graffiti revolution starts so I can move to Afghanistan or Rwanda, please!'. Deep stuff, eh? On the same page you can read the words to the rap 'Illegal Aliens' by the Convicts, which is basically a long and pathetic racist chant against Hispanics/Iranians/Koreans/Nigerians and others. It just serves to prove that black racists are just as moronic as white ones, and it leaves me wondering why the white editors would chose to include such drivel in their magazine.

Other highlights include an interview with 'blood sucking freaks Ink and Dagger', a band from Philadelphia. I was kept awake reading this only because I was trying to work out who was the most stupid — the band or the interviewer. In the end I figured it was a draw as nobody had the remotest bit of intelligence or originality. A big chunk of the magazine consists of collages of graffiti tags interspersed with bits of porno magazines — and the porno pictures were way more interesting then the graffiti.

I could go on (it's so easy), but I've already devoted more time and energy than this dross merits. It's hard to believe that anyone would really pay for shit like this. Avoid it like the plague, it doesn't deserve to make it to Nº 4. **Pan Pantziarka**

DAINTY VISCERA
VOL 4 Nº 6

$3 48pp; Sean Beaudoin, 537 Jones St., #2074 SF CA 94102, USA; email: headSNAP@aol.com

Ah, America. Land of the free, home of the brave. Home, too, of the First Amendment, guaranteeing freedom of speech, and leaving people more or less able to publish what they like (Mike Diana notwithstanding). Hence the existence of Loompanics Unlimited, *ANSWER Me!* magazine, and Paladin Press, crazed survivalist purveyors of such 'information only' gems as *Ragnar's Guide to Home and Recreational Use of High Explosives* (I'm not making this up!). Hence, too, *Dainty Viscera*. This small-format b&w zine contains, amongst other things, an interesting interview with Jim Blanchard, AN-SWER Me! cover artist and inker of Peter Bagge's *Hate!* comic in its latter-day, much-unloved colour incarnation. Also a strange piece of fiction(?) entitled 'The Feraliminal Lycanthropizer'. So far, so uncontroversial. The First Amendment-stretching doozy of this issue, however, is a two-page article at the back by one 'Bob Arson', called 'Butchering the Human Carcass for Human Consumption'. This is an informative and technical piece about, well, killing and eating people, illustrated textbook-style by Sergio Posada. The tone is largely dry and non-judgemental, although not entirely devoid of a certain lip-smacking relish:

> *WE PERSONALLY PREFER FIRM CAUCASIAN FEMALES IN THEIR EARLY TWENTIES. THESE ARE 'RIPE'. BUT TASTES VARY, AND IT IS A VERY LARGE HERD.*

Not having even killed, much less eaten anyone myself (though don't think I haven't been tempted), I can't really judge the quality of the advice offered on skinning and butchering, but it all seems pretty sensible. Believe me, I'm more than happy to be wrong about this! Serving suggestions are largely absent, apart from some tips on what to avoid:

> *THE FEMALE BREAST IS COMPOSED LARGELY OF GLANDS AND FATTY TISSUE,*

TEAM OF REVIEWERS

DARREN ARNOLD
ANTON BLACK
TOM BRINKMANN
MIKITA BROTTMAN
MICHAEL CARLSON
EUGENE CARFAX
RICK CAVENEY
SIMON COLLINS
MARK DEUTROM
DUKE FRETSCORCHER

DAVID GREENALL
JAMES MARRIOTT
PAN PANTZIARKA
RIK RAWLING
JACK SARGEANT
STEPHEN SENNITT
SARAH TURNER
CHRIS VAILLANCOURT
JOE SCOTT WILSON
WILL YOUDS

ALL REVIEWS NOT CREDITED ARE BY
DAVID KEREKES

SEND MATERIALS FOR REVIEW TO
HEADPRESS, 40 ROSSALL AVENUE, RADCLIFFE, MANCHESTER, M26 1JD, UK (see submission guidelines on p.144)

AND DESPITE IT'S [sic] APPETISING APPEARANCE IS RATHER INEDIBLE.

So, essential reading for all you budding Geins, Dahmers, Nilsens and Albert Fishes out there. **Simon Collins**

BLUE BLOOD Nº7

$7.95 60pp; Blue Blood, 2625 Piedmont Road, Suite 56-332, Atlanta, GA 30324, USA; www.hallucinet.com/blueblood

This is a little surprising. It looks like any one of a number of glossy horror and 'vampire chic' magazines currently in vogue (most of which seem to be emanating from the US and Australia). Well, while the calibre of the writing is on a par with those publications — *I've just never been that big a fan of torture murders (although I know some of you are,)* [sic] *but I've always wanted to try cannibalism'* — its content is decidedly more risqué, with *Hustler*-type photo spreads, but switching the sexy secretary scenario for shaved-blonde-piece-with-fangs and her curiously coiffured boyfriend. It ends with him being butt-fucked with a strap-on. So long as you don't stray into the text, you might get a rise out of it...

Blue Blood — a non-humour magazine that has on its cover 'The Trade Mag of Cool'.

CARPE NOCTEM Nº13

£2.95 (incl p&p; Europe add 20%) 80pp; payable 'Chris Reed', BBR, PO Box 625, Sheffield, S1 3GY, UK; www.bbr-online.com/catalogue $5.00; 260 S.Woodruff Avenue Ste. 105, Idaho Falls ID 83401, USA

With a title that, I presume, means bats that seize the pleasure of the moment, this could be nothing else but a Goth magazine. Glossy and well produced, *Carpe Noctem* is fodder only for those children of the night still trapped within the black-eyed, black nail varnished, lager-and-black drinking Gothic Rock days of the mid 1980s. I am amazed there is so much interest in this stuff, I thought this lot had died off with the *Batcave* and the Virgin Prunes! But no, the entire magazine is crammed with advertisements from companies flogging black vampire fetish clothing, skulls and bones jewellery,

Gothic CDs and 'accessories'. Maybe I am out of touch, or just too old, but this stuff really bores the pants off me!

Music reviews and fiction aside (I am not even attempting to read the fiction!), there are a few... well... three points of interest here. The centre pages, which are irritatingly inserted upside down, deal with the oriental art of foot binding. This beautifully designed colour insert deserves a better after-life. As does a pretty good article on the artistry and manufacture of gravestones. But best of all is the cringe-inducing 'Cinematic Autopsy: The Artistry of the Giallo Film'. Dario Argento's anus must be clean enough to eat your dinner off after this sycophantic scrawl. *Opera* is described as 'a stunning display of camera pyrotechnics and fluid motion utilised within the fabric of a seductive mystery' and 'truly inspired'. But I am saving the best bit till last. Lamberto Bava is 'every bit the film-maker his father was'. Need I say more? **David Greenall**

THE NEW BONDAGE FAIRIES

KONDOM

$2.95 24pp; Eros Comix (Fantagraphics) Japanese adult manga — often referred to as 'Hentai' (pervert) or H-manga — can be shocking to Western eyes accustomed to the type of vanilla porn found in most European and American comics. The more extreme of the adult manga can make the kinkiest of Crepax or Manara look like family entertainment. Such is the case with the *Bondage Fairies*, a series of comic books by the mysterious Kondom, which is the most bizarre, twisted and head-scratching manga to have a release outside of Japan.

Bondage Fairies tells the story of the sweet but not very bright Pfil, and her kinky, sarcastic lover Pamila. Both patrol the forest, making sure the myriad insects and rodents that populate the area don't run amok. Pfil and Pamila aren't doing a very good job, as in nearly every issue, some creature will do a dirty deed, usually sex related. It's up to our two buxom, scantily clad and horny fairies to punish them.

The original *Bondage Fairies* was

published in the early Nineties by the now defunct Antarctic Press, and dealt with Pfil's capture and torture at the hands of rival fairies. *The New Bondage Fairies* picks up the story some time later, and is decidedly less sadistic than its predecessor — though it will still send any reader looking for hot comic book babes to whack their pud to screaming in terror. *New Bondage Fairies* wallows in scenes of degradation, kinky sex, S&M and violence, as good-natured but incredibly naïve Pfil is endlessly tortured by a parade of lovingly rendered, grotesque critters. Most stories have a similar plot: Pfil fights with Pamila over Pamila's unfaithfulness, they have sex (usually quite tender, and erotic), and go on their patrol. Pfil ends up, either by trickery or force, at the wrong end of a bug's twisted penis, and after pages of rape and torture (peppered with bizarre asides and jokes) Pamila comes to the rescue and enacts bloody revenge (usually, castrating the rapist insect). Throughout each story, Kondom shows his fondness for bugs and rodents, drawing them realistically and in a decidedly uncartoony manner, as opposed to the cute and stylised fairies. The sex is extremely graphic, with no opportunity to show spurting bodily fluids wasted, and is almost as violent — it's not uncommon for a story to end with Pamila holding up a bloody, severed penis while its owner whines in the background.

Kondom frequently tosses in surreal bits that serve only as in-

Cherry and Rich have a bloody snog. *Blue Blood.*

jokes, such as a little nature lesson interrupting a graphic sex scene, or Pamila making reference to the fact that they're in a comic book. *The New Bondage Fairies* is not for all, but it's got more craft, wit and warmth than most other adult comics out there. **Chris Vaillancourt**

TALES FROM THE IDIOT BOX
£3 / A$4 15pp
MORE TALES FROM THE IDIOT BOX
£3 / A$4 17pp; email:
darrenarnold@hotmail.com

This xeroxed-and-stapled fanzine from Queensland is dedicated to Australian cinema of any genre. It's a basic affair that would have looked amateur 10 years ago. Dated by design, each issue contains 50 brief reviews and a handful of actor and director profiles. Of the reviews, most are scribed by editor Darren Arnold with a few culled from the likes of *Headpress* and *Samhain*.

Its intentions may be well-meaning, but *Tales from the Idiot Box* (named after David Caesar's 1996 heist film *Idiot Box*) suffers one major flaw: a lack of information! The profile and filmography of Peter Weir for instance takes up less than half an A4 page. Poor design and photocopying I can forgive, but if the text contains nothing you can't find in your average film guide then why bother. The whole thing smells of teenage film-fan vanity.

Stick with the seventh edition of the *Time Out Film Guide* which reviews 114 more Australian films than these two publications.
David Greenall

THE EROTIC REVIEW
£2.50 (subs £20/10 issues); 5-7 Carnaby Street, London, W1V 1PG
Spin-off publication of the Erotic Print, this key player in the increasing gentrification of porn — or 'erotica', as I'm sure they prefer to think of themselves — is on the up and up, changing from a quarterly to a monthly, adding more pages and getting 'raunchier' (they promise), and enjoying critical praise from the mainstream press. Nevertheless, I will not be renewing my subscription, which has just run out, and here's why.

I originally subscribed in response to a special offer whereby you got a free sub if you bought the Erotic Print Society catalogue for £5 (more on the catalogue later). As soon as I saw the mag, I knew it was not for me. The adverts it contained were a dead give-away. Dear oh dear! Paunch concealers, baldness remedies, impotence cures… Without wishing to brag, I felt the advertisers were missing their target market with me. I may be a degenerate, but I'm not such a decrepit degenerate as that (yet)!

Nor was the editorial content much more beguiling. *The Erotic Review* has made much of their use of big-name writers, and indeed there are many (Arnold Wesker, Simon Raven, Philip Hensher, Michael Bywater, Susan Crosland, Martin Amis, Auberon Waugh — a veritable plethora of the great and not-so-good). But this is not necessarily a guarantee of steaminess. If you want to know about Naim Attallah's interest in knickers, or the intimate ins and outs, so to speak, of Peter Stringfellow's fantasies (he wants to exile himself in a tropical hotel with 25 young girls to dance attendance on him for the rest of his life), then, mister, you're a sadder perv than I'll ever be.

Visually, the mag resembles *The Spectator*, but with more tits. The pictures are consistently more interesting than the text, but it just isn't enough. *The Erotic Review* bills itself as 'the fastest-growing magazine in the UK', and I have no reason to suppose that this isn't true, but it's certainly never caused any fast growth in my underpants. Not even

a little bit. It's aimed fairly and squarely at the sort of crusty old twat whose idea of a sexual fantasy is some posh Sloaney bird wearing jodhpurs and pearls eating oysters in Paris, so unless you're a Young Conservative (the last one in captivity?) or over 50, forget it. Though if you have a randy old uncle, a gift subscription might be just the ticket for Christmas.

The Erotic Print Society catalogue is an entirely different proposition. Now in its third edition, and niftily presented in a dinky A6 format with glossy paper and full-colour throughout, the 108-page catalogue is jam-packed with trouser-arousing imagery of excellent stuff that you probably can't afford, but is nice to look at anyway, and at a fiver is a bargain purchase — for the price of a couple of issues of *Razzle*, you could show a bit of class about being an unrepentant filth-hound. Or you could wait for another promotional offer and get some crap magazines as well. **Simon Collins**

SWEET SMELL OF SICK SEX N° 2
US$10 (incl p&p) 88pp; payable 'Sophie Cossette', PO Box 41, Place du Parc, Montreal, Quebec, Canada, H2W 2M9

Sweet Sophie — who would think you'd have such a filthy mind? Absolutely anything goes in Sophie's gag cartoons and comic strips, and this giant collection of material doesn't skimp on the cum quota as stars from stage and screen rub schlongs alongside royalty and presidents. Kurt Cobain holds a pistol to his head while porking Courtney. 'C'mon Kurt,' she hollers, 'do me a

Al Goldstein as portrayed by Sophie Cossette, *Sweet Smell of Sick Sex N° 2*.

104

big favour and blow your brains out already! I can't wait to go from grunge to GUCCI!' Also included in *Sweet Smell* N° 2 are features on a great-looking Canadian crime tabloid from the Fifties called *Allo Police*, which often ran lurid sketches on its covers when lurid crime scene photographs weren't available. (It appears to be still running today, but as a smut paper.) And the supposedly true tale of two murderous madams from Mexico, as recounted by Ramona, 'slave-whore' and 'lone syphilitic survivor'…

> OH! / COULDN'T STOP MYSELF. / KEPT LICKING AND SUCKING ON HER CUNT EVEN THOUGH / KNEW IT WAS RIDDLED WITH THE DEADLY CURSE OF SYPHILIS… YEAH, / BURIED MYSELF IN ILENA'S STINKY SNATCH AND / TRULY RELISHED EACH NEW DROPLET OF HER DEATH-DRENCHED CREAM ON MY LIPS.

There's even a sensitive illustration by Sophie running alongside.

Danny Hellman, Al Goldstein, The Cramps and Phil Liberbaum number among the interviewers and interviewees also featured herein.

DRACULINA N°s 29–33
(no order info; try comic shops)
GAUNTLET 14
Porn in the USA 2
$6.95 (+$7 p&p outside US) 128pp; Gauntlet, 309 Powell Road, Springfield, PA 19064, USA

Draculina has an identity problem. Is it a horror comic, showcasing a rather poor comic strip about a sexy female vampire? This would be a waste, as it seems like there should be a niche for a magazine devoted to contemporary schlock horror and thrillers, featuring photo spreads from imaginative B-movies and enthusiastic pictorials of naked stars. Or is it historical? The high point of these five issues is a feature in N° 29 by editor Hugh Gallagher, chronicling the deaths and lives of porn suicide Savannah and perennial problem starlet Margaux Hemingway.

On the other hand, Gallagher's similar feature on Seventies B-queen Claudia Jennings in N° 31 adds lit-

tle that is not already available to her film legend, or to the details of her highway *Crash*-style death. Even the pix are uninspired.

There are signs that Gallagher is tempted to take *Draculina* down the soft-focus silicone path that *Scream Queens* and *Femme Fatales* have already staked out (so to speak). This would be a mistake. The positive side of *Draculina* is its raunchiness, its authenticity, and its real position outside the commercial mainstream.

Thus it's a little surprising that the main feature in the so-called Special Vampire Issue (N° 33), which otherwise offers nice pieces on the remarkable Sasha Graham and talented Tina Krause, is an interview with Annie Sprinkle that strives for a sort of mainstream respectability, rather than delving at long and degrading depth into the pre-performance art phase of her career. This is the sort of stuff that would be better left to magazines like *Gauntlet*.

Which, strangely enough, it was. The same interview, word for word, appears in *Gauntlet*'s second 'Porn in the USA' issue. Writer Don Vaughn probably discovered *Draculina* doesn't pay any better than *Headpress*! But *Gauntlet* is a better place for Annie Sprinkle, even if 'Porn in the USA 2' is tame by their standards. *Gauntlet* runs out all the usual suckspects, including Nina Hartley at her most academic. As one of the few porn stars who gives more than lip-service to the idea that the mind is the most erogenous zone, Nina's 'serious' stuff is remarkably bland. Smoother than the cheeks of that amazing bubble-butt! Vaughn checks in with another whitebread and vanilla interview with porn scripter Cathy Tavel that doesn't live up to the pix of her being tortured with flame. In fact, about the only stuff with any juice in this issue is Al Goldstein's rant about the decline of porn standards and Wes Trails' look at amateur porn videos. Maybe the internet is making *Gauntlet* redundant, or maybe the mainstream just ain't paying attention. A better cover photo of Nina might help!
Michael Carlson

EYE N° 17
£2.95 (incl p&p UK; Europe add 20%) 58pp; payable 'Chris Reed', BBR, PO Box

625, Sheffield, S1 3GY, UK; www.bbr-online.com/catalogue $3.95 (plus p&p); 301 S.Elm Street, Suite 405, Greensboro, NC 27401-2636, USA

Somewhat left wing, right-on and strangely irritating, *Eye* is one of those (generally short-lived) glossy publications that is itself rooted in origin to other small press publications. Picture *Headpress*, *Fortean Times*, *High Times*, *Body Play* and *Factsheet Five* moulded into one. It's more mainstream than those listed above, more palatable to the masses, and as a result lacks direction; there is no core to *Eye*, no binding theme. The sort of magazine you buy but find yourself reading only ten per cent. Shame — it looks good and reminds me of our own *Bizarre* magazine without the *FHM*-style T&A. Also like *Bizarre*, it acts like a jumping-off point for those interested to seek out some really interesting publications (eventually discarding the host).

With articles on kitsch, lounge music, pink dolphins and underground videos, *Eye* is interesting, but not interesting enough. Geared towards the Public Access TV/*South Park*/drug culture generation, it fails to reveal anything truly subversive.
David Greenall

BOMBA MOVIES N° 6
£1.95 (+ £0.30 p&p) 32pp; payable: 'Dark Carnival', Dark Carnival, 140 Crosby Avenue, Scunthorpe, South Humberside, DN15 8NT
This sleazy little item has been around for quite a while now, but times have changed and *Bomba Movies* now costs £1.95 more than

it used to. With early issues bearing a resemblance to those great American zines of the Eighties — such as *Gore Gazette* and *Subhuman* — cut-and-paste production has made way for professional composition of image and text, and glossy paper. But do not for one minute think that this means the Bomba boys have traded in their damaged brains for more sensible models. *Bomba Movies* is still a riot; it's just easier to read now.

This issue is an all-review issue, 29 in all. A typical Bomba movie being one crammed full of strong violence, gore, and hardcore sex — *Emanuelle in America*, *Porno Holocaust*, *Entrails of a Virgin*, *The Killing of America*... Just don't mention horror-comedy, *Bomba Movies* hates these with a vengeance (so do I). Some of the reviews are up-dated reprints from earlier issues, but even if you have all these, don't let this put you off, it's worth buying just for the amazing (unrelated) stills and illustrations that accompany the reviews.

But the real fun to be found here is in the writing style: vulgar without being juvenile.

Bomba Movies is required reading for all. I steal the following quote from the *Bomba* review of Joe D'Amato's *Porno Holocaust*: 'junk movie fans in search of that ultimate fix of mayhem, mutilation and glistening twats'. **David Greenall**

79 REASONS WHY HITCHHIKING SUCKS
ANDREA WYCKOFF
$1.00 (include something for p&p)
Andrea Wyckoff, PO Box 19554,
Portland, OR 97280, USA

Two female friends decide to go off on a hitchhiking tour across the US. After travelling from Portland, OR, down to LA and over to Colorado, they give up and head back home. This slim booklet — printed on different coloured paper stock — offers an annotated insight into what caused Andrea Wyckoff and her pal to change their minds. In other words, 79 reasons why they think hitchhiking sucks. Reason #1 is having to

> LISTEN TO PEOPLE GO OFF ON THEIR LIFE STORIES, LIKE HOW THEIR WIFE LEFT THEM, HOW THEY LOST THEIR VIRGINITY IN COLLEGE TO SOME RED HEAD, AND HOW THEY THINK THE GOVERNMENT SUCKS.

The booklet is divided into equally short and concise pointers, running through a whole bunch of vaguely humorous non-events and dippy on-the-road characters. There are two photo montages (one of which constitutes the cover), offering the opportunity to try and match a blurry Polaroid to relevant folk mentioned in the text. Unfortunately the guy who makes up Reason #49 — the Cub scout dad — isn't one of them. He lectured the girls on 'how bears are attracted to the scent of a girl "at that time of the month".'

Pity the whole bum trip is over all too quickly.

COP PORN
Lively Essays for the New Police State
DAN KELLY
$5.00 84pp; 1573 N. Milwaukee Ave. #481, Chicago, IL 60622, USA

Kelly writes concise essays in a pleasing style. This collection of his — culled from a variety of publications printed over the years — covers an enormously broad array of subjects. Everything in fact, from the Art and Practice of Cadaver Display, to the Physical Properties of the Stigmata. Elsewhere, he provides an historical discourse on the eating of one's own dog and a Top Ten of White Supremacist book titles (*Hollywood Reds Have Acquired Strange Protectors* by Myron Fagan is at the bottom of the list). The articles average about two pages apiece.

DELIRIUM
A Guide to Italian Exploitation Cinema, 1975–1979
ADRIAN LUTHER-SMITH (Ed.)
£10.95; UK: Media Publications, 1997; ISBN 1 901759 00 8
(Available through Headpress, see p.70)

Four years may not seem an awfully long time, but in terms of Italian exploitation films of the mid-Seventies it's a frighteningly dense period, arguably Italy's golden age in which filmmakers constantly pushed at the boundaries of taste and decency with nary a backward glance. There are literally hundreds of titles contained in this special book-sized edition of *Delirium*, with most accompanied by informative reviews, full credit details and rare illustrations.

The primary motivating force in these films was money, and the easiest way to make that was to drown your movie in kinky sex and gratuitous violence. The result? A shameless and exciting era, wallowing in *Dirty Harry* rip-offs and *Omen* cash-ins. Nunsploitation, Nazi atrocity, Black Emanuelle, Mondo, hardcore, tacky comedies, they're all here. The only gripe with this book is the layout, and non-existent page numbers.

SUTURE
The Arts Journal, vol 1
JACK SARGEANT (Ed.)
£14.95 192pp; UK: Creation, 1998; ISBN 1 871592 70 4

I really wanted to like this. The book looks great, with colour Trevor Brown illustrations on front and back, set against a matt black cover, and the first article I've seen on Suehiro Maruo, creator of *Mr Arashi's Amazing Freakshow*. It's a real shame, then, that it just doesn't live up to expectations.

The stated purpose of the collection is to examine and explore those zones which 'have been largely neglected'. A laudable aim, for sure, but I hardly think Lydia Lunch has been underexposed, or even Joe Coleman for that matter. Ironically one of the most interesting pieces is

$5

Es la Ley!

LIVELY ESSAYS FOR THE NEW POLICE STATE — BY DAN KELLY

on John Hillcoat, director of *Ghosts... of the Civil Dead* and *To Have and to Hold*, but who, with two features to his name and probably a couple of *Sight & Sound* pieces, can hardly be considered 'underground'. He has some interesting things to say, though, and is allowed to say them by the interviewer, Billy Chainsaw, who fortunately employs a minimal interviewing technique far removed from that of editor Jack Sargeant. Jack seems to hold his own agenda to be more important than that of the interviewees. The other pieces are on Dame Darcy, Romain Slocombe, Marne Lucas/ Jacob Pander, Mark Hejnar, Trevor Brown and James Havoc.

The book suffers from a lack of variety in terms of format, being (with only minor exceptions) a series of articles followed by interviews. Illustrations are minimal, and it would have been good to see more of them and (considering the £14.95 price tag) a colour section. This problem's exacerbated by the fact that most of the interviews are overlong and often repetitive, and some of the

material is of severely limited interest. A tighter edit would have been very welcome. Of the illustrations, Lydia Lunch's recent photos look excellent. The Joe Coleman repros look a little murky, though, and the screen grabs used to illustrate the piece on Mark Hejnar, director of *Affliction*, are terrible.

Although generally well-researced, some of the writing in the essays, I'm afraid, is risible. It often reads as though Sargeant has swallowed a dictionary of critical theory and is bringing up what he can't digest. Almost all of them feature 'what the fuck?' passages such as the following:

> IT DOES NOT SEEK TO REPRODUCE A MIMESIS OF 'REALITY', RATHER IT CREATES A PHANTASMAGORICAL TROPE BASED ON THE BIO-PHYSICAL RESPONSE OF THE BODY TO STIMULATION. *THE FILM IS AN EXEGESIS OF FUCK MANIFESTED VIA A THERMO-PHYSIOLOGICAL CARTOGRAPHY OF THE BODY.*

Trevor Brown is the only person featured who draws attention to Sargeant's over-determined interpretations, and comes across all the better for it. Here the distance between the aims of interviewer and interviewee is most clearly defined, with Brown's disarming modesty and down-to-earth manner in violent contrast to Sargeant's humourless, theory-ridden prose. Sargeant's footnote on the Chapman brothers made me laugh out loud and wonder whether it was a piss take: after describing their work as 'characterised by a morphogenic eruption in which bodies are distorted becoming twisted chimera', he writes, 'These distortions are made all the more strange due to the fashionable sporting shoes the figures are wearing.'

There's a telling quote during the Mark Hejnar piece, in which Sargeant states:

> *IT* SEEMS TO ME THAT MAYBE THAT [sic] THERE IS A 'TREND' IN THE UNDERGROUND BY PEOPLE TO DOCUMENT THE UNDERGROUND, BUT THE DOCUMENT IS IN ITSELF PART OF AN UNDERGROUND MODE OF EXPRESSION. *M*AYBE *A*DAM *P*ARFREY AND *A*POCALYPSE *C*ULTURE STARTED IT.

Suture collection wants badly to be a document on the scale of Parfrey's book. Parfrey, however, drew attention to a whole host of unknowns — the truly marginalised — while here there are no surprises. It doesn't open any new doors. In a way that's a problem which dogs a lot of the underground (I hate the word, but it's a convenient shorthand) press: the same people, the same obsessions recycled again and again. Looking at this collection and at the material on display at a lot of underground outlets, you could be forgiven for thinking the underground more narrow-minded and conformist within its ranks than any more dominant culture. You'd also be forgiven, looking at this, for believing that the underground is an almost exclusively North American domain. There are people doing interesting work who have been ignored by the underground press — who has seen a piece on Arthur Lager? — and a

CULTURE GUIDE

collection like this should be a forum for introducing them to a wider audience. It's a pity that it's not.
James Marriott

EROS IN HELL
Sex, Blood and Madness in Japanese Cinema
JACK HUNTER

£14.95 228pp; UK: Creation, 1998; ISBN 1 871592 93 3

Books dedicated to Asian cinema are rife at the moment. Most devote themselves to the subject of latter-day Hong Kong Action flicks. The surge of popularity in these types of films means that I, for one, don't want to see them. Fortunately, there is another side to Far Eastern cinema, one that Jack Hunter explores in his book *Eros in Hell*. This is the realm of the New Wave, underground films and extreme films — alien landscapes and phantasies, often driven by the equally alien concept of a unison between sex, art, and commerce.

Eros In Hell commences with a history of Pink cinema (the Japanese equivalent of the Blue movie), the first film of which is generally considered to be Tetsuji Takechi's *Daydream* (1964), whose theme of an anaesthetised girl being molested and raped by a dentist caused the Japanese government some embarrassment when released during the Tokyo Olympics. A whole chapter is devoted to an essay by Rosemary Hawley Jarman on *Ai No Corrida* (1976), Nagisa Oshima's landmark film about two enraptured lovers whose increasingly passionate bouts of lovemaking end with one of them dead. Jarman explains how the director initially intended the film to be hardcore porn, processing it in France so as to avoid the Japanese tradition of exorcising images of genitalia. Other chapters move into darker waters, discussing the films of the prolific Hisayasu Sato (who claims he wants to drive his audience mad), the pseudo-snuff of the *Guinea Pig* series, and the appalling-sounding *Death Women*, the latest in a long line of Asian 'shockumentaries'. Hunter notes that *Death Women* is comprised of 'nothing but real-life studies of dead females... ranging in age from infancy

upward'. The footage comes from accident scenes, official sources, and actual autopsies (but autopsies in which the deceased can be dressed in pure white cotton panties). *Death Women* is currently up to volume eight, is believed to be of Taiwanese origin, and has editors who remain anonymous.

You need more than one book on Asian cinema. *Eros in Hell* ought to be one of them.

END-TIME VISIONS
The Road To Armageddon?
RICHARD ABANES

H/BK £13.99 428pp; US: Four Walls Eight Windows, 1998; distributed in UK by Turnaround; ISBN 1-56858-104-1
(Available through Headpress, see p.70)

At some point in the near future our world will be destroyed... Throughout history, civilisations and cultures have been creating their own unique belief systems based upon the idea that the world would end and be born anew. Today's religions are no different, but it is the apocalyptic teachings of Christianity that have had the greatest influence on western society and around which Richard Abanes concentrates his book, *End-Time Visions*. As early as 150 AD, prophets were foretelling the return to Earth of Jesus Christ and of the anguish that would befall sinners. Just as millions will flock to Jerusalem at the turn of this Millennium, so was there a mass exodus the last Millennium, when people gave up all their belongings and travelled to the Holy City in anticipation of the Second Coming. When the end didn't come, the dates were simply reshuffled.

And they're being reshuffled to this day — a plethora of end-time prophets, seers, and cults, all promising hellfire and damnation someday soon. For the Korean *Hyoo-go* movement, the end-time was scheduled to start on October 28, 1992; that was the day of Rapture, when all good Christians would be whisked up to Heaven in the blinking of an eye, leaving millions to suffer the Tribulation — seven years of unparalleled destruction — after which the world would be destroyed. Cult members prayed so loudly through the nights in the run-up to the big

day that spitting blood became a sign of salvation. Many believers quit their jobs or schools, sold their homes, and abandoned their families. Pregnant women had abortions so that they wouldn't be too heavy to be lifted up to Heaven. Others simply committed suicide. Minutes after the deadline passed, the senior pastor of the cult announced, quite simply, 'Nothing has happened. Sorry. Let's go home.'

The Amazing Criswell, friend of B-movie director Ed Wood, also gets a look-in, thanks to some strange end-time predictions: 'pressure' from outer space,' he wrote in *Criswell Predicts*, will 'cause all solids to turn into a jellylike mass... the people who attempt to escape in wild panic will be unable to move through the gummy streets.' (Criswell's career in predicting the future started quite by chance. He was a TV newscaster in New York when, one evening, he ran out of news 15 minutes early and decided to fill the remaining air time with his thoughts on what *might* happen the next day.) Nostradamus gets a whole chapter to himself, as author Abanes takes to systematically debunking several of his most highly regarded prophesies. He claims that these have been badly translated from the French, juggled about, and in some instances even fabricated outright in order that Nostradamites — fans — can fit them to major events in world history. What's more, Abanes suggests they're not even prophesies, but 'contemporary political lampoons' of the day (an interesting explanation but not a wholly convincing one).

Then there is the curious story of William Miller, and how 'the great disappointment' of his prophesised world end in 1843 didn't deter followers from establishing their own apocalyptic cults. Out of the Millerites sprang the Adventists, and later the Jehovah's Witnesses — a group Abanes describes as 'one of the most deceptive and dangerous of today's apocalyptic cults'.

End-Times Visions covers a lot of ground in a thoroughly satisfying way (so long as you overlook the silly little typos). Written by a Catholic and former cult member, it applies logic, common-sense and hard-research to a very mad subject.

CINE EAST
Hong Kong Cinema
Through the
Looking Glass
MILES WOOD

£9.95 160pp; UK: FAB Press, 1998;
ISBN 0952926024
(Available through Headpress, see p.70)

This is a fascinating look at Hong Kong cinema from an Eastern perspective, which escapes the typical concentration on martial arts, gunplay and ghost movies to give an overview of what the industry's really like. There are interviews with 12 prime movers, chosen partly for their importance within the industry (rather than appeal to the West) and partly because they have not yet had much exposure in English language publications. Which means that unless you're an hardcore fan, most of the names here will probably not be familiar. I've only seen a handful of the movies mentioned in *Cine East*, but didn't find the fact, or the lack of familiarity with the interviewees, a problem. It's intriguing to get the insiders' view of how their industry works, especially as most of the interviews appear to have been conducted immediately before the 1997

handover. There are also some acute observations on other film industries, particularly Hollywood. All in all, I would have welcomed a longer introductory essay (which is concise to say the least), and an endpiece describing what has happened to the HK film industry since the handover. That said, I've yet to see anything bad from FAB. **James Marriott**

PORN KING
Autobiography of
John C. Holmes
JOHN C. HOLMES with LAURIE HOLMES & FRED E. BASTEN

$19.95 192pp; Johnny Wadd Publications, 8200 Montgomery Blvd. NE Suite 210, Albuquerque, New Mexico, USA

John Holmes falls into the same category as freak shows, car wrecks and special effects, in as much as most people would not admit wanting to look at the former, but do, and love the wide screen spectacle of the latter. But as with the now-popular 'freak', Holmes was only human, while at the same time being unlike most. This of course caused his fame and fall. On one level he served as shock value and on another as a tool

Apocalypse when? Protesting against the Jehovah's Witnesses. *End-Time Visions.*

(pun intended) for many a voyeuristic, vicarious fucking.

The first chapter in *Porn King* gives the story of his days at UCLA as student, art class model, and

TASCHEN!

THE ART OF PLEASURE
TOM OF FINLAND

H/BK £29.99 350pp; Taschen, 1998; ISBN 3-8228-8598-3

A big book of big men with big cocks (and a couple of ladies too). For anyone who's not familiar with Tom's work — very few Headpress readers, I imagine — this could indeed be a bit of an eye-opener. Immaculately drawn masculine men (no queens allowed) having uninhibited sex in scenarios which involve fisting, fucking, sucking, pissing, bondage, uniforms, CP and S&M. For those who are familiar, I can only say that this is the most complete collection of Tom's works I have ever COME across, starting with Tom's early Forties work (strangely, the only colour pictures in the book, the rest being black & white or sepia toned), and working its way chronologically to his sad death in 1991.

Tom has always been a big part of the Art/ Pornography debate, but that is because his motives are lower than art — if Tom doesn't get a hard on when he's drawing then he knows its crap. This is indeed far hornier than Inches or Advocate, **and pound-for-penis it works out a far better deal.**

Tom also has a great sense of humour, illustrated brilliantly in the cartoon strip 'Threesome,' taken from the Adventures of Kake series. It relates the tale of a huge-dicked sailor and large breasted lady, who get down to some fucking in the woods, only to be interrupted by an even bigger dicked leatherman. As the sailor and leatherman get off together, the poor lady is shown furiously pointing at her empty pussy, while shaking a clenched fist at them. She then goes off and finds a huge dicked cop who, after putting a smile on our lady friend's face by letting her fuck his truncheon, joins the other two for the 'Threesome'.

As well as the drawings there's a section on Tom the man by Micha Ramakers, which includes lots of Tom's personal pin-ups and a personal recollection from Dirty Dirk who has 'discovered through Tom's work that he was as much a man as his heterosexual counterparts'. There's also a

The Art of Pleasure © Taschen

PORN KING

The Autobiography of
John C. Holmes

by John C. Holmes
with Laurie Holmes & Fred E. Basten

eventually his introduction into the world of stag film loops. In subsequent chapters we learn of his childhood — starting in rural Ohio — his lack of a positive father figure, and his closer relationship to his mother and three siblings. The book, not being an in-depth objective biography, skims over much of his life in the service and at UCLA, and could be termed an insider's overview of the porn industry from the late Six-

ties onward.

According to the book, Holmes wants to set the record straight and separate fact from fallacy regarding events in the last years of his life — a life cut short at age 43 by his contraction of the HIV/AIDS virus. He does go into more detail and explanation about his involvement in the mysterious bludgeoning deaths of four people on Wonderland Avenue on July 1, 1981. Also discussed are his battle with cocaine addiction and finding the love of his life and wife, former porn actress Misty Dawn (Laurie Holmes).

But most of the slim book is about the events leading up to the murders and his life thereafter. In an interview for *Hustler* (Vol 9 N° 12, June 83), with his then 'autobiographer' Barbara Wilkins, given while incarcerated for 110 days in a LA County jail, he told the same tale of being caught between a wealthy freebasing night-club owner and a gang of drug dealing junkies. In the same interview he answers questions about his life in jail, which he only mentions in passing in the book.

This is not *Boogie Nights*, a movie

whose soundtrack could serve as a late night info-mercial for Seventies and Eighties wallpaper music. A more 'documentary' film — although certainly not objective — is *Exhausted* (1981), the last movie he made before the murders, which Holmes himself has admitted was made when he was at his lowest point. In it we see an at times jittery, sweating, uneasy Holmes being interviewed by someone off-camera. This is sandwiched between film clips from his movies, 'person on the street' interviews, and behind the scene looks at porno shoots. He went on to make more movies in the Eighties — according to him even after he found out about his HIV-positive status, but does make the point that none of the actresses he worked with came down with the disease. He also tried, unsuccessfully at the time, to get mandatory HIV tests for the actors in the porn industry. He and his wife both question the government as to the source of his getting the disease. Ms Holmes, in the epilogue, sets the rumours straight and states that her husband did not get the virus from using dirty needles — which makes sense since he talks of

---

bit of bumph about the Tom of Finland Foundation and The Tom of Finland Company.

Don't be put off by the sheer size of this book — it's amazingly light and easily transported by hand. Yet another great cutting edge, affordable book by Taschen.

Rick Caveney

1000 DESSOUS
A History of Lingerie
GILLES NÉRET

£16.99 766pp; Taschen, 1998; ISBN 3-8228-7629-1

Taschen don't do things in short measures. This pictorial history of lingerie is part of their door-stop series and weighs in at over 760 pages. Starting with the first pair of briefs, circa 3000 BC, right through to current trends in fetish wear, the study takes in the changing forms of underwear as depicted in film, advertising, and pornography. The largest section is 'Through the Ages', and shows the preposterous extravaganza of crinolines (the big birdcage contraptions supporting room-devouring dresses, popular at the turn of the century), and the asphyxiating qualities of the wasp-waist corset, in which 'the requirements of fashion often proved fatal'. Also on display is a patent for

armoured undergarments, which were to 'protect ladies from being pricked by passing sadists in the street'. Elsewhere, the female propensity for layers and layers of heavy clothing, helped to make 'academic journals' containing nude studies — like Le Nu Esthétique (circa 1903), supported by the Institute of France — enormously popular. Indeed, it was the French Academy who invented the first 'artistic' briefs in the form of a dinky metal fig leaf.

Any book that starts with a Siné cartoon showing a pageboy lifting up a bride's wedding dress and having a wank has got to be worth at least one look.

SERGE JACQUES
GILLES NÉRET

£16.99 768pp; Taschen, 1998; ISBN 3-8228-7880-4

More *ooh la la* from Gilles Néret and Taschen. Here the subject is blacklisted photographer Serge Jacques, who was raided and arrested many times for his shots of women displaying pubic hair — a serious offence in 1950s France. He was led away in handcuffs when a photo of his appeared depicting a female tennis player with a few stray pubic hairs peeping out of her underwear, and was successfully sued over a picture whose theme was a naked girl pouring

Serge Jacques © Taschen

freebasing cocaine throughout the book.

Porn King also contains a partial filmography, listing the main body of his work on film and video (1969–1997). According to the blurb on the back cover, it contains some 2200+ productions.

Nobody can really judge as to whether Holmes is guilty or innocent concerning the murders, because we were not there and those that were are not talking. But I doubt one person could subdue four others while beating another to death.

The man, the myth, the legend — read the book, see the movie.
Tom Brinkmann

OUT-TAKES
STEWART HOME & 'FRIENDS'
£3.75 68pp; Sabotage Editions, BM Senior, London, WC1N 3XX

I read this, but I don't really feel qualified to comment… It's a collection of pieces largely by or about Stewart Home — some previously published, some not — consisting mainly of people slagging other people off for not having the right critical attitude to some C19th text or other. Contemporary anarchist thought, from the evidence on display here, seems to resemble Christianity in its fractures and factions and in-fighting over what appear to be cosmetic differences. If you're interested, topics of debate include the Art Strike of the early Nineties, the K Foundation (who thankfully aren't as humourless as most of this bunch), and odds and sods too numerous/uninteresting to mention.

There's what might be construed as a veiled warning at the end of the collection during an interview with Home:

IF A CRITIC WISHES TO WRITE ABOUT 'MY' TEXTS AND/OR ACTIVITIES, THEN THEY CANNOT ASSUME THAT THEY ARE EQUIPPED A PRIORI TO DO SO. IT IS NOT MY RESPONSIBILITY IF HAVING APPLIED THE WRONG THEORETICAL TOOLS TO THE TASK, A CRITIC MAKES A SERIES OF CATEGORY ERRORS AND IS THUS TRANSFORMED INTO A LAUGHING STOCK.

Not a laughing stock — please, anything but that! To be fair, this is, as the title has it, a collection of out-takes, and is probably not a good introduction to Home. Actually, I quite like the tactics of disinformation and confusion on display in what I've seen of Home's works, and suspect that 'Stewart Home' doesn't exist at all, but is simply a 'multiple name' like those others described here. For Home completists and pamphlet addicts only. **James Marriott**

FLESH AND BLOOD BOOK 1
HARVEY FENTON (Ed.)
£12.95 246pp; UK: FAB Press, 1998; ISBN 0 952926 03 2
(Available through Headpress, see p.70)

Flesh and Blood has always been one of the better horror/sex/exploitation film zines, primarily because most of the people associated with it could actually write and are knowledgeable about their given topic. Now, at last, the zine has emerged in book form — which, I believe, will be published on an annual basis. [*Editor's note: That schedule now appears to be twice-yearly.*] Most *Headpress* readers will no doubt be familiar with the format,

engine oil into her car. The oil manufacturer noticed their brand name on the can…

Serge Jacques sold his early work to Paris-Hollywood, **an under-the-counter publication that featured some rather average-looking girls captured in various states of undress, all exhibiting unnatural skin tones on account of the cheapskate reproduction process utilised in printing. But the models who appeared in** Paris-Hollywood **were hopeful that they might make it one day to the pages of two cinema-based magazines from the same publisher, the altogether more respectable** Le Film Français **and** Cinémonde. **Maybe some did.**

The images that go to make up this book were all taken during the Fifties and Sixties, and show a bevy of the photographer's favourite models — pubes and all. Some of the girls are strikingly beautiful; most look like they might live next door. At least one wears a headscarf.

THE COMPLETE REPRINT OF 'EXOTIQUE'
The first 36 issues, 1951–1957
£29.99 2444pp; 3 volumes in slipcase; Taschen, 1998; ISBN 3-8228-7436-1

Leonard Burtman, scientist and keen amateur photographer, left the government not a happy man when his close proximity to A-bomb tests in the California desert in the mid-Forties made him sterile. The blast may also have buggered up some brain cells, too, because shortly afterwards he turned his talents to creating and publishing Exotique. **These slim booklets out of NY, devoted themselves to depicting the 'bizarre and the unusual' with drawings and photos of scantily clad women, women in heels and hose, and — reflecting the rapidly growing fetish scene — 'damsels in distress'. Some fine comic strips by Gene Bilbrew and Eric Stanton are scattered throughout; short fiction (that shamelessly covers a lot of pages) and letters that smack of whimsical fabrication, were also regular features. In** Exotique **No 5, for instance, an escapologist's female assistant writes in to regale readers with her description of a routine that has her acting like a house maid while donning a black leather straight-jacket and velvet panties.**

Serge Jacques © Taschen

which hasn't changed too much with the new look, being a mix of reviews, interviews, and articles. One thing that is different, however, is *F&B*'s expansion into other areas of interest... manifested here in a massive interview with Rock Bitch. For the uninitiated, Rock Bitch sound like bad heavy metal, spout an essentialist, and thus thoroughly dull and reactionary paganism, and — gasp! — have sex on stage. They are the kind of crap you watch on *Eurotrash*, and would probably be upstaged by a Belgium who can spit live fish into a basketball net if they ever appeared on the show together. But, whilst I would question editor Fenton's musical taste — and perhaps point out that Psychic TV and their ilk did similar pagan/sex/music performances more than 15 years ago — I have to say that I read the entire piece (every goddamned line of it). I am no closer to caring about Rock Bitch, though. Point being: regardless of your interest — or otherwise — in Schlock Rock, *F&B* still delivers.

Jack Sargeant

SCREAMS AND NIGHTMARES

The Films of Wes Craven
BRIAN J. ROBB
£16.99 191pp; UK: Titan Books, 1998;
ISBN 1 85286 945 3

At first sight, this looks like just another glossy coffee table book from Titan, but actually turns out to be quite a substantial (200 page) guide to the work of writer, producer and director Wes Craven, including lots of b&w photographs, a full filmography, and a detailed overview of his many TV projects. The earlier chapters detailing Craven's 'low-budget beginnings' are the most interesting, but then, these low-budget films are themselves far more fascinating than the later 'box-office triumphs'. We learn that Craven is an ex-English teacher with a master's degree in philosophy, who was heavily influenced by childhood fears and experiments with recreational drugs in creating film sequences. Much of the text gives us the film-maker's own words on the subjects of film-making, commercial cinema and violence in the movies. He claims, for example, that he walked out of *Reservoir Dogs* 'because I felt at a certain point that the film-maker was just getting

off on the violence' — and this from the man who directed *The Last House on the Left* with its protracted rape sequence, and who, in *The Hills Have Eyes*, brought us 'the closest the movies have ever come to wasting a baby', according to cult movie reviewer Joe Bob Briggs.

Craven also discusses the fact that people wouldn't leave their children with him after the release of *The Last House on the Left*, and the influence on his work of comicbook styles, noting that at one point he was working on a movie project based on the Jonestown massacre. Robb claims that the success of *A Nightmare on Elm Street* in 1984 'turned Craven's career around', enabling him to make films that were commercially successful, but — I would argue — much less interesting, since nothing he's made since 1972 even comes close to the compelling violence of *Last House on the Left*.

Although Robb quotes a fascinating (bad) review of *Elm Street*, which essentially criticises the film for breaking the 'implicit contract between a horror film director and his audience that dreams don't kill', the chapters after the one on *Elm Street*

Although still being published today, come the Sixties the sheen had been taken off Exotique with the arrival of Playboy. Taschen presents Leonard Burtman's pride and joy as it was in its heyday — the first 36 issues, bound as an exquisite three-volume box set. Sarah Turner

THE PLAYBOY BOOK
The Complete Pictorial History
GRETCHEN EDGREN (Ed.)
H/BK £19.99 368pp; Evergreen (Taschen), 1998;
ISBN 3-8228-7607-0

Hugh Hefner launched Playboy magazine in November 1953. On the cover of the debut number was Marilyn Monroe; inside was the celebrated, but previously unpublished shot of the blonde bombshell reclining against a red backdrop. The new title shifted 50,000 copies.

Of all the top-shelf magazines in circulation, Playboy is arguably the only one to which the phrase 'I read it for the articles' can legitimately be attributed. Over the years they've carried original work by such luminaries as Ray Bradbury, Norman Mailer, Harvey Kurtzman, Lenny Bruce, and Ian Fleming (who had three new Bond novels serialised in its pages over the years), and have interviewed everyone from Fidel Castro, through Groucho Marx to Burt

Alex Haley interviews self-appointed leader of the American Nazi Party, George Lincoln Rockwell for *Playboy*'s April 1966 edition. Rockwell had checked that his interviewer wasn't Jewish. "I didn't tell him I was a Negro," admitted Haley. *The Playboy Book* © Taschen

Reynolds.

The prestigious Playboy **Rabbit Head symbol was, by the late-Fifties, established the world over. A pair of Rabbit Head cuff links on a plain white cover — not a semi-naked lady in sight — was enough to sell in excess of a million copies of the magazine. By the Sixties, the symbol was being incorporated into covers in a variety of**

— just like the films — get increasingly less interesting. There's a chapter on Robert Englund and the marketing of Freddy Krueger, detailed accounts of the production of each of the *Elm Street* sequels, and some discussion of special effects. Analysis gives way to quotes from *Fangoria* and *Cinefantastique*, along with lots and lots of detailed descriptions, which, while interesting in their way, never seem to address the issues behind Craven's ongoing fascinations with suburbia, the broken family, and children in peril.

Incidentally, as the film posters in this book reminded me, Craven's films always seem to be tagged with some of the best and most original movie marketing slogans of all time: 'Don't bury me... I'm not dead!' (*The Serpent and the Rainbow*); 'If Nancy doesn't wake up screaming... she won't wake up at all!' (*Elm Street*); 'Not recommended for persons over 30' (*Last House on the Left*); 'A nice American family. They didn't want to kill. But they didn't want to die' (*The Hills Have Eyes*); and, for the miserable *Scream 2*, 'Someone has carried their love of sequels one step too far'. I'll say. **Mikita Brottman**

THE REDNECK MANIFESTO
JIM GOAD

$11.00 274pp; US: Touchstone (Simon & Schuster); available from Mark Pawson for £7.95 (+ £0.80 p&p), PO box 664, London E3 4QR; www.mpawson.demon.co.uk

I never saw any of the original issues of *ANSWER Me!*, and only came across the writings of Jim and Debbie Goad in the recent *First Three* collection. For the uninitiated, their stock-in-trade is the furious, vitriolic debunking of myths surrounding taboo subjects. Not just your average, run-of-the-mill taboos, either — the Goads knew what kind of people would read their rants, and focused on the topics which produce knee-jerk reactions in the most 'liberal' and 'enlightened' of readers: racism, sexism, rape, suicide, etc. They were also not only unafraid of attacking their audience, but positively delighted in it. Whoever you are, you're a target for indiscriminate but acute Goad rage and hatred.

The Redneck Manifesto is the first book-length project from Jim Goad, and kudos should go to Simon & Schuster, a mainstream publishing house, for putting it out. It's basically a polemic in defence of 'the cultural clan variously referred to as rednecks, hillbillies, white trash, crackers and trailer trash', to quote from the back cover blurb. The book's obviously very US-centric, but a lot of its ideas are applicable here too, and it's interesting to note how we've swallowed wholesale American cultural assumptions about class in the States. I don't think the USA has a Ken Loach or a Mike Leigh, or much idea of class pride for the underprivileged, compared to the often inverse prejudice in the UK media.

The word 'redneck' is used dismissively for poor American whites. And it's Goad's basic premise that poor American whites are prejudiced against, both economically and in terms of media representation, and blamed for a range of sins they never committed. He argues convincingly that class and wealth distribution rather than race are the key dividing factors in American society, and that institutional racism was established by the ruling elite during slavery as a divide and rule tactic — Goad shows that the volume of European

---

increasingly novel and cryptic ways (creating a kind of antithesis of Mad magazine's self-depreciating Alfred E Newman in the process), and Playboy would often be inundated with letters from readers unable to find the bunny.

In many ways, Playboy's photo spreads only serve to 'get in the way' of the rest of the magazine. In an age where the ubiquitous 'top shelf' is rife with quality-free, sexually explicit magazines, the airbrushed Playboy model seems a pretty wholesome option. As writers and artists clamour to be associated with the award winning Playboy, equally actresses and pop starlets clamour to appear nude in it. It's a sign of having made it.

Gretchen Edgren's book is a full-colour picture history of Playboy magazine. (And who better qualified for the job than the person who interviews the Playmates for their photo-spreads?) Excerpt pages from major articles are reproduced, as well as some of the more striking covers and notable models, each one sourced and accompanied by a fascinating sliver of information. A section at the back of the book folds out to reveal thumbnails of every Playboy centrefold, from Monroe in 1953 to Anna-Marie Goddard in January 1994. A trivia section recalls every interviewee and imparts such

factoids as 'Biggest selling issue ever' (November 1972) and 'Date of the first Braille edition' (July 1970).

An excellent volume.

A quick note about the frontispiece, which comprises of a hand-tinted photograph showing a young Hugh Hefner surrounded by Bunny Girls and smiling up at the camera... it doesn't half remind me of Jack Torrence at the end of Kubrick's The Shining, another guest trapped inside the dated photograph that hangs within the Overlook hotel.

THE DOMINANT WIVES & OTHER STORIES
ERIC STANTON

£16.99 704pp; Taschen, 1998; ISBN 3-8228-7435-3

It's my firm belief that wives and girlfriends should be spanked as often as possible, for every last little misdemeanour...! So you can imagine my shocked amazement at this latest offering from Taschen which comprises 768 pages of Stanton's female-domination comic strips in which women literally take the upper-hand — forcing shamed husbands, sneaking voyeurs and many a young innocent to undergo severe strappings, canings, beltings and — in some cases — outright bloody beatings for around 720

113

slaves imported into the country far outweighed that of African slaves, which is news to me, and that most 'rednecks' now are descendants of these slaves; not really 'the oppressor', or able to experience any of the much-vaunted white privilege. He debunks myths about the Civil War, — specifically about it being a war to free black slaves — and offers an acute analysis of media representation of both poor whites as 'rednecks' and as militia members, exploring the extraordinarily biased reporting on militias and the legitimacy of their concerns. He also deals at length with inverse racism and white guilt, and the absurdity of a situation in which racial pride is encouraged in all groups except whites, pointing out that white racial pride is usually seen as a fascistic tendency. It certainly can be a fascistic tendency, but that doesn't mean that Nation of Islam can't.

The first few chapters are taken up dealing with these issues, which can be a little dry at times — Goad is, after all, seeking to show that a number of historical assumptions are built on false premises, and backs up his argument with liberal quota-

tions from contemporary documents. To offset this, though, Goad writes extensively about himself, 'a proud member of the White Trash Nation', his community, and 'trailer trash' culture. Goad's arguments are more convincing and credible than I can do credit to here, and as an added bonus you get some prospective reviews written by the author, such as the following:

THIS BOOK IS A PSYCHOTIC, SELF-PITYING, ONE-SIDED, HISTORICALLY REVISIONIST SCREED. *W*HAT AN ACCOMPLISHMENT — MAKING PEOPLE *FEEL GOOD* ABOUT RACISM AGAIN.

Goad's sawn-off shotgun approach to the reader might not win him many new friends, and it is easy to see this book being misinterpreted. It killed a few assumptions of my own, and made me think about the situation here more clearly — it's refreshing to have someone cut through all the sensitive tiptoeing and be unafraid to offend everyone with a giant 'fuck you'. Angry? You should be. **James Marriott**

LUSTMORD
Sexual Murder in
Weimar Germany
MARIA TATAR

no price listed; US: Chichester: Princeton University Press, 1995

Weimar Germany is to serial killers what the Italian Renaissance is to poisoners, an early golden age. Unfortunately, Maria Tatar is more concerned with the artistic representation of sexual murder than in the murders themselves, and by narrowing her focus thus — by being willing to confuse the act and the art — she winds up dodging the chance to analyse what it was about the conditions of Germany in the 1920s that made it such a fertile breeding ground for what has resurfaced today like a modern murder epidemic.

Tatar's thesis is that German men, disempowered by the loss of the Great War and by the growing emancipation of women, sexualised murder, turning crime against women in a manifestation of revenge for women luring men into their seductive evil. This is both simplistic and misguided: using the mores of late 20th Century feminism to misread something which should bear a far

of those pages, with only the merest hint at similar up-endings for the girls! Outrageous!

Despite this situation, these 'Stantoons' are genuinely erotic and for the most part, exquisitely detailed forays into S&M, emerging from a period (mostly Sixties and Seventies) when this type of material still seemed fresh, exciting and somewhat disturbing, having yet to be appropriated and rendered bland by mainstream fashion associations. This is no more in evidence than in the very first story, 'Bound in Leather' and its sequel, 'Bound in Leather 2' in which every sort of kink in the bondage fetish is covered, including the unsettling visage of 'a beautifully made face mask in flesh coloured suede' (an image worthy of someone like Thomas Ligotti!). More knockabout fun is in evidence in stories like 'Marriage at Stake', 'She Dominates All' and 'Partners in Punishment' which examine in detail the battle of the sexes with victory, as per usual, going to the 'ladies'. Some of Stanton's scenarios are more outlandish, taking place in genre settings like westerns, crime, or espionage, and these tend to be crueller still... in 'Bonnie and Clara' the male protagonist has a target painted on his arse whilst our heroines throw full-size heavy darts at him! The western story includes scenes of branding and thrash-

Eric Stanton's 'Bonnie and Clara',
The Dominant Wives & Other Stories © Taschen

ings with cacti... youch!

All in all, The Dominant Wives is, I suppose, as sick a turn-on as you're likely to find, whilst still seeming 'fun'. This is due to Stanton's appealing, colourful artwork and his ability to exaggerate just enough without descending into gross caricature. This hefty sampling of his work depicts a master of the genre at the top of his form. One tip, though... don't try to read this very heavy, well-produced volume with one hand unless you're capable of mastering one of those busty Stantoon chicks... In other words: not for limp-wristed wimps! Stephen Sennitt

broader analysis.

It seems to be taking its cues from the work of Ann Douglas, whose *The Feminisation of American Culture* and *Mongrel Manhattan* see the modern movement as a male attempt to destroy a feminine culture, and the Great War as a fit of testosterone madness aimed at revenge against Victorian mothers.

We could draw intriguing parallels between Weimar Germany and post-Vietnam America for example, or between the Roaring Twenties of 'come to the Cabaret, old chum' and the Eighties highlife which Reagan and Thatcher brought to the yuppies. Is there a breeding ground for serial killers? *Lustmord*, however, isn't interested in making bigger connections. Tatar opens her book with references to a German children's rhyme based on Fritz Haarmann, executed in 1925. She never mentions the fact that Haarman's victims were exclusively male, which wouldn't fit into the violence against women thesis.

Looking at serial killing as a 'defense against male fantasies about sexually seductive women' may be valid as far as it goes, but it doesn't go very far. Tatar knows that W.W.I marked a symbolic loss of masculinity (check the symbolic significance of Jake Barnes in *The Sun Also Rises*, for example), but traditionally men had gone to war to protect, as it were, a civilisation which was symbolised by its female aspects. The Great War brought into question the whole concept of civilisation being something worth dying for. A generation was being sent, lemming-like, to suicide in the service of a newly mechanised, impersonal, homogenous death. There was no civilisation to die for, there was just death.

Men might reclaim their masculinity by revenging themselves on civilisation by attacking the women who symbolise it, but even Tatar also recognises 'the belief that men might be able to reconstitute themselves through art'. She sees the art of Dix, Grosz, Beckman, Fritz Lang, and Doblin as needing to kill women to do that. But she never grasps that the major art movement of the period, cubism, was all about deconstruction, or even destruction, and offered in its explosive realities

a reconstituted humanity full of non-murderous loss.

Violence against women is certainly a part of the art of Weimar Germany, and certainly a part of the serial lustmord that partly characterises the era. But it is more a symptom than a cause, and the causes run far deeper than Tatar, for whatever reason, cares to look.

Michael Carlson

DESTROY
Pictures of the Sex
Pistols and the others
DENNIS MORRIS
£19.95 155pp UK: Creation books, 1998; ISBN 1 871592 74 7

'Nostalgia for rejects to come'... Twenty years on and the nostalgia has well and truly arrived. No sooner have we recovered from the Sex Pistols' rather sad reformation, than we're getting regurgitated *NME*-type photos from the Seventies and asked to pay £19.99 for the dubious pleasure.

Destroy is a book of paparazzi photos dealing with the Sex Pistols, that boat trip with Richard fucking Branson and gigs in Sweden, Coventry, Wolverhampton, Brunel university and Penzance. If you were at any of these gigs, or indeed, on that boat you may give a fuck about this book. I wasn't and I don't.

There are a couple of good pics: a nice one of Trojan looking fucked-up and the ever-beautiful Jordan (Amyl Nitrate) relaxing next to a friend; Nancy, doing impressions of that-dead-bloke-from-Nirvana's-widow. Also it proves that both Malcolm McLaren and Vivienne Westwood have always been pig ugly. Oh yes, and Sid's actually quite fuckable — anyone know where he's buried? **Rick Caveney**

FLOOZY
JANE GRAHAM
Illustrated by XTINA LAMB
£5.00 100pp; UK: Slab-O-Concrete Publications; ISBN 1 899866 11 6; Slab-O-Concrete Pubs., PO Box 148, Hove, BN3 3DQ; email: mail@slab-o-concrete.demon.co.uk

Jane Graham is aka 'Jane S. Stamp', creator of *Shag Stamp* zine (reviewed *Headpress 17*). *Floozy*, her first book, is a picaresque autobiographical jaunt through strip shows,

lap dancing, life modelling, hitching, and generally skirting the fringes of the demimonde, doing whatever it takes to avoid getting a 'proper' job. Jane is evidently what the Victorians called an 'adventuress' — not really a committed tart, not really respectable, living for kicks. It has to be said, though, that the relentless shabbiness of her surroundings, and of the uniformly revolting male punters she comes into contact with, leave her more jaundiced than full of the 'up-for-it' quality she starts the book with. Although there is little coherence or connecting narrative to the vignettes which make up the text, *Floozy* charts a consistent trajectory of increasing weariness and disillusionment that make the latter part of this little book rather more poetic and interesting than the first. There are moments of real pathos:

I CAN'T WRITE MORE THAN A COUPLE OF LINES ABOUT THEM ANYMORE. WHERE'S THE VARIATION? I PUT MY MAKE-UP ON, DO MY HAIR NICE, AND YOU PUSH ME DOWN, SHOVE IT IN, COME AND LEAVE.

Whilst the likes of Peter Sotos may get off on this kind of thing, most people, most men, even, will see it as pitiful. One's sympathy for Jane, however, is tempered by the knowledge that she has the intelligence and resources to leave this life whenever she likes. What about her co-workers who don't have her advantages, who really don't have a choice? Jennifer Blowdryer's introduction compares Jane Graham to Kerouac, but I think better comparisons can be made with the William Burroughs of the *Junkie* and *Queer* period, Orwell's *Down and Out in Paris and London*, or Jack London's *The People of the Abyss*. Like these, *Floozy* is a report from the shady side of the street by someone who's been there, but isn't actually from there. This is not to say that Jane Graham is as good a writer as Burroughs, Orwell, or London. She's a perfectly adequate one, though. My favourite chapter is 'The Tattooed Lady', in which she describes getting a large tattoo, and then having sex wearing the new design, with tenderness and verve:

115

AS SHE WATCHES HIS COCK
TEASING AT THE ENTRANCE
SHE WATCHES THE DRAGON
ALSO, ITS WINGS AND
CLAWS TIGHTENING AS SHE
LURES HIS COCK INTO ITS
LAIR, WATCHES THEM
UNFURL AS HER BELLY LETS
OUT SMALL SPASMS OF
ECSTASY.

This is the only point in the book at which the sex act is described in pleasurable terms. It is also one of only two chapters written in the third person — make of that what you will.

Jane's stories are nicely set off by Xtina ('Christina', presumably) Lamb's clean-limbed pen and ink illustrations. Add to this a nifty square format, and the modest price tag, and Floozy is a recommended product. **Simon Collins**

17% HENDRIX WAS NOT THE ONLY MUSICIAN
BILLY CHILDISH
and his FAMOUS HEADCOATS
£10 94pp (Book & CD); UK: Slab-O-Concrete (details above);
ISBN 1 899866 17 5

Billy Childish comes across as a man on a mission. Now at 39-years-old, Billy has a full and creative life. Self-confessed punk poet, he also turns his skills to painting, literature, mu-

Floozy. Art © Xtina Lamb

sic and, believe it or not, woodcarving! All represented here in his new book — a retrospective look over Mr Childish's career.

The journey begins with Billy's school report card, from which the title of the book is taken (being a comment made in 1972 by an obviously frustrated music teacher). It then moves on to a selection of his paintings, the subject for most of which, I guess, is himself. These images remind me of the work of Salfordian artist, LS Lowry: stick-like, brightly coloured people doing what comes naturally.

After the paintings, we move on to 'Communications from Group Hangman,' a sort of artist's bible on how to approach the world of art and deal with the ramblings of the artistic elite. If that doesn't get you excited, quickly move on to the photo-booth pages, where you can reflect on Billy's life via the medium of photography (does this man have no end to his talents?). We see angry (but quite cute) Billy as a young teenager in 1979, with punk attitude and all. Marvel at the passing of time from one photograph to another, finally ending with his last photo taken in 1988. I guess the punk movement played a sick joke in that it made no provisions for reaching old age.

We then head for the land of poetry. Here is my favourite part. With titles like 'Dissection' and 'Strange Bravery', we see the real Billy Childish, and by far the most entertaining part of Billy's work.

At the back of the book is a 14-track CD, which includes a cover of 'Teenage Kicks' (The Undertones) and 'Pinhead' (The Ramones). This CD certainly has its moments, and takes us back to the heady days of Punk Rock. Together with his group, Thee Famous Headcoats, Billy has released a staggering 80 records in total!

I like this book. I enjoy artists stretching their limits and getting into new fields (unless it's David Bowie trying to revive his acting career). It's a journey through mixed feelings, like spending the afternoon in a mental hospital with a sick relative. An entertaining, multi-tasking book that I am sure will interest even the most cynical Punk Rocker. **Will Youds**

AN UNSEEMLY MAN
My Life as Pornographer, Pundit and Social Outcast
LARRY FLYNT
with KENNETH ROSS
£6.99 292pp; UK: Bloomsbury, 1997

Look for this one in your local bargain bookshop (I think my copy cost £1.99), though it would certainly be worth paying full price for this compulsive little page-turner. Arriving hot on the heels of Milos Forman's excellent film *The People vs. Larry Flynt* (superior, I thought, to the overrated *Boogie Nights*), this is the ghosted autobiography on which the film was based, and this edition contains no less than four forewords — from Oliver Stone (producer), Milos Forman (director), Woody Harrelson (star), and Al Goldstein of *Screw* magazine — all running along the lines of what a surprisingly affable fellow Larry Flynt is when you get to meet him, and why his story is required reading for all those interested in defending the First Amendment. The book's political and cultural credentials established, let's get down and dirty.

An Unseemly Man energetically recounts Flynt's dirt-poor Kentucky hillbilly upbringing, including his early sexual experiences with a 'neighbor girl' at seven, and with a chicken at nine. In his mad-tycoon phase, Flynt immortalised the latter by having a three-foot high replica chicken installed (with a mock-up of his shotgun-shack childhood home) in the basement of his mansion. Also discussed are his careers in the armed forces, his three failed marriages (or was it four? I lost count, and no doubt so did Larry) and sundry illegitimate offspring. Then we're in more familiar territory with the founding of the Hustler go-go clubs in Ohio, and the launch of *Hustler* magazine. The latter half of the book is largely taken up with accounts of his bizarre conversion to born-again Christianity at the hands of President Carter's sister Ruth Carter Stapleton, the lengthy legal battles he fought on *Hustler*'s behalf, the white supremacist assassination attempt in Kansas that left him permanently wheelchair-bound and in constant pain for years (but at least it destroyed his religious faith), and the death from AIDS of his consort Althea (played with great bravura by Courtney Love in the film). There is plenty of entertaining incident along the way, and, as you'd expect, lashings of sex.

Flynt evidently possessed an overwhelming interest in making the beast-with-two-backs long before he got into the skin trade. He recounts an incident in Cannes during his Navy days when, on shore leave, he hired the entire staff of a brothel — 20 girls — lined them up naked, and proceeded to play musical dick. He had to be carried back to his ship. Finding himself running a string of topless clubs in the late Sixties, he was indeed a happy camper:

I WAS INSATIABLE, SOMETIMES HAVING A DIFFERENT WOMAN EVERY FOUR OR FIVE HOURS. THERE MAY HAVE BEEN SOMEONE WHO HAD MORE WOMEN THAN I DID, BUT I SERIOUSLY DOUBT IT. IT GOT TO THE POINT WHERE I COULDN'T REMEMBER WHO I'D SCREWED.

Nor did this behaviour diminish after he met the love of his life, Althea Leasure, an underage dancer who was swiftly promoted to managing the clubs whilst Flynt nursed his nascent magazine, and who eventually ran the magazine whilst Flynt spent all his time in court.

It is clear that Larry Flynt's astonishing rags-to-riches-via-rudeness story happened because Flynt possessed several invaluable personal qualities — a flair for publicity, a ruthless instinct for profitability, a pugnacious enthusiasm for baiting the bourgeoisie, and an uncanny sense for what would appeal to the blue-collar readership he courted (although he makes the interesting point that *Hustler* also proved popular with the intelligentsia, highly educated people evidently being 'less hung up on conventional morality' than the amorphous middle-class masses who were his real bugbear). It is also clear that the fury and animosity that *Hustler* aroused had as much to do with its social and political outspokenness as it did its sexual explicitness. Flynt had a genius for making enemies, and a righteous unwillingness to back down.

You have to admire a man who appears in court wearing a T-shirt emblazoned with the words 'FUCK THIS COURT', and who screams at the Supreme Court of the United States of America, 'You're nothing but eight assholes and a token cunt!' *Hustler*'s most protracted court case was fought over a Campari ad parody in which Flynt depicted TV evangelist Jerry Falwell reminiscing about screwing his drunken mother in the outhouse, but my personal favourite *Hustler* prank was the spoof ad they ran headed 'JESSE HELMS — PHONE SEX — BLACKS PREFERRED', and giving his home and office numbers.

First and foremost, though, all red-blooded men owe a profound debt to Larry Flynt for being the man who brought us the split-beaver shot, the man who had what seems in retrospect an obvious realisation:

TO PUT IT BLUNTLY, IF YOU GOT THE MODELS TO SPREAD THEIR LEGS A LITTLE WIDER, YOU'D SELL MORE MAGAZINES. I MADE A MENTAL NOTE OF THAT.

Thanks, Larry. **Simon Collins**

THE LONG ROAD OUT OF HELL
MARILYN MANSON
with NEIL STRAUSS
£12.99 288pp; UK: Plexus, 1998

...Brian Warner: The Not So Long Teenage Angst Filled Road Out Of Canton, Ohio...

Let's face it. Whether we like it or not, the world at this point in time is Marilyn Manson's oyster. Unfortunately for Marilyn/Brian, that oyster appears to be a week-old putrid, effluvial, cancerous pustule of a bivalve, brimming with apathy, hatred, and hypocrisy, despite his fame, fortune and adulation. Or at least that's what he wants us to think.

Curiously, his literary life only begins at age 13 (scary!). Could it be that Brian has the terrible secret of a happy childhood to keep hidden from his legion of adoring pubescent middle-American vampires? Certainly the childhood photos scattered throughout the book in which he looks pleased as punch, and cute as a button, would tend to support this theory. The only really terrible thing he can attribute to his parents

is his mother's application of a home-made remedy for acne, and that hardly places her in the Rose West category. He infers that his perverted grandfather poisoned his dog, although admits that there was no real evidence to prove this. We get the standard American small city adolescent obsession with all things dark and scary, and teenage alienation by the truckload: smoking pot, listening to Judas Priest and Ozzy Osbourne, and of course, toying with demonic forces beyond our control. As a teenager in Texas, I personally knew at least 30 people who attempted to make pacts with the horned one, just because, well, that's what we did on the weekends.

The big change comes in 1989, when after moving to that white trash Mecca known as Florida, Brian decides to form a band 'to see if a white band that wasn't rap could get away with acts far more offensive and illicit than 2 Live Crew'. Granted, this is a tall order when up against a couple of guys wearing baseball hats that use the words 'pussy' and 'bitch' frequently. The character of Marilyn is born amidst much metaphorical psychobabble about Milton and the validity of Charles Manson — whom, we are told, is a 'gifted philosopher'. This proves beyond a shadow of a doubt that all musicians are frustrated comedians.

He gets a band. He does drugs. He gets a girlfriend. He treats her bad. They break up. He meets Trent Reznor. He does drugs. They make a record. They fall out. He goes on tour. He does drugs. He makes another record. He gets another girlfriend. He believes he is the Antichrist. He does drugs. He goes on tour. I was all ready to receive a sacrament of the damned and what I got was bland tales of backstage and hotel tomfoolery amongst sycophants and roadies straight out of the pages of an Aerosmith or Led Zeppelin biography. Can't these guys think of anything new to do? Now, if I were Antichrist Rock Star for a day, I'd be making trousers out of newborn puppy ears and building up my mummified vulva collection.

The most interesting moments occur when the real person that is inside Marilyn peeks out, and tries to reconcile true emotion with the façade that he has created for himself. He finds himself genuinely uncomfortable when witnessing some of the more extreme entertainments that are provided for him, and even strays dangerously close to being poignant when describing his girlfriend's flu and subsequent abortion.

His jealousy of Axl Rose recording a Charles Manson 'song' before he does is revealing, although laughable and immediately pathetic. It appears even the Antichrist just can't help feeling human every once in a while. Despite all of his transgressions, there is certainly a duality at work, and that's where the real story is. He's actually a nice guy.

I really wish that I would have been shocked, offended and outraged by what I read, but in the end Marilyn turns out to be as threatening as a vanilla milkshake. The biggest outrage for me is the chilling admission that he would not cheat on his girlfriend. If I was a confused 14-year-old in Witchita, I would feel infinitely betrayed, but then a lot of 14-year-olds are going to think he's the cat's pyjamas because their parents don't like him, and they are exactly who this book is for.

Marilyn kind of jumped the gun on this autobiography thing. I think he should have waited until he was 60 to write it, because the last 30 years are not nearly as interesting as the next thirty are going to be.

Mark Deutrom

OSWALD TALKED

118 RAY and MARY LAFONTAINE
$25 454pp; US: Pelican Books, 1996;
1101 Monroe Street, Gretna, LA 70053, USA

Accepting that Lee Oswald was indeed a 'patsy' in the Kennedy Assassination, and that there was indeed a conspiracy, the question of what exactly Oswald was doing, or thought he was doing, has prompted years of informed guesswork.

This books ends all the guesswork. Working with Dallas police records released in 1992, in the wake of the furore surrounding the film *JFK*, the LaFontaines have reconstructed Oswald's stay in custody, and proven both the existence of a conspiracy and his status as its patsy.

Dallas Police kept no records of their interrogation of Oswald, but Mary LaFontaine discovered that Oswald had actually shared his cellblock with two other prisoners. One of those men, John Elrod, testified that police brought a badly-battered prisoner into the cell for Oswald to identify, and that Oswald said he had met that man along with Jack Ruby.

Tracing the identity of that prisoner proved more difficult, but he turned out to be Lawrence Miller, arrested on 18 November after a high-speed chase involving a car laden with weaponry stolen from the US Army base at Fort Hood. Miller's partner was Donnell Whitter, an occasional employee of Jack Ruby, and it was with Ruby that the two had earlier met Oswald. Why? The FBI, contrary to policy, destroyed the informant report that led to Miller's arrest, but the LaFontaines make a credible case, including testimony of an FBI file clerk, that Oswald was that informant.

Oswald would have been ratting out both the mob-linked gunrunners and an anti-Castro Cuban organisation, the Student Revolutionary Directorate (DRE), both of which were linked directly to the CIA. The likelihood that Oswald blew his cover would make him a perfect candidate to serve as a patsy, and the fact that he was on the FBI payroll helped ensure that J Edgar Hoover's G-Men showed no real interest in investigating the actual facts of the assassination on behalf of the Warren Commission.

This explanation resolves a lot of the contradictions in Oswald's pseudo-Marxist behaviour, and his multiple appearances within the Cuban exile movement in Texas and

Louisiana. This is probably the single most important work on the Kennedy assassination to have appeared in the past decade, and demands far more attention than it has thus far received. **Michael Carlson**

RFK
A Candid Biography
C. DAVID HEYMAN
£20 596pp; William Heinemann

SHADOW PLAY
The Murder of Robert F Kennedy, The Trial of Sirhan Sirhan, and the Failure of American Justice
WILLIAM KLABER
and PHILIP H. MELANSON
£6.99; St. Martin's Press

The publishers of David Heyman's biography promoted it with the line 'this book will make President Clinton look like a choirboy', which is probably something no book deserves. Now I wonder if C David Heyman might be available to ghostwrite the next volume of Kenneth Starr's memoirs. Because until we learn that Clinton got more raised than just campaign funds by the likes of Barbara Streisand, Carly Simon, and Sharon Stone, Heyman's disingenuous publicity remains sadly accurate.

Bobby Kennedy played the hard-working family man to his brother's Camelot playboy, but anyone who looked just a little below the surface recognised a hard and vicious politician, with a cold calculating ruthlessness. Those of us working on Eugene McCarthy's campaign against Lyndon Johnson's war machine saw as much when Bobby muscled him out of the way after McCarthy had proven an anti-war candidacy was viable. He had earlier trampled Senator Kenneth Keating in New York, and a look further back would show Bobby's face smiling behind Senator Joe McCarthy and Roy Cohn during the famous trials that gave an era's repression its name. So to many people, Bobby was never a saint, though to many others, he was.

Heyman works hard to disabuse the latter of their delusions, mostly by assembling an array of circumstantial and anecdotal evidence to show that little brother was getting

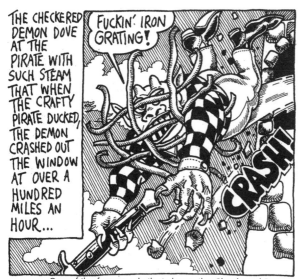

THE CHECKERED DEMON DOVE AT THE PIRATE WITH SUCH STEAM THAT WHEN THE CRAFTY PIRATE DUCKED, THE DEMON CRASHED OUT THE WINDOW AT OVER A HUNDRED MILES AN HOUR...

FUCKIN' IRON GRATING!

CRASH!

One of the few panels that shows the Checkered Demon with his pecker still in his pants. © S. Clay Wilson

more pussy than Jack Kennedy and Frank Sinatra put together. The Kennedy political machine was like a travelling *Animal House* frat party, with Jack as Otter and Bobby as Boone. A whole array of starlets who brightened my adolescence engaged in the famous Kennedy touch football: Marilyn Monroe, Lee Remick, Kim Novak, Jayne Mansfield, Candice Bergen, Claudine Longet (killer of the skier Spider Sabich), etc etc.

Most intriguing are the details of Bobby's affair with his brother's widow, and the revelation that he and Rudolf Nureyev made out in a phone booth. Heyman's sources may not be the world's most reliable (Gore Vidal admits he was — next to Jimmy Hoffa — the man Bobby hated most), but it does make for good gossip.

Bobby also had a thing for young and impressionable campaign workers, the Mary Jo Kopechnes of their day. All the Kennedys did. It's hard to see what the point of a gossipy tabloid bio like this is, except to whisper behind wet palms all the nasty details. Heyman doesn't delve very deeply into anything: he recounts the tale of JFK's affair with Mary Pinchot Meyer without ever mentioning that her husband was a high official in the CIA, which became relevant when her brother in law, Ben Bradlee, editor of the *Wash-*

ington Post, gave her diary to the CIA's James Angleton.

The Kennedys were protected from the kind of scrutiny which has blighted Bill Clinton by the ethos of the times and by the family's mon-ied influence. You could look at Chappaquiddick as marking a turn-ing point in the private lives of poli-ticians in America; Teddy's late night ride with Mary Jo pushed his pri-vate life into the public domain.

I know from experience that the next generation of Kennedys, Bob-by's children, carried the same sort of arrogance, ruthlessness, and abil-ity to indulge their personal desires while maintaining a public face of respectability — but with far less success. They fell victim to drugs, to allegations of rape, and to scan-dal, doing their best to dissolve what-ever image remained of Jack and Bobby as American heroes.

Martyrdom helped keep that he-roic image alive, and the question of Bobby Kennedy's assassination has never drawn the massive question-ing that accompanied his brother's. Although Sirhan Sirhan was in ef-fect caught in the act, the fact re-mains that the shot that killed RFK was fired from point-blank range di-rectly behind him, while Sirhan stood in front of him, no closer than half a yard away. There is also ample evi-dence that more shots were fired than can be accounted for from

Sirhan's gun.

Philip Melanson is chair of the RFK Archive at UMass-Dartmouth, and has written previously about the possibilities of conspiracy in the RFK killing.

This book, written with documen-tary film maker William Klaber, comes almost as a response to Dan Moldea's *The Killing of Robert F Kennedy*. Moldea, who had been a leading critic of the Sirhan-acted-alone theory, reversed his opinion in this book. In an eerie echo of Gerald Posner's *Case Closed*, Moldea de-cided that Kennedy had been lean-ing backwards and to the left, thus presenting his right ear to Sirhan's gun. Posner had attempted to explain the 'magic bullet' by using a similar Kennedian contortion.

While reiterating the evidence that argues in favour of Sirhan hav-ing been a pre-programmed decoy for the actual killer, Melanson and Klaber are actually more concerned with detailing the way the legal proc-ess ensured that no consideration would be given to any possibility other than Sirhan as the classic lone crazed assassin. While this in and of itself does not prove a conspiracy, it certainly does little to restore any-one's faith in the system's ability to reveal one if it did exist.

With the LaFontaines providing new evidence in the JFK killing; in the wake of the death of James Earl Ray, and Martin Luther King's fam-ily calling for a re-opening of his as-sassination, the real story of the Six-ties remains not that these leaders indulged their libidos, or that we were or weren't better off not know-ing. The real story is that all were murdered, and that none was killed by a lone crazed assassin. Or a jeal-ous husband. **Michael Carlson**

THE COLLECTED CHECKERED DEMON, VOL 1

S. CLAY WILSON

$19.95 (+ $7 p&p outside US); US: Last Gasp, 1998. ISBN 0-86719-384-0; Last Gasp of San Francisco, 777 Florida Street, San Francisco, California 94110, USA

Believe it or not, this is the first major retrospective of Underground Comix's most controversial and un-compromising figure. We've had

Crumb up to here; Robert Williams, Gilbert Shelton, even Spain's Agitprop *Trashman* has been collected, so this bumper grimoire of Wilson's demonic drawings is more than welcome...

The Checkered Demon, deranged delinquent that he is, first featured way back in 1967 in Wilson's self-published *Grist* before his 'public' debut in the Crumb-edited *Zap* Nº 2 the following year. *The Collected Checkered Demon* follows the course of his 'progression' from atrocity to atrocity in chronological order, featuring all his appearances in *Zap* through to the notorious 'banned in the UK' issue of *Weirdo* Nº 17, and beyond. On the way we take in all the demented sexual perversions and apocalyptic landscapes of surrealistic nightmare (this is not mere hyperbole, I promise you!). With tales like 'Thumb and Tongue Tales' and 'The Swap', and incredibly detailed drawings with titles such as 'Spoonful of Maggots', 'Toast to the Severed Head' and 'Baby Sitting The Little Carnivorous Cyclops Child'. First announced (to my baited breath!) in a S. Clay Wilson issue of *The Comics Journal* three years ago, finally the ultimate Wilson tome has arrived. I can only say that while the waiting has seemed eternities, it's been worth it! Buy this NOW!
Stephen Sennitt

MALICIOUS RESPLENDENCE The Paintings of Robt. Williams

$79·95 / £60; US: Fantagraphics, 1998; $125·95 / £100 (Limited Edition); distributed in UK by Turnaround

Self-defined 'lowbrow' artist Robt. Williams has influenced a couple of generations of similar kitschy, scuzzy artists whilst always remaining several (thousand!) steps ahead. This is testified nowhere better than in this present, huge volume which showcases an exhaustive retrospective of the unparalleled artist's work. The whole gamut is covered, ranging from early drawings, paintings and sculpture (how come Robt.'s work in this area looks so much like that of Stanislav Szukalski, who he apparently didn't meet until years later...? Hmmm...) to the hot-rod stuff in conjunction with Ed 'Big

Sex Murder Art.

Daddy' Roth, underground comix work for *Zap* and the notorious *Felch*, and, of course, the full scale, brain-rotting canvases, of which there are around 200 full-colour plates — the most detailed viewing you will get of Robt.'s work outside a gallery! The production of the volume is stunning; the design exquisite. Fantagraphics should be congratulated on spending so much time and effort in giving this Dalí of the Underground Comix Culture a fitting platform. Resplendent works on a grand scale!
Stephen Sennitt

SEX MURDER ART The Films of Jörg Buttgereit

DAVID KEREKES
£11.95 192pp; UK: Critical Vision;
ISBN 0-9523288-4-4
(Available through Headpress, see p.70)

Given that Jörg Buttgereit has only made a handful of films, it might seem strange that people want to write books about him and his work. But then for those of us in the UK, suffering the harshest censorship laws in Western Europe, reading about his films is about the only thing we can do. So far only one of Buttgereit's films is legitimately available on video release in this country — *Der Todesking*, courtesy of those nice people at Screen Edge.

Sex Murder Art provides not only a detailed analysis of Buttgereit's work, including excellent synopses, but also a wealth of back-ground material. Kerekes gets to grips with the films and with the disparate (and occasionally desperate) cast and crew.

The book is extremely well-produced and the photographs and graphics serve to give a taste both of the films and the milieu on which they traverse.

Why Buttgereit's films — which veer from a haunting *artiness* to crass splatterama — should attract so much controversy is beyond me. His themes of death, decay and sexuality are the stock products of horror cinema, though they seem to lack the exploitational cheap thrills of many Hollywood productions. The only one of his film's that I've seen is *Der Todesking* (being a law-abiding sort), and I found it intensely moving, lyrical and genuinely disturbing. The film is made up of seven segments — one for each day of the week — in which we are presented with characters who are isolated, alone and apparently ordinary. Each segment ends with a death, and again there are none of the pyrotechnics which we associate with Hollywood. This bleak realism is deliberately thrown back at us on several occasions, forcing us to acknowledge that this is film, breaking up any incipient complicity between the characters on screen and those of us watching.

Perhaps it is this handling of death which is the problem. In a Western world in which youth is everything (a world in which death is sanitised and hidden away), perhaps an honest mediation on the facts of death is unwelcome. *Der Todesking* opens with a body uncurling from a foetal position until it is flat on its back, dead. The gradual decay and putre-

120

faction of the body through the film is the motif which links together the different segments, and it is as haunting an image as any that you'd see on film today.

Sex Murder Art manages to capture all of this, as well as chronicling the reactions that Buttgereit's work has managed to garner. And, despite the grim subject matter, the book is an enjoyable read. Highly recommended. **Pan Pantziarka**

THE ART OF THE NASTY

NIGEL WINGROVE
and MARC MORRIS

£19.99 (+ £1.50 p&p); Salvation Films, BCM Box 9235, London WC1N 3XX

Working in a video shop in this day and age is a depressing experience. Blockbuster, the McDonald's of the entertainment industry, is full of multiple copies of identikit Hollywood mindrot. Look hard and you might find a copy of *Nikita* or *Cyrano de Bergerac* lurking in a dusty corner — the tokenistic 'world cinema' section. But to get there you'll have to fight your way through the lobotomised masses staring gormlessly at the covers of *Terminator 2* and *Home Alone*.

Flashback 16 years. There are no multiplexes, and the cinemas may be showing *Axe*, *Frauleins in Uniform* or *One On Top of the Other*. In Regent Video, my prepubescent eyes are wide with wonderment. My dad has just bought a video player and we're looking for something to watch on it. Hmmm, *The Blood Spattered Bride*, perhaps? How about *The Headless Eyes*? Maybe *I Spit On Your Grave* or *Zombie Flesh Eaters*? — they must be good, because they've been in the Top Five Most Rented Films for a good few months. Do we plump for Nazis torturing naked women or for psychotics slicing up co-eds? So many films, so little time.

The shop was just down the road from St Marie's RC Church, which I attended every Sunday. I'd end up impaled upon Satan's pitchfork just for thinking about these films, let alone for watching them. What the fuck was all this stuff? *Dracula's Virgin Lovers*? *Werewolf Woman*? *Beast of Blood*? Who made them? Where did they come from? Did the priest know about this? My dad let me see

them, and the films themselves were as great as the covers. Even when they were crap they were great. *City of the Living Dead* gave me nightmares, but that was great too. (He wouldn't let me watch *Grange Hill* in case it made me violent, but that's another story…) It's hard to believe now, but in the very early Eighties you could barely find a Hollywood movie in a video shop. These places were plastered wall-to-wall with porn, grindhouse trash and Eurosleaze. Hell's bells, it makes me misty-eyed just thinking about it. So please tolerate this self-indulgent interlude; I read *The Art of the Nasty* in a haze of blissful nostalgia.

The book is fundamentally a coffee-table volume, reproducing approximately 350 of the choicest covers from video's golden age in fairly arbitrary categories, which include the official 'video nasties', those that the DPP eventually dropped from the list, and 'The Good, The Bad And The Vomit-Inducing' — every sleeve from the Wingrove archive that didn't fit into any of the other categories.

Also provided are capsule notes on each title, with some details on censor cuts and obscure trivia (did you know that *The Burning* marked the debut appearance of Holly Hunter, or that Sandra Bernhardt provided one of the voices for the dubbing of *Shogun Assassin*, or that *Pink Flamingos*, 'could be obtained by sending a blank tape and some cash to Palace video and they'd send you the film by return post'?). Also included are sidebars on what was happening in the world beyond your VCR: '*1982. Neighbourhood Watch introduced. Householders agree to look out for dodgy geezers in their area.*'

I'd forgotten just how much sleeve

designers used to get away with in those happy-go-lucky days, and it's astonishing to witness in the VPRC-ridden 1990s just how gruesome and misogynistic video wrappers used to be: would a film called *Violation of the Bitch*, boasting the tag line, 'She asked for it!' get shelf-space today? I think not. And neither do I think we'll be seeing the return of *Blood Vengeance* ('Tortured by his lust for two women!'), its cover proudly depicting a demented George (*Anthropophagous*) Eastman, meat-cleaver raised above head, about to hack up a blood-drenched nubile. Of course, the come-on covers preserved for posterity in this volume were largely what all the furore was about. Video company owners, being one part film distributor to four parts carny barker, knew that to sell any screaming shitflick you needed plenty of blood, breasts and sharp knives up front and visible, and a healthy disregard for Trading Standards practices. The films themselves were almost an afterthought: Is *Savage Terror* any good? Who the fuck cares? The cover is GREAT! It's a huckster tradition as old as Christianity: sucker the rubes by using their own repressed desires against them. If you can get some good controversy going, all the better for sales. If not, invent some. Such showmanship would eventually backfire: a Go Video promo man anonymously complaining to Mary Whitehouse that *SS Experiment Camp* was obscene may have shifted a shitheap of copies to a suddenly interested populace (who would never have seen the film if not for tabloid outrage), but the snowball effect that such tactics produced would drive his company out of business.

The Art of the Nasty is mostly

comprised of visuals, but for your £20 you also get a contextual introduction by Wingrove. Grammatically dubious and a little cursory, this intro places nasty-ism over the backdrop of 1970s Britain: post-hippies, contemporaneous with punk rock, three-day weeks, riots in Brixton and Toxteth, and a world-wide desire on art's part to shock, shock, shock. All of these and more were laid to rest by Margaret Thatcher during her unprecedented stretch as leader of the country, leaving the UK the joke of Europe, an anally retentive Victorian back-alley of a country — a reputation which it enjoys to this day. Your coffee table will look naked without this tome. **Anton Black**

THINKING OF ENGLAND
A Consumer Guide to Sex in a Cold Climate
KITTY CHURCHILL

£6.99 292pp; UK: Abacus, 1996

In 1994 or thereabouts, Kitty Churchill, freelance veteran of the women's magazine circuit, decided to immerse herself in the kinky depths of English sex culture, bringing back jaw-dropping revelations of suburban seediness for her prurient readership... but it didn't quite turn out that way. In fact, she barely got her toes wet. For, as participant-observation field studies go, this one contains a lot more observing and a lot less participating than most. Despite her early declaration that, 'there were several fantasies I was keen to try out,' when it comes down to shit-or-get-off-the-pot time, Kitty bottles out time and again. Thus, we accompany her to famous fetish clubs like the Torture Garden and Submis-

sion, to dodgy nudist clubs, to Westward Bound, a B&D B&B in Cornwall (no, really!), to private swingers' parties, to weird Tantric sex therapists, and... nothing happens! Or rather, she stands in the corner like a latex-clad wallflower, drinking too much and being bitchy about the physical shortcomings of the pathetic men who make advances to her. Her companion on most of these forays is Ben, and together they pose as a 'couple', thus cravenly avoiding any possibility of interaction with the people she meets. I'm pleased to report that her solo visits to the Muir Reform Academy, a 'real school for adult boys, girls, and "boys who would be girls"' left her with a very sore bottom. But by the end of the book, I was feeling that Kitty Churchill actually wasn't that much into sex in the first place. In fact, she admits as much:

IN OVER SIX MONTHS, I AMASSED A GRAND TOTAL OF TWO ORGASMS DIRECTLY RELATED TO MY RESEARCH AND, AS ONE OF THEM WAS WITH MY HUSBAND, I DON'T THINK THAT ONE REALLY COUNTS... MONTHS AND MONTHS OF TREATING SEX AS A NON-CONTACT SPORT HAD RUBBED OFF IN MY BEDROOM.

In addition, *Thinking of England* is written in a breezy you-don't-have-to-be-crazy-to-work-here-but-it-helps style that would be fine for a magazine article, but becomes arch and tedious over the course of the book. For a book about sex, this book is remarkably unsexy. I don't know why Kitty Churchill bothered, and you shouldn't bother reading this, even if you find it in a bargain bookshop, as I did. *Thinking of England* left me with a sour taste like a mouthful of cum, though evidently *Cosmo* and *The Daily Express* liked it. Which tells you a lot.
Simon Collins

PSYCHOTROPEDIA
A Guide to Publications on the Periphery
RUSS KICK

£15.95 576pp; UK: Critical Vision, 1998; ISBN 1-900486-03-2

(Available through Headpress, see p.89)

More than 'a guide to publications on the periphery', *Psychotropedia* is your skeleton key to books most often sniffed at by your high street bookstore. From this book I have discovered the paintings of Judson Huss, and the essential British horror comic. I know why I get ratty when I chew too much sugar-free gum, and what Clinton's really saying when his speeches are played backwards. I know what Thomas Pynchon might look like. Oh, and I know where to get erotic furniture and what happens when bedbugs mate. So with all that, tell me, what else is there WORTH knowing?

Thanks to Russ Kick's diligent research (how I'd love his bookcase), I am no longer pissed off that I can't walk to the Compendium bookshop, because this book, with it's browse-by guides to well over a thousand *shade-culture* titles, is the next best thing. Fourteen sections covering sex, art, conspiracy, comix, drugs, the body, politics, etc., document a fair slice of some of the best and strangest titles out there, often with quoted extracts and bullet-point factoids from the books. Russ Kick writes crisply and without the taint of judgement, whether he's outlining a book on how to succeed in topping yourself, the conspiratorial writings of David Icke or Alex Constantine, or one of the many titles on taboo and marginalised sex. Too heavy for you? Then take *All I Needed To Know I Learned From My Golf-Playing Cats*. I kid you not, that book exists and you'll find it in here.

As publishers and their outlets roll together like blobs of mercury, increasing — so it would seem — the pressure on the survival skills of smaller publishers, the messengerial role of the peripheral presses is moving ever further towards front of stage, filling the vacuum created by the few who gratify what they assume to be the needs of the many, and in so doing deepen mass trance and restlessness. The worst sins of the mainstream, their blandisation of culture, feed the fires of many of those writing and being written about in the books outlined here. So not all vicious circles are as savage as they seem, and I am not inordinately disappointed to see that the balance

AP photo of an extremely controversial form of protest. *Psychotropedia.*

in *Psychotropedia* weighs down on the side of American titles. The United States' hyper-accelerated culture has created the hottest subcultural dynamo in these terminal years of the millennium. The author acknowledges the greater amount of US books. Perhaps future editions will see him look towards redressing the balance with more publishers from Europe and the East.

Russ Kick's great achievement in crafting the close-on 600 pages of *Psychotropedia* is to prove — if proof were needed — that you're not as messed-up or marooned as the mainstream would have you believe. There's other ways of thinking, of being, and how inspiring it is to dip into this volume and be reminded so. As Russ Kick writes, 'it's nice to know that some things will never be co-opted by the Spectacle'. Or as someone else once had it: gravity doesn't work on mutants. The unwitting legacy of the mainstream's timid steps towards a cookie-cut society is the creation of more sovereign mutants. As long as there are more channels of looping, rolling, repeating television — as long the bestseller lists are stacked with tasteful tat — as long as there's magazines existing only to feed off everyone

else's ideas — and even if the Internet becomes the boot system for Bill Gates' Xanadu 1.0, there will be enough jewels to fill a hundred *Psychotropedia*s.

A box of gold stars to Headpress for this addition to their range of provocative titles. *Psychotropedia* is both the Devil's library index and a stand-alone feast for your mind. (And the back-pages contain full publisher's details and a complete index of titles.)
Eugene Carfax

PSYCHOTROPEDIA
A Guide to
Publications on
the Periphery
RUSS KICK

(details above; Available through Headpress, see p.89)

It's difficult to write this review because every time I pick up *Psychotropedia* I lose another hour or so. This 'guide to publications on the periphery' is readable, interesting and difficult to put down. Open the book at random and chances are you'll find something that catches your attention, and one page becomes two becomes...

Psychotropedia — a conjunction of the words 'psychotropic' and 'encyclopaedia' — is a massive compendium of book and magazine reviews, organised into 14 categories. The range of material covered is phenomenal, and suggests that Russ Kick is a socially dysfunctional print junky of the worst kind. He's got a habit, but he can control it, honest.

With so much to chose from deciding what to highlight ought to be tricky, but then I've got my own obsessions to pander to: the Sex section of the book is pretty extensive and covers most bases, from foot fetishism to SM to scat to porn. Where else can you read about the *American Sphincter Society*, de-circumcision, solo oral sex and the fine art of vaginal fisting? No matter how obscure or deviant, chances are that someone somewhere writes about it, and that it's reviewed here. A book like *Alternate Sources* might be more comprehensive in this department, but *Psychotropedia* is not a listings

directory and it's a whole lot more readable and informative.

Another favourite area is the No Compromises chapter, which includes an eclectic and sympathetic section on Anarchism. Also covered are Animal Liberation, The Patriot/ Militia Movement and Nazism (amongst others). Of course there's a degree of arbitrariness involved in these categories, and material from the Freedom section could quite easily fit into the No Compromises chapter. Similarly there's a certain amount of cross-over between the sections on Sex and The Body. Luckily there's an index included to help you navigate should you lose your way.

If there's one conclusion to be drawn from *Psychotropedia* it's that print has an enduring appeal that no amount of new technology can touch. No matter how many people get connected to the internet, and no matter how cheap web publishing becomes, people are still writing, publishing and reading books, magazines and pamphlets. *Psychotropedia* itself is the perfect example of this; the information's probably all there on the internet, but a book makes more sense and is a lot more useable than any number of HTML pages.

Reading this book is a pleasure, and even if you have no intention of tracking down a single one of the goodies that it describes, it's a pleasure you shouldn't deny yourself. **Pan Pantziarka**

LORDS OF CHAOS
The Bloody Rise of the
Satanic Metal
Underground
MICHAEL MOYNIHAN
and DIDRIK SØDERLIND

£10.99 / $16.95 378pp; US: Feral House, 1998; ISBN 0 922915 48 2; distributed in UK by Turnaround (*Available through Headpress, see p.70*)

Hot off the infernal presses of Adam Parfrey's Feral House imprint, comes this scorcher about rock'n'roll damnation in the frozen fjords of Norway. For those of you not up to speed on the events this book recounts, I'll briefly recap. In the late Eighties and early Nineties, a number of mostly well-educated middle-class young metalheads, mostly from Scandinavia and particularly from Norway (and why this should have been so is one of the most interesting questions exhaustively explored in *Lords of Chaos*) took the cod Satanism of such bands as Venom, Slayer and Mercyful [sic] Fate way, way too seriously. At first they were content to form bands — Burzum, Mayhem, Emperor and Bathory amongst others — that pushed the already-frenzied Black Metal sound to new extremes of intensity, unintelligibility, and unlistenability. But because the established Church of Norway failed to fall beneath this sonic onslaught, the frustrated headbangers hit on the idea of setting fire to churches. Mediaeval Norwegian 'stave' churches being of a unique (and beautiful) all-wooden construction, they burnt very well, and soon ancient monument arson became quite the fashion — nearly 100 churches were torched, warming up the icy Norwegian nights no end. Some of the more articulate Black Metal types saw this as a process of reclaiming their Viking heritage from the 'alien' creed of Christianity. The next logical step in this Satanic jihad would have been to start killing priests, but being crazy mixed-up kids they mostly turned instead, to killing (*a*) themselves, and (*b*) each other. Dead from Mayhem shot himself. Varg Vikernes aka Count Grishnackh, the whizkid behind Burzum, stabbed Oystein Aarseth aka Euronymous from Mayhem, apparently in a conflict over unpaid royalties (although a struggle for control of the Oslo scene seems also to have been a factor). And so on.

So you thought you were a bit of a rip in your so-called misspent youth? Well, sucker, read this and find out what real juvenile delinquents do. Gasp in wonder as picturesque churches explode in fiery homage to an atavistic retribution! Chuckle at the exquisite irony of a photo of a guy called Dead who's, well, fuckin' dead in the picture, having taken a shotgun to his head earlier in the evening! His homeboy Euronymous (later to die himself at the hands of Varg Vikernes), upon discovering the body, hastened out to buy a camera in order to take some album sleeve shots, informed the authorities, and then bustled around picking up skull and brain fragments

to turn into necklaces for his friends and a nutritious stew. Piss your pants (in mirth rather than fear) at the sight of hordes of skinny young lads made up to look like the living dead and waving mediaeval weaponry around, for *Lords of Chaos* is copiously and hilariously illustrated.

Most of the leading lights of the Scandinavian Black Metal scene are now either in Valhalla, Hades or some other afterlife-type situation, or else they are busy biro-ing pentagrams and inverted crosses on the walls of their cells. Varg Vikernes became a favourite media *bête noire* whilst standing trial for murder, due to his boyish good looks, his outspoken defence of his actions and his remarkable lack of remorse. He is now as much a national pariah in Norway as, say, Charlie Manson in the States or Myra Hindley in Britain, and, ever the trend-setter, has abandoned Satanism as passé, advocating instead both Fascism and an Odinic revival, signalling this shift by shaving his girlie locks off and cultivating a goatee. Ásatrú or Viking paganism is a rising force, and the combination of this religious atavism with a growing nationalism (bands singing only in Old Norse and rediscovering ancient instruments) forms a natural foundation for an interest in Nazi philosophies.

This book is as thorough, as well-researched and as well-written a look at this fascinating and sorry saga as it is possible to imagine. The authors (one American, one Norwegian) have talked to all the involved parties who are still alive, and not only dish up mounds of helpful background info on Heavy Metal, the Nazi occupation of Norway, and the influence of Odinism on early Nazi thinking, but also delve into tangential issues like the resurgence of interest in Viking religion mentioned above, the international neo-Nazi scene, and Black Metal-inspired crimes in other countries — not only the USA and Britain, but also Russia, Poland, the former East Germany, France and many others.

This is a far more literate and serious book than the subject matter would lead you to expect. There are exhaustive footnotes, a bibliography, and several appendices on occultism in Scandinavia. Only the lack of

an index mars its scholarly credentials. And it is better written than any book on rock music has a right to be. The authors maintain an admirably impartial tone — they are clearly not apologists for Satanism, but neither are they outraged moralists, nor prurient sensationalists. *Lords of Chaos* is one of the most important books on alternative/youth culture ever written, and the fact that it's about such a bizarre, marginal subcultural phenomenon does not alter this at all. Only *The Family* by Ed Sanders (admittedly a very different kind of book) rivals it as an account of youth culture-inspired crime. Anyone with any interest in Heavy Metal, occultism, Fascism, crime or Scandinavia will lap it up. I cannot praise *Lords of Chaos* highly enough, and may you burn in Hell if you fail to buy it!
Simon Collins

KILLER FICTION

GJ SCHAEFER, as told to SONDRA LONDON
£10.99 / $14.95 308pp; US: Feral House, 1997; ISBN 0-922915-43-1; distributed in UK by Turnaround
(*Available through Headpress, see p.70*)
Gerard John Schaefer's brutal, repellent short stories were one of the highlights (or low points) of the excellent 1996 Bloat Books compilation of the writings and artefacts of murderers, *Lustmord* (reviewed *Headpress 13*), though I was already aware of his work from the 1993 book *Knockin' on Joe: Voices from Death Row* (Nemesis Books, edited by Sondra London). Schaefer was, until his death in prison in 1995,

serving time for the 1972 murders of two young women in Florida. A serving policeman until his arrest, Schaefer was convicted partly on the evidence of writings found by the police in his room — writings that dwelt obsessively on fantasies of torturing, hanging and strangling women, and on the mechanical details of committing crimes and disposing of the bodies and weapons. These stories, under the heading 'Actual Fantasies', are included in *Killer Fiction*. Schaefer protested that these were merely 'realistic horror fiction', but the courts didn't believe him, and neither should you. Following his conviction, Schaefer continued to write, and in 1989, Sondra London's Media Queen company published the original edition of *Killer Fiction*, following a correspondence between Schaefer and herself in which he sent her manuscripts. It's fair to say that Ms London had a special interest in Schaefer's work — not only had she lost her virginity to him whilst they were (briefly) high school sweethearts, but she wound up marrying Danny Rolling, another serial killer doing time with Schaefer. The relationship between London and Schaefer is exhaustively, even boringly, documented in the present volume — from their first kiss to the death threats and paranoid rants he started to send her after their Media Queen arrangement turned bad. In America, Sondra London has been roundly (and rightly) excoriated for her grandstanding celebrity-killer-chasing groupie antics, but the original printing of *Killer Fiction* swiftly became an impossible-to-find-but-must-have collector's item for murder junkies everywhere. With this greatly-expanded reissue from Feral House, owning a copy is now within everyone's grasp. But do you really want it? Well…

Schaefer never copped to being a serial killer, nor indeed a killer of any sort, although the authorities believe that he may have murdered up to 34 more people than the two he was convicted for. Instead, he adopted a teasing Ted Bundy-like attitude: whereas Bundy would ruminate hypothetically in the third person on his crimes, Schaefer would write about his own depredations in the most intimate, visceral, first-person

reportage style, and then claim it was all fiction. No-one reading these hellish documents, however, will doubt that Schaefer was as guilty as sin — his evil mindset drips off the pages. In story after story, young women are stalked, kidnapped, humiliated, tortured, executed and dismembered. And why must they die? Because they're WHORES, dammit! The little minxes have the temerity to reject poor Gerald's fumbling advances, and for this crime they deserve to be hung by the neck until they poo in their pretty pink panties (this physiological phenomenon is dwelt on at gloating length in *Killer Fiction*, and appears to have been the chief motive behind Schaefer's modus operandi). The titles of the stories — 'Whores: What to DO About Them', 'Gator Bait', 'Blonde on a Stick', 'Flies in Her Eyes' — offer a fair indication of their contents, but don't even begin to hint at the awesome hatred, misogyny and rage of Schaefer's prose. Check it out:

/ APPROACHED HER, KICKED HER SMARTLY IN THE RIBS, AND LISTENED TO THE SUPPRESSED SCREAM BEHIND THE GAG. IT HARDENED MY COCK. / UNBUCKLED MY PANTS… THEN SLICKENED HER CUNT AND ANUS WITH A HANDFUL OF SPIT… / AROSE AND RETURNED TO THE TRUNK OF MY CAR. FLUNG THE PLASTIC-WRAPPED CORPSE OF THE BLONDE OUT ONTO THE EARTH AND REMOVED IT FROM THE BAGS. / COULD FEEL BETSY'S EYES FOLLOWING ME… / SEVERED THE BLONDE'S HEAD, CARRIED IT TO A STEEL SPIKE AND MASHED HER HEAD DOWN UPON IT. THERE WAS A CURIOUS SQUISH AS THE ROD WENT UP INTO HER BRAIN, AND GOO BEGAN TO DRIP ON THE GROUND.

/ RETURNED TO BETSY. 'Y WANT SOME ASS,

WHORE, OR YOUR HEAD WILL BE ON THE OTHER STICK.' BETSY MADE LOVE LIKE A DREAM.

Equally unpleasant are the 'Starke Stories', tales of doing hard time in Florida State Prison at Starke. The worst of these, 'Nigger Jack', serves up a potent brew of racial hatred, gloating misogyny, necrophilia and nihilistic terror, as Schaefer regales the hapless reader with every minute detail of the electrocution of a female prisoner and the subsequent sodomising of her corpse by the black orderly assigned to prepare the body for burial. This story caused a permanent rupture in the relations between Schaefer and his editor, London.

It is relatively rare for serial killers to meditate in print on their horrid deeds at such length, and this in itself makes *Killer Fiction* essential reading for True Crime buffs and shameless gorehounds alike. Be warned, though, this is a seriously fuckin' unpleasant book — the only items I've come across that rival it in intensity are Carl Panzram's memoirs (also extensively extracted in *Lustmord*), and *Final Truth: Autobiography of a Serial Killer* by Donald 'Pee Wee' Gaskins (Mondo Books, 1993; reviewed *Headpress 9*). Schaefer's literary career has been cut short by a prison shiv making

Assault victim Nancy Trotter posing for a police re-enactment, ordered and paid for by the state, but curiously submitted as evidence on behalf of Schaefer's defence. *Killer Fiction.*

Ghost World © Dan Clowes

little holes all over him in his cell in 1995 — it couldn't have happened to a nicer guy. But it seems unlikely that he would have produced anything startlingly different to the 50 or so pieces collected in this volume. His writing is way too obsessional and fixated for that. Schaefer fancied himself to be a great realist crime writer, telling it the way it really went down (or the way he wished it did).

Reading *Killer Fiction* gave me bad dreams. Seriously. More risible are Schaefer's claims to be serving both God and mankind by writing as he does. I for one have no doubt that the composition of these grim little tales gave Schaefer endless hours of spunky-fingered joy, as he relived his crimes and imagined others he'd have gotten around to if only he'd had a little longer in which to prey upon co-eds and hitchhikers. And his claims to being a great writer are bullshit. In fact he totally lacks the kind of objectivity and critical distancing that makes for good art. The stories are raw, brutal, crude, unpolished and as intense as hell. Reading *Killer Fiction* is as close as I ever want to come to being at a murder scene. If you didn't have it before, reading *Killer Fiction* will give you the thousand-yard stare for keeps. **Simon Collins**

THE CORPSE GARDEN
The Crimes of Fred and Rose West

COLIN WILSON

£5.99 256pp; UK: True Crime Library

There is a serial killer writer on the loose in Cornwall. He preys on tabloid accounts of grisly crimes, of grisly schlock purveyed by true crime writers, and disguises it under a veneer of psychological and historical background that gives it an air of respectability. At the same time, he cannot hide his fascination with sexual detail, and he is adept at reporting it both salaciously and scientifically. 'Stop me before I write again,' ought to be at the end of Colin Wilson's author bio.

Actually, Wilson is a deft summariser of evidence, able to sift through varying accounts, point out contradictions, and resolve them. He's very convincing on the issue of Rose West's undoubted guilt. He's also very good at getting into the various points of views and agendas which earlier chroniclers have brought to the case. As you'd expect from someone who's been on the serial killer path for nearly 40 years, Wilson conveys a depth of knowledge and is able to make connections that most writers might miss.

Of course, many of these connections are old hat if you've read Wilson before. Maslow's theories of dominance, the divided brain, the sexual superman, all this has been rehashed many times. And as Wilson drifts off into synopses of various serial killings from around the world, you feel sort of like you're listening to your granddad tell the same family story for the umpteenth time: 'tell me again how Gerald Gallego sodomised his daughter.'

Life also seems to have passed him by. He remarks on the unusual sadistic cruelty Canadian serial killer Paul Bernardo showed when he forced his lover/accomplice Karla Homolka to write 'I must never forget to record *The Simpsons*' a hundred times. For a guy who raped and murdered at least three women, including Karla's younger sister, this seems pretty mild… especially when we recall that each episode of *The Simpsons* begins with Bart being punished by having to write some penance on the school blackboard. Post-modern irony from a serial killer. What'll they think of next?

Wilson's fascination has always been with the area where the sexual impulse and the violent impulse cross over. This makes his compendia both useful reading and quality schlock. Rest assured you'll get plenty of the good stuff here, and it might make you think as well. Or pretend you do. It just could've done with some pictures. But don't worry about this one. Somewhere out there there's a killer waiting to provide Wilson with another book. **Michael Carlson**

BATMAN
OTHER REALMS

BO HAMPTON, SCOTT HAMPTON & MARK KNEECE

£8.99 135pp; UK: Titan, 1998; ISBN 1 85286 977 1

Yet another in a long, long, way too fucking long line of attempts to 'reinvent' the Batman character. Word Up Fellas! Frank Miller's *Dark Knight Returns* still stands as the *ultimate* take on the mythos of the character, and that's because Frank has respect for what has gone before and a clear understanding of the inherent symbolic power — not to mention the cold-light-of-day silliness — of the idea of a man dressed as a bat. The fools involved in the two strips featured in this hastily and lazily assembled collection have presumably read *Dark Knight* but have never tried to take on board many of it's exemplary lessons in how to treat a genre as ludicrous as the superhero. This is most clearly illustrated in the first strip 'Destiny' which — I shit ye not — features the Bat Man of Norse legend! What the fuck?!? At the very least they could've had loads of 'Praise Odin' dialogue and much smiting with huge fuck-off-axes but, no, they haven't even got the wits to play it for laughs… Justifying the setting by embroiling the present-day Batman in dirty dealings with evil corporations looking to dump toxic waste in Scandinavian fjords is as lazy as it gets and the rest of the story, what there is of it, is played

A FEW MINUTES LATER...

Buddy's dad gets a haircut.
Buddy Go Home © Peter Bagge

out in such a pedestrian fashion, with all its Norse legends reference worn on its sleeve, that it makes any episode of the *Batman* TV cartoon look like a Thomas Pynchon novel. And barely a wench with ripped bodice in sight. Piss poor.

But, at least the first strip is so ridiculous that you're propelled along by its car crash logic. 'The Sleeping' is as pointless a comic strip as you could possibly imagine. Batman/ Bruce Wayne ends up in a coma and the rest of the story is played out in his mind. You would think this would have given any writer/artist the rare opportunity to go whole hog and chuck in all kinds of crazy shit. But no, just lots of moody black ink, a brief deadly giant eel encounter and a gut with a beard who looks like everyone's idea of a child molester. Only some dynamic Corben-esque panels featuring Bats twatting a huge demon thing are worth looking at twice. The rest of it is shite.

The comics industry is in decline right now and anyone observing from outside of slavish fandom would not be surprised based on this evidence. STOP making comics like this. Go do charity work or get pissed and cruise for chicks instead. The world will be a better place. **Rik Rawling**

GHOST WORLD
DAN CLOWES

£9.99 / $9.95 80pp; US: Fantagraphics, 1998; ISBN 1 56097 299 8; distributed in UK by Turnaround

'Unusual and wonderful'... 'An amazing piece of literature'... 'Le plus bel album de l'ane'e'... These are just some of the hyperbole-gushing recommendations on the back of Dan Clowes' latest release. For those

unfamiliar with his work, Clowes originally became popular thanks to his drawing style and design sensibilities appearing to adhere to the recent 'kitsch' and 'retro' infatuation with 1950s Americana. His character, Lloyd Llewellyn, grooved through a world of Tiki lounges, cocktail bars and cod-weirdness. There were occasional flashes of his sardonic wit and jaded misanthropy but it wasn't until he started the ongoing anthology title *Eightball* that he began to develop his strongest abilities — a simple but potent art style and a disturbingly keen insight into peoples' true feelings and motivations.

In previous book collections — like *Pussey* (an unrestrained assault on comics fandom and the industry itself), *Like A Velvet Glove Cast In Iron* (an overindulgent, but truly bizarre series that David Lynch would have given his left nut to dream up), and the best-of-*Eightball* books — it's clear that Clowes has been holding back the sauce, pissing about with pointless one-pagers like 'Needledick the Bug Fucker'. But, in getting that shit out of his system, it's clearly allowed him to make *Ghost World*, his most impressive and, I've got to say, *intelligent* piece of work to date.

The story, such as it is, can be summed up in one sentence: Enid and Rebecca, two teenage girls in modern America, face up to the impending horror of adulthood. That's it, and told like that it sounds no different to so many other books that are doomed to wind up in the Waterstones sale. What makes this different is the comics medium used — allowing Clowes to turn in a wonderfully sparse art job — and the sheer depth of insight and empathy in the writing. The sense of alienation, of mundane polarisations, is subtly but brilliantly achieved. The girls talk, sit in diners, play pranks on strangers; barely animated but utterly desperate. The target audience — that 'Gen-X Post-Literate' demographic — will probably want to run and hide under the stairs when they see their culture and it's flotsam and jetsam of nostalgic ephemera exposed in such howlingly stark detail. Clowes is never judgmental though; he simply shows what he's seen and lets the reader decide.

There are some disturbingly accurate depictions of everyday losers — minimum wage slaves, nihilistic zine writers, neighbourhood oddballs — but they serve only to add what little substance there is to the world of Enid and Rebecca. The title says everything, or, nothing at all.
Rik Rawling

BUDDY GO HOME!
Vol IV of the Complete Buddy Bradley Stories from Hate!
PETER BAGGE

£9.99 122pp; US: Fantagraphics, 1998; ISBN 1 56097 276 9; distributed in UK by Turnaround

This is the tale of slacker Buddy Bradley, who travels back to his home state of New Jersey to live with his parents and start his life over again. Lisa, his volatile girlfriend, rides along with him. And if that isn't enough, Bradley's childhood buddies start to crawl out of the woodwork — all of whom are either too stoned, too dumb, too uninterested or too incarcerated to realise he's been gone for several years in the first place. Buddy's daily adventures consist of him buying a ridiculous car, minding his sister's brattish kids, driving Lisa for a job interview and, best of all, going into partnership with Jay and opening a Collector's Emporium which deals in toys, records and cheesy ephemera of yesteryear. Peter Bagge is in his element with sending up the Fan Boy mentality, the sweaty asscrack types and the weird middle-aged men who argue the toss over the packaging on a *Star Wars* Princess Leia doll. But then, you'd need to be something of a sweaty asscrack yourself to figure some of the jokes. A funny book.

HÔPITAL BRUT № 2/3

£13.50 (incl p&p) from Mark Pawson, PO box 664, London E3 4QR; www.mpawson.demon.co.uk

I first met Mark Pawson at the London Small Press Book Fair a couple of years ago. Standing out from the other stalls selling self-published poetry and lower-end fanzines, he stocked a variety of eye-catching material, including garish Panter-style French comics, printed in a variety of weird formats and looking unlike anything I'd ever seen before. I asked him about them and was stunned by the price — they don't come cheap. But he explained that they were really a labour of love, coming in print runs of 100–150, and with an attention to detail almost unheard of in anything so resolutely uncommercial. I bought some. And then more. Mark runs a mail-order service, selling cool toys, good fanzines, weird books, and these French comics, published in Marseilles by Le Dernier Cri.

Le Dernier Cri is a loose-knit collective of comic artists who grew out of the Paris punk scene of the early Eighties. They moved to Marseilles a few years ago and publish principally material by their members: Yves Blanquet, Bruno Richard, Caroline Sury and Pakito Bolino, to name a few. They've also published work by Gary Panter and Mike Diana, which should give you some idea of where they're coming from. Ratty, fucked-up lines and extreme, offensive imagery beautifully presented, usually silk-screened, in Day-Glo colours on thick, high-quality paper. This kind of attention to detail given to this kind of material seems a peculiarly European subgenre of comics. In Lambiek last year, Amsterdam's premier comics shop, I saw a load of silk-screened comics, including a huge, beautifully produced A3 book of silk-screened comic art by our very own Savage Pencil — going for about £100. Le Dernier Cri stuff's cheaper than that, although some of their comics go for £25. *Hôpital Brut*, the most recent Dernier Cri effort that I've come across, is a good introduction to what they do, being two thick A4 comic magazines featuring all the regulars. Mark had a couple of them seized by Customs, who probably objected to, among other things, the ridiculously offensive blood, guts and porn photo-comic about the death of our beloved Princess. The layout and presentation is amazing — foldouts, all sizes of pages, every space filled with bizarre illustrations — and the content no less so. It seems that every imaginable graphics style is represented here, with an emphasis

128 on the extreme — Romain Slocombe's illustrative work wouldn't look out of place here, and there's a clear embrace of things

ABBEY ROAD/LET IT BE   The Beatles
PETER DOGGETT
£9.95 151pp; US: Schirmer Books (Simon & Schuster), 1998; ISBN 0-02-864772-6

On January 1969, only months away from an ugly split embroiled in monetary disputes, public animosity and petty backstabbing, the Beatles entered Twickenham film studios to prepare new material for a proposed live concert. It was a far cry from the close-knit confides of Abbey Road No 2 studio, where the group was used to working; Twickenham was the size of a aircraft hanger. The band were now only perfunctorily a working unit, each member essentially producing solo compositions on which the others — often begrudgingly — played. At Twickenham it got much worse (and it stayed worse when the band moved over to their own Apple studios after two weeks). Conflicts within the Beatles were accelerating, thanks in part to the band being unable to agree on a business manager and ending up instead with two: one for Lennon, Harrison and Starr, and one for McCartney, both working in opposition. Another conflict was that Lennon — either strung out on heroin, or trying to kick the habit — would bring his girlfriend, Yoko Ono, to the sessions, insisting that she should have as much say in the group as he. That was when Lennon bothered to turn up at all.

And the icing on the cake? The whole thing was being recorded by a film crew for the contractually obliged new Beatles film — instead of bothering the group with an actual script, it was to be a documentary on the Beatles rehearsing to go on the road and perform live for the first time since 1967.

It quickly became apparent that the gig was not going to happen, and the project switched in mid-production to being a film about the making of a Beatles album. With less than a week to go to the projected live concert date, the Beatles not only had conflicting ideas as to where such a concert should take place — i.e., in which country — but couldn't yet agree on whether to bother with a gig at all.

Day-in, day-out, the band bickered. A typical dialogue has McCartney warning Lennon that the band are facing a "crisis", and when would his musical-other-half come up with some new material? "I think I've got Sunday off," Lennon flippantly replies.

Amidst the cameras, lights, and conflicts, the Beatles managed to lay down a handful of fresh songs, and jam endlessly on useless Rock'n'Roll standards. Every bitter word, every bum note seems to have made it onto magnetic tape — what wasn't caught by the sound engineer recording the band, was captured by the sync-tape operated by the film crew. More than 120 hours of it.

Michael Lindsay-Hogg's completed film, Let It Be, is a dull, mournful experience (alleviated only in the closing minutes, with an impromptu decision by the Beatles to take their amplifiers to the rooftops of Apple and play their live concert to no one in particular). If Peter Doggett's excellent book is anything to go by, however, the documentary is a positive Walnut Whip compared to the real air of hopelessness and desolation that permeated the Let It Be sessions. The film lasts for 81 minutes, but the sessions — and back-stabbing — went on for weeks.

After the live concert angle dematerialised, the intended album — Get Back as it was then known — became one in which the Beatles would play raw music, free of overdubs and stripped of extraneous production. The tapes from the sessions were given over to Glyn Johns, an engineer with the thankless task of arranging the bits and pieces of songs, to come up with an album package. The Beatles washed their hands of any further input.

The result, together with the whole Get Back experience, has become a bootlegger's wet-dream.

Johns came up with an album that — not surprisingly — no one liked very much. Doggett, in his book, derides the engineer-producer's inclusion of several tracks, when more complete and better versions of the same songs were recorded and available. To be honest, it's all subjective and Johns no doubt was trying to balance the general awfulness with good humour.

The Get Back acetates were 'leaked' to American radio stations, and soon after became probably the only album in history to be bootlegged before receiving an official release. But it never did get released, and at the Beatles' behest, Johns was forced to compile a second and third Get Back album, each with a different track listing, each getting a thumbs down.

Such was the delay, however, that the Beatles had recorded and released a subsequent album — Abbey Road — still without any sign of Get Back making it into the shops.

Ultimately, the project was handed over to Phil ('Wall of Sound') Spector, and the intended spontaneous 'back to basics' album — now titled Let It Be — came out swamped in strings and choirs. McCartney thought it was a travesty, while a relieved Lennon — who deemed the raw material to be "the shittiest load of badly recorded shit... ever" — said of Spector's effort: "I didn't puke." Some commendation.

Let It Be and Abbey Road are inexorably linked, and Doggett tackles the recording of both albums in his book. However, it's the former that is of most interest, given that the film cameras and audio tapes offer a fascinating notebook of the world's biggest and most influential band at work. That the band was fast burning up, seems only to give the endeavour an even keener edge.

Given that the book is part of a series called 'Classic Rock Albums', whose editor is Clinton Heylin, author of Bootleg, it comes as no surprise that Abbey Road/Let It Be keeps bootleg recordings a stable part of its itinerary. Indeed, one must question whether such an insightful behind-the-scenes book would even exist without access to bootleg recordings, surely the source for some of the alternate takes and band member banter discussed in its pages.

You don't want to know how many clandestine record releases have materialised out of these sessions, but on bootleg you'll find everything from the complete rooftop live set, through Glyn Johns Get Back albums, to every taped minute of Twickenham dialogue (favourite moments of which include McCartney suggesting to other parties that Lennon ought to shoot Yoko Ono; director Lindsay-Hogg constantly bringing up the subject of a live concert, and confusing the band with dry-runs of codenames he himself has allocated; Harrison meeting with apathy every time he comes up with a new number of his own he'd like the band to try.)

Other books in the same series include the **Sex Pistols'** Never Mind the Bollocks **and Cream's** Disraeli Gears**.**

Japanese throughout. There are also text pieces on a variety of themes, from art brut (Dubuffet's term for the work of self-taught artists, particularly the institutionalised) to interviews with artists, via pieces on the Angoulême comics festival. I can't really recommend this — or other Dernier Cri products — enough. In a world in which fewer and fewer worthwhile comics seem to be made, there's at least one source of quality material left.

If you want to have a look, Mark Pawson — as well as running a mail-order service — has a stall at Camden market, which is well worth a visit anyway. **James Marriott**

THE EXIT COLLECTION
GEORGE PETROS (Ed.)

$25; US: Tacit; 1341 W. Fullerton Ave, suite 182, Chicago, IL 60614-2134, USA; email: TacitPubs@aol.com

Exit was a 'zine' produced in the Eighties under the guidance of George Petros and — for the first three issues — Feral House's Adam Parfrey. The publication gave voice to many of the key artistic figures to emerge from the dirty underbelly of the underground subculture: John Aes-Nihil, Kim Seltzer, Jim Blanchard, Richard Kern, GG Allin, Nick Zedd, Nick Bougas, Lung Leg,

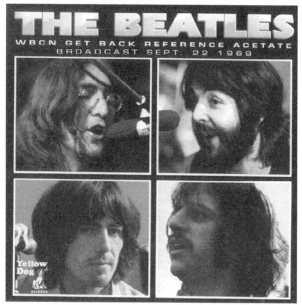

129

The Get Back acetate that was surreptitiously broadcast by WBCN radio in Sept. '69. The whole broadcast (including DJ commentary) later turned up on this bootleg by Yellow Dog.

CULTURE GUIDE

Boyd Rice, various members of Cop Shoot Cop, Genesis P. Orridge, etc. All of whom contributed work to what Petros describes in his introduction as the magazine of 'Outlaw Liberal Fascist Sci Fi Pop Art'. Now, some four years since the last issue of *Exit*, Tacit have published this lavishly produced 384-page collected edition — which includes work from all six issues as well as unpublished works executed for the magazine.

Exit was predominately a graphic and visual publication, and the book includes the large, symmetrical contstructivist-manga of JG Thirlwell, which, with its harsh chiaroscuro, looks as powerful as the quasi-industrial propaganda on which it is at least partly based. Also included is Joe Coleman's beautiful *The Dance of Death*, some great pictures by Steven Cerio, and some Mark Mothersbaugh strips. RN Taylor includes detailed pictorial anthropological and artistic histories of both The Swastika, and the Pentagram, tracing their usage across cultures and continents. While John Aes-Nihil co-ordinates a series of Charles Manson and Fredrich Nietzsche quotes, each of which is suitably (mis-) interpreted by an artist. On a literary front, contributions come from Henry Rollins' *Love Life*, and Lydia Lunch's *Meltdown: The Gun Is Loaded*, whilst non-fiction is provided in Adam Parfrey's *Eugenics: The Orphaned Science* (a version of which was published in *Apocalypse Culture*), and Carlo McCormick's *L(aw), S(cience), D(isorder)*.

This collection is an insight into the early work of some of today's underground luminaries, and contains several interesting pieces. For the archivist, or enthusiast (who hasn't seen *Exit* previously), it is a valuable source. It should be noted, however, that it does represent only a small selection of many of these artists' work, who, in most cases, have progressed since first contributing to *Exit*. **Jack Sargeant**

THE LIFE AND TIMES OF R. CRUMB
Comments from Contemporaries

MONTE BEAUCHAMP (Ed.)
£11.99 / $17.95 192pp; US: St Martin's

Griffin, 1998; ISBN 0 312 19571 0;
distributed in UK by Turnaround

An impressive array of hip movers and shakers make up the 'contemporaries' who offer their thoughts, opinions and personal reminiscences on R Crumb, Underground artist extrodinaire. It's a formula Monte Beauchamp utilised to equally good effect in the acclaimed *Blab!*, the first edition of which had comic artists fondly recalling EC comics. For Crumb, however, Beauchamp has been able to recruit such names as Terry Gilliam, Matt Groening, Roger Ebert, and Ralph Steadman, to run alongside the appreciations of these lowly comic artist types. The entries range from a half-page to 20 pages. Don Donahoe recalls his forays into publishing Crumb's early comics, *Zap* and *Mr Natural*, and the pornographic *Snatch Comics*, which were 'distributed in an atmosphere of secrecy and caution'. Comic artist Trina Robbins reflects on how seeing the first issue of *Zap* in the Sixties was an experience akin to being 'born again'. Her condemnation of Crumb's later work as being hostile to women earned her ostracism among fellow artists, but she stands by that claim today (she refers to Crumb's early work as 'sweet', which alone necessitates any hostile change Crumb may have exhibited). On the other hand, Ralph Steadman reckons Crumb has 'never influenced me in the slightest', while Robert Armstrong, fellow musician in Crumb's band The Cheapsuit Serenaders, provides an insight into an aspect of the artist that is rarely touched upon: 'his deep affinity to certain styles of music.' Eric Sack, Underground art collector, discusses the rising value of Crumb's original artwork and laments that certain early pieces can now command prices ranging anywhere from $6,000 to over $50,000!

One of the most fascinating, less obituary-like, entries comes from Tom Veitch, who tears into Straight Arrow Press — the book publishing arm of *Rolling Stone* — for burning so many comic artists with their book, *A History of Underground Comix*. The author of that heavily illustrated tome, Mark James Estren, wanted to pay everyone for using their artwork, but the publishers re-

fused point blank. Crumb was the exception. As Crumb had invented Underground comics, Straight Arrow Press had to play by his rules or there couldn't be a book. Outside of a few renegades — S. Clay Wilson, Greg Irons and Tom Veitch — everyone else, after being plied with free booze at a 'preview party', signed releases for their work. The three protestors were told, in no uncertain terms, 'Either you sign or you're out of the history of underground comix.' They didn't sign.

The book was a success and has been reprinted several times over. In it, there are two tiny pieces of art by Greg Irons, which he had failed to copyright (the publishers originally intended to use 57 pages of Irons' work); Veitch has one piece; Wilson has several. All lacking a copyright.

INDEX

PETER SOTOS

£7.95 164pp; UK: Velvet (Creation Books), 1998; ISBN 1 84068 000 8

MY TASTES RUN VERY SIMILAR TO THOSE OF IAN BRADY AND I ENJOY HIS WORK BECAUSE IT IS 100% HONEST AND SELF-CONCERNED.

FEMALES ARE DOGS WHOSE ONLY WORTH IS AS PAWNS FOR MY PLEASURE. ALMOST EXCLUSIVELY, THIS INVOLVES PHYSICAL VIOLENCE.

Remember Peter Sotos? His interview with Paul Lemos, from which the above bons mots are taken, was one of the more startling inclusions in Adam Parfrey's seminal *Apocalypse Culture*. Sotos, an advocate for what may best be described as an 'alternative' morality, produced a zine in Chicago in the mid-Eighties called *Pure*, which extolled the virtues of child molestation and sexual murder. Its third and final issue landed Sotos in court on a kiddie porn possession charge (he had cut-and-pasted images from a magazine called *Incest IV* into *Pure*). Did being placed on probation cause him to mend his ways? Did he get therapy and find out what made him so fucked-up in the first place? Did he become a born-again Christian and devote his life to the service of oth-

Background *The Life and Times of R. Crumb* © Crumb

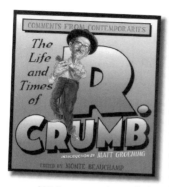

ers? Well, no, no and no — he has been far too busy with his other projects. Following *Pure*, he produced a short story collection, *Tool*, and a new magazine, *Parasite*. All three were collected (without the offending pictures, natch) in *Total Abuse*, an elusive 1995 volume published by Jim Goad, of *ANSWER Me!* notoriety. He has also become a permanent member of extreme electronic noise-terrorists Whitehouse, and samples of his prose have appeared in the excellent 1997 Velvet Books anthology *Heat* (see above), and Rude Shape's *Funeral Party vol II* (reviewed *Headpress 16*). 1998 has seen the publication of two more books by Sotos: *Index* and *Special*, another one from Rude Shape.

So what is *Index* like? Well, it's every bit as intensely nasty as you'd expect, given its pedigree. Sotos dwells on all kinds of exploitative sexual relations — peep shows, anonymous gay sex in toilets, gang bangs, porn videos etc. The paradigmatic act is the blow-job culminating in facial cum-shot — all take, no give, sexuality stripped back to a commercial transaction. This is the authentic voice of a man who's completely rejected the idea of any human interaction not predicated on either money or violence.

The writing style is terse, arid, and adapted like a predator to the harshness of the territory it inhabits. The only contemporary authors I know of who write stuff this bleak and despairing are Michael Gira of the Swans (who shares Sotos' fascination for peep shows), Henry Rollins in his more nihilistic moments, and the late Jesús Ignacio Aldapuerta, whose most disturbing collection *The Eyes* (pub: Critical Vision) was reviewed in *Headpress 13*. Sotos seasons his stew of misogyny, misan-

thropy and child-lust with a fat dose of racial hatred too. All in all, then, I wouldn't recommend you buy *Index* for your dear old mum this Christmas, unless you have a very scary mum. Like de Sade, Sotos situates himself at a terminal point of unwillingness to compromise his rage for the sake of an easier life. I really feel sorry for people who paint themselves into such a wretched corner of alienation — there just seems to be no way back in from the cold. The mind of Peter Sotos — an interesting place to visit, but I definitely wouldn't want to live there.

> *I'M SORRY TO HAVE HAD TO ADD TO THIS SORT OF NOISE, THIS SORT OF FILTH, THIS SORT OF DEMEANING CONSIDERATION... I'M SORRY, JUST TRULY SORRY, FOR ALL OF IT.*

Yeah right, Peter, I'm sure you are.
Simon Collins

CHARLES BUKOWSKI
Locked in the Arms of a Crazy Life
HOWARD SOUNES
£16.99 354pp; US: Rebel Inc

Although Charles Bukowski achieved a cult status in America — which seems to be growing all the time — for most of his career he was actually more popular in Germany. Perhaps this was because he had been born there, though his American father soon moved him back to the USA. More likely it was because Bukowski's autobiographical stories, poems, and novels struck a chord with Germans:

> *BUKOWSKI WAS A MAN WHO WROTE BILDUNGSROMANS ALL HIS LIFE. THERE IS AN ADOLESCENT QUALITY WHICH HIS WORK NEVER LOSES, AND IT SEEMS TO APPEAL TO THE ADOLESCENT WHICH LIES BURIED UNDER MANY ADULT SELVES.*

Charles Bukowski was ugly. He drank. Boy, did he drink. He sorted letters in a post office. He went to the track and played the horses. He chased easy women. He got into fights. All that made him different from thousands of other wasted souls in flop houses and skid rows across

America was that he wrote about it. Fuelled with a sort of hard-boiled romanticism, he wrote in a bare, straightforward style which gave an air of reality to his tales, and turned much of their adolescent world-view into self-deprecating humour. It is his way of coming out on top, of maintaining faith in a romantic view of the world, even when seen through a haze of smoke, drink, and rejection. It is not that the life Bukowski presents to us is false, it is that it is presented through eyes that are never as bloodshot as they seem, a sensibility never as lost or cynical as it appears on the surface.

Through the unlikely avenue of two small-press publishers, Bukowski became famous in a fashion, and through his fictional alterego of Henry Chinaski, his bottled dreams came true. All the booze he could drink, pretty women throwing themselves at him, and his work being taken seriously.

Writing a biography of someone who has constructed such a vibrant existence through fiction is a challenge which Howard Sounes meets head-on, and battles at least to a draw. He is particularly good on the realities of Bukowski's childhood, and on his progression to loser status. Detailing the nature of his relationships, and seeing in particular the three women who made up the bulk of his life, before his writing became successful, rounds out the more romantic picture Bukowski draws in his work.

Strangely enough, Sounes is less revealing about how it was that Bukowski's work eventually caught the public's eye. Although he turned against most of the small-press people who aided him in the early days, it is not a common thing for someone to move from the mimeographed magazines where he began his career, to financial success. It can be argued that Bukowski made Black Sparrow Press, but there isn't a good sense of just how that came to happen, of whether Bukowski's ultimate popularity 'just happened' or whether John Martin or someone else played the Buk card deftly. He's also not very interested or adept at analysing what it is that makes Bukowski's stuff work, or not. What are the differences between the poetry and the stories, if any?

Given that, this biography cries out for more space and more salacious detail. Perhaps not surprisingly, Sounes is one of the many writers to produce books on the West killings. His *Fred and Rose* is one of the most reticent of the genre, unwilling to dwell on prurient gore. This is understandable, perhaps, when dealing with murder. But when you're relating the life of a man who tossed the intimate details of his own life onto the page with a seemingly casual disregard, this is more surprising. Sounes pointed out that severe head trauma may have helped transform Fred West into a sex fiend and sadistic killer. Bukowski's cranium certainly absorbed its share of poundings, which might help explain the sex part.

Bukowski was a classic drunken fuck-up, crying in his beer the next day. In classic juicer behaviour, he turned against many of the people who loved him or helped him. Becoming successful gave him more opportunity to indulge, and to screw-up more spectacularly. As the situations get more and more bizarre, you long for more detail. I wish Amber O'Neil's 'Blowing My Hero', an account of being sickened by having sex with Bukowski, could have been reprinted as an appendix. The recollections of the various women who now found Bukowski-the-successful-

GODS OF DEATH

Around the World,
Behind Closed Doors,
Operates an Ultra-Secret
Business of Sex and Death.
One Man Hunts the Truth About
SNUFF FILMS.

YARON SVORAY

with Thomas Hughes

writer attractive and romantic stand in sharp contrast to his early life; yet almost all the stories seem cut off before they get to the gut-wrench stage. The tension between Bukowski the romantic, and Bukowski the cynical love machine, lies underneath almost all of them, and needs to be brought to the surface. Even the potential absurd hilarity of Hollywood tough-guy types like Sean Penn paying homage to a small-press poet doesn't get played out for all it is worth.

In the end, Bukowski got to indulge his adolescent fantasies of priapic power, not just in the pages of little magazines, but in life. No matter how bad the night before, Bukowski was back at the typewriter the next day. Few of us can literally work and make our dreams come true, but he was able to. In that sense, Bukowski's life was far less crazy, and less tragic, than people think. Was he, in the end, heroic, or were the readers who believed in Henry Chinaski simply taken for a giant con, and wound up buying the drinks for the guy telling funny stories at the bar? That's the question Sounes doesn't ask, and it stops this engrossing biography just short of the final hurdle. **Michael Carlson**

HOT OFF THE NET
Erotica and Other Sex
Writings from the
Internet
RUSS KICK (Ed.)
$14 (+ $3 p&p; outside US $9) 239pp;
US: Black Books, 1999; Black Books, PO
Box 31155, San Francisco, CA 94131,
USA; email: Info@BlackBooks.com (all
major credit cards accepted)
THE BLACK BOOK
5th Edition
BILL BRENT (Ed.)
$17 (+ $3 p&p; outside US $11) 222pp;
US: Black Books, 1998 (details as above)
Call me a Luddite, but I find it satisfying that a collection of the 'hottest sex on the internet' requires the medium of hard print to present itself in the real world. 'De-digitalized' by editor Russ Kick (see reviews of his book *Psychotropedia* above), the stories by 'unknown' authors in *Hot Off the Net* are rounded out by Kick's customary attention to minutiae (like plenty of contacts and links) for those readers who wish to pursue more

smut. But for that you'll have to have a computer.

More contacts in Bill Brent's *The Black Book*, a directory for sex-positive publishers and organisations across the US and Canada. A brief description accompanies each of the 700+ entries, while sections at the back of the book organise the entries geographically and by subject.

GODS OF DEATH
YARON SVORAY
with THOMAS HUGHES
H/BK £16.99 306pp; US: Simon &
Schuster, 1997; ISBN 0-684-81445-5;
distributed in UK by Turnaround
(Available through Headpress, see p.70)
After infiltrating the neo-Nazi underground in Germany — the subject of an earlier book — ex-paratrooper and Israeli detective-turned-writer Yaron Svoray claims to have witnessed a film which has haunted him ever since. Screened to a select audience of the masturbating far-right, it depicted the rape and murder of a little girl. Svoray had encountered a Snuff movie. Years later, still waking in the night to the terrible images in that film, Svoray concluded that to exercise his demons, he had to prove to the world that Snuff films do exist. *Gods of Death* is the result.

It hasn't yet made the *News at Ten*. But then, Svoray's cause isn't helped any by the fact his platform is a book which reads like a two-bit novel, full of cliff-hanger type prose, and a note at the beginning which informs the reader that 'the story you are about to read is essentially a true one'. That's a pretty telling statement for a supposed work of non-fiction.

Svoray's investigation took place over a several year period, but in order to provide a 'cohesive narrative', as he puts it, the timescale has been compacted and some details have been changed. All of which is a shame for anyone who is less inclined towards a good thriller and more interested in absorbing Svoray's proposed investigation of the 'truth'.

The first part of the investigation takes the author to Bangkok, where Svoray pays a visit to a dodgy geezer running a bar. That trail gets him nowhere, and Svoray returns to Israel where he meets a Russian arms dealer with a chain of porn shops. Nothing. Then to Germany, and England, from one country to the next and back again, with little to show but a string of empty promises, and a wife and family pleading for him to come back home.

But Danger is Yaron Svoray's middle-name. To try and infiltrate the Snuff underground, first he poses as a buyer of Snuff movies and later as a dealer of them. Most everyone he speaks with claims to be able to get hold of such films, or will put him in touch with someone who can. Svoray takes all of this at face value and as affirmation that there is indeed an industry out there peddling murder on tape for sexual gratification. Not for a moment does he stop to think that these 'low-lifes', who he knows full well hustle for a living and will do anything to turn a quick buck, might say anything that he wants to hear if they think there might be something in it for them.

He gets into a screening of a snuff film, the audience for which is comprised of professional-looking people aged between 30 and 50. Svoray pays the $1,500 entrance fee and watches as two men cut a woman's throat as she is being fucked. But Svoray needs hard evidence — he needs a copy of a snuff film himself.

The way the story develops, it would be reasonable to suggest that the whole thing is more grounded in Svoray's fantasy than it is in hard reality. It has all the dynamic of a Hollywood movie adaptation and more than once Svoray talks of film rights, even contemplating who might portray him on the big screen! People get murdered; Svoray does a hard-man act; there are gangsters and clandestine meetings; there is a sting on a Mr Big... But then, when all seems like out-and-out bunkum, Svoray deals a hand there can be no arguing with (short of landing the publishers with a multi-million dollar lawsuit): he enlists the help of Robert DeNiro.

When a snuff film is finally offered to him, the $50,000 asking price shoots it completely out of Svoray's reach. However, through a fortuitous set of circumstances, Svoray is able to interest megastar DeNiro into posing as a rich client for whom he is working — the deal being that DeNiro will see some of the film, announce to the dealer that

he has seen it before and isn't interested in buying it, and then go on public record stating that snuff films do exist. With DeNiro's name attached to it, the world's press couldn't fail to take notice.

Although the actor does attend the screening, things don't go quite according to plan. Consequently, DeNiro has never announced that he has seen a snuff film, and Svoray remains yet another frustrating handreach short of coming up with the hard goods.

Gods of Death milks its subject matter for every ounce of sensationalism. As snuff film detective stories go, you could do worse; then again, you'd do a whole lot better to pick up a copy of Robert Campbell's *In La-La Land We Trust*, which has no aspirations to get to the 'truth'.

COWS
MATTHEW STOKOE
H/BK £11.95 118pp; UK: Creation, 1998; ISBN 1-871592-39-9

In the scheme of losers, Steven, the 25-year-old narrator of *Cows*, rates less than Absolute Zero. He lives with the Hagbeast, his mother, who loathes and is loathed by him in turn. At the abattoir where Steven works, the butchers get their kicks from rapping cows before firing bolts into their heads. Well, did you honestly think they *didn't anyway*, Headpress reader? One of these bovine cupids, Cripps, takes Steven under his tutelage, showing him how to kill the cows — then giving him a buggering as payment. From there it gets... well... it gets *interesting*, with slaughter and corporeal disgust being explored in detail. Oh, and there's the hipster-talking Guernsey cow. Shame about those bits. This work has been compared to Ian Banks, not entirely fatuously, although the shades of Stokoe's particular nightmare are not as persuasively rendered. Indeed, the gothic and somewhat effluvial style, whilst turning up gems from time to time, is devoid of romance. Vegetarianism has been suggested as a stance, yet Stokoe is too preoccupied with exploring the limits of his own twistedness for any 'message' to be else but a tease for pseuds. Allegorical, well yeah, of course, 'nuff said... If only someone would persuade Dis-

ney to option the animated version.
Eugene Carfax

METAL SUSHI
DAVID CONWAY
£7.95 201pp; UK: Oneiros, 1998; ISBN 9-781902-197005

This is the first offering to come from Oneiros Books, and *if* subsequent Oneiros projects are anywhere near as good as this, they will soon become a publisher of real importance.

Not that David Conway's *Metal Sushi* will suit everyone. It is a very extreme book. Extreme, not in the sense that it tries to emulate the sexual ferocity of, say, Peter Sotos or Jesús Ignacio Aldapeurta, or that it plunges headlong into splatterpunk horror or Kenneth Grant-style occultism. In actual fact it does all these things. Where it is extremer than the aforementioned is in its pyrotechnical and brutal use of *language*, borrowing phrases and neologisms from the cutting-edge of Quantum Physics, Cybernetics, Virtual Reality and the micro-sciences of cloning and biological engineering to devastating effect. The resultant word-carnage is truly apocalyptic in its impact, and totally unlike anything else you will ever read.

In 'Eloise' we are introduced to Conway's recurring theme of the destruction of the body's boundaries, coupled with the mutational expansion of consciousness to its original pristine cosmically primal level. This theme is continued in both the blackly comic 'Metal Sushi' — in the guise of a deranged pulp racial supremacy thriller — and in 'Black Static', where these biological/metaphysical complexes meet Lovecraft's mythos at the apex of their expression. The more meditational 'Omegaville' explores this theme in terms of a more recognisable human omniscience, while 'Manta Red' is a purely hellish vision of all these possibilities in their most decadent, voyeuristic forms — and is one of the most unrelenting, ferocious pieces of fiction you will read. Only 'Zuprader Boulevard', a science-fiction meditation on the Kennedy assassination, fails to entirely convince, due, in parts, to some ham-fisted, stereotyped dialogue.

Rumour has it that *Metal Sushi* has received rather a cool reception

133

on 'the scene', but this is to be expected. Conway refuses to press the recognised buttons beloved of the current 'counter-culture', even though all the obsessive themes are present: horror, occultism, snuff-porn, bizarre ritualised sex, gender-bending, etc, etc. It's just that when Conway has finished with these themes, they seem to turn out strangely unrecognisable, strangely transmuted into something less definable. If Conway has been rejected it's because he has made it *easy* for the reader to reject him; he obviously writes for *himself* and is unwilling to make any concessions in terms of 'trendiness'. Don't worry if you don't 'get' Conway yet — he's several years ahead of his time.

Stephen Sennitt

METAL SUSHI
DAVID CONWAY
(details above)

'*In his final days*', opens 'Omegaville', one of the short stories in David Conway's collection, '*Verlaine would spend endless hours wandering the abandoned proving grounds of the derelict research station on Zhorakesh, ponderously contemplating the distant image of the Terminal City, the enigmatic symmetry of its haunted monoliths*'.

Personally, that sentence is enough to make me abandon the book — but then, I'm not much of a fan of futuristic short stories, especially not those dealing in 'metamorphic delirium, millennial depravity and misanthropic carnage', as the blurb describes *Metal Sushi* — subtitled 'Quantum Psychosis and Holocaust Theory'.

These six stories, written in Conway's 'superheated, superdense prose', are meant to be 'part Lovecraft, part Manga, part post-human porn', but I didn't make it through enough of them to be sure about that. It's hard (for me, at least) to visualise concrete images of 'stigmata colonies', 'protoplasmic organisms', 'embryonic hybrids', 'hyperreal mutations', 'turgid menis-cuses' or 'hyperspace entities', and, difficult as it is to conjure up this landscape in my mind, it's even more difficult for me to follow an abstract narrative whose protagonists are either 'Lovecraftian entities' or a 'her-maphrodite-amphibian detective'.

But I can imagine some (mostly male) people might really get a kick out of these stories — fans of Burroughs, Lovecraft, Alan Moore and Ray Bradbury, maybe. And in his enthusiastic introduction, Grant Morrison describes them as 'something not too far removed from eczema', which I'm sure is intended as a great compliment. **Mikita Brottman**

NIGHTSHIFT
PETE MCKENNA
£5.95 122pp; UK: ST Publishing, 1996; ISBN 1 898927 40 5; ST Pubs, PO Box 12, Lockerbie, Dumfriesshire, DG11 3BW
Predating Punk Rock by a couple of minutes, a youth culture erupted in the North of England that was every bit as intense in its devotion to an altogether different form of music. In this instance, the music was Soul and the movement became known as Northern Soul. Like Punk, Northern Soul appeared to be more a reaction to the times than it was about liking music. It looked to have come from nowhere, but in fact has a history woven into street gangs, Mod and Ska revivals, and an efflorescent drug culture. Clubs catering to the scene quickly sprang up — The Torch in Stoke and the Twisted Wheel in Manchester, for instance — but none captured the spirit and heart of the scene as much as the Casino Soul Club in Wigan.

Before we go any further, I'd like to point out that I'm not approaching this book as a fan of the music, or — godforbid — someone who was once a part of the scene. Soul music does nothing for me. Despite Pete McKenna's enthusiasm throughout *Nightshift*, not for a minute did I ever feel I wanted to hear a single note of any of the records he was gushing over; I knew exactly how they'd sound, and that is *bad*. But, I am interested in 'movements', and I can appreciate the record collector mentality that leads hardcore fans to pay extortionate amounts of money for rare 7" platters.

Wigan Casino ran regular Soul nights from September 1973 up until December 1981, at which time the organisers were unable to renegotiate their lease and the club was forced to close. (The club alternated between Soul nights and Punk bands.) During this period, Wigan established itself as a Mecca for Northern Soul fans, who made the trip every weekend from all over the country to attend the Casino's All-Nighters. (Why All-Nighters should have become a requisite of the Northern Soul scene is never explained in the book.)

Needless to say, McKenna is a fan and writes about the ritualisation of his social life, how everything revolved around those eight-or-so hours spent in the Casino: The travelling from his hometown in Blackpool each Friday night (first by coach and then later by any means necessary), the drugs that were an integral part of the scene for most people, but which ultimately eroded it, and the 'coming down' and the void felt waiting for the next weekend.

McKenna relates many horror stories. Some of these are drug-related, but not all. As the book progresses, it seems that the bad times outweigh the good ones, but not once does McKenna's devotion to the scene falter. Ultimately, he gets Wigan-fever so bad that when one day he discovers his father lying on the stairs suffering from a stroke, he steps over him and goes to bed, hoping that someone else will deal with it — should it mess up his plans to get back to his beloved club.

Nightshift is not particularly well-written. It doesn't aspire to be a facts-and-figures historical chronicle, but rather a rites of passage recollection for McKenna. The blurb on the jacket says, rightly, that *Nightshift* is a fast-paced read. With some tighter editing (or any editing at all), it could have been a much faster one.

ROAD RAGE!
TONY WHITE
Price? 125pp; UK: Low Life (ST Publishing) (details above)
Will Goodman, crusty hero of this odd little tale, is a man with a cause: to stop the road builders in their tracks, to destroy Babylon and to show us the way to freedom. And, on the other side, is evil Sir Marcus Farkus, head of Roads 4U, out to destroy nature and who builds roads over ley lines in order to out-magick the crust pagan hordes. The story's

too silly to describe, it's pure tosh, with frequent, unerotic sex scenes, plenty of anarcho-crusty mysticism and the occasional laugh (not all of them intended I'm sure). If one of the aims of the book is to build sympathy for the road protests than this fails dismally — by the end of the book I didn't really care what happened, even though I think Reclaim The Streets are one of the most interesting groups to emerge in recent years. Somehow nothing of the politics behind the road protests emerges from the story, though there's enough detail in the descriptions to suggest that the author's probably a crusty himself. The only other thing worth mentioning is that Sir Marcus, shit-eating industrialist deviant, is by far the most interesting character in the book, certainly more interesting than young Will who deserves to be knocked down by a speeding BMW next time he ventures out of his squat. **Pan Pantziarka**

CRASH COURSE FOR THE RAVERS
A Glam Odyssey
PHILIP CATO

£6.99 136pp; UK: ST Publishing (details above)

This is an amiable and harmless little memoir of the early Seventies Glam Rock era. Nothing much happens in the book apart from the author building up his record collection and putting together some tapes himself. Expect no insights into Glam, no inside information about the groups and not much in the way of analysis. You can also forget trying to relate what was happening in the music to what was going on in the wider world at the time. This is

When the crusties take on the road builders, Mother Nature decides to lend a helping hand.

Tony White's
ROAD RAGE!

a 12-year-old boy's view of the world, and it's relayed pleasantly enough in those terms and no more. What more can you say about a book where the most exciting thing that happens is that young Philip's dad gives him a hair-cut that goes horribly wrong? **Pan Pantziarka**

MANCHESTER SLINGBACK
NICHOLAS BLINCOE

£9.99; UK: Picador

In a particularly apposite instance of synchronicity, I came across a copy of the biography of James Anderton (the religious zealot who used to run Manchester's police force), whilst reading Nicholas Blincoe's latest — *Manchester Slingback*. Not that I'm saying you need to read *God's Cop* (Michael Prince, New English Library) to enjoy or understand Blincoe's book, but rather that it serves to remind us of the real mania of the man who had been at the helm of Britain's second biggest police force. Anderton is the man who launched a crusade against filth, pornography and political subversion, which meant raids on gay bars, bookshops, publishers, and collusion with the National Front. Blincoe's book is set in that same era, though thanks to our libel laws God's Cop is here transformed into an acolyte of John Anderton — one John Pascal to be exact. And although the names have changed, the atmosphere comes across as depressingly authentic, the routine harassment of gays and pornographers a reminder of those days back in the Eighties. And, just as it was then, while Pascal/Anderton sees Sodom and Gomorrah in the grimy streets of Manchester, the real horrors are taking place in the children's homes outside the city. Rentboys, outrageous queens, Bowie clones and kids running away from institutionalised abuse; Blincoe paints a vivid picture of life in the dark underbelly of our second city. The story is all the more harrowing at times because Blincoe doesn't make a big deal of what was going on in the kids homes. He doesn't revel in the horror to the detriment of his story or its characters, and the book's stronger because of it. The abuse is just another fact of life...
Like all of Blincoe's books, this

Pete McKenna's
NIGHTSHIFT

one is shot through with a humour so black it almost makes you choke. This doesn't have the same edge of weird inventiveness that featured so strongly in *Jello Salad*, but somehow this is a stronger book. If you really want darkness, then this is the place to find it. It's everything that crime fiction ought to be.
Pan Pantziarka

NEVER HIT THE GROUND
KIRK LAKE

£10 218pp; UK: Pulp Books, 1997

Ray Gardner is a petty crook looking for a grubstake so that he and Lisa can quit the urban wasteland of South London for sunnier climes. Unfortunately, Ray is not only broke, he's also in the shit with Rudi — an altogether more heavy duty crook — for selling bad drugs in Rudi's club, Hades (it's supposed to be called Shades, but the neon sign's bust). Rudi is not a nice man. Rudi has an ashtray made out of a hand on his desk. That's the kind of man Rudi is. Ray finds himself coerced into taking Rudi's prize Siamese fighting fish over to Amsterdam for an important bout, and he decides to try to turn the situation to his own advantage after his old mucker Loose Joints tells him about a bloke he knows who's looking for someone to mule Es back to London. Even though the whole deal stinks worse than a dead fighting fish, Ray gets on the ferry. Lisa goes along for the ride. Loose Joints goes along to effect introductions. Harry and Rootboy, two other companions in villainy of Ray's, are flown over by Rudi to keep an eye on his fish

135

(which, natch, turns out to be no fish at all). Meanwhile, Absolutely Sweet Marie and Queen Jane Approximately, a pair of transsexual drag queens financing their hormones and operations via shoplifting and prostitution, see a big break coming their way when Queen Jane is offered a plum part in a porn flick. The location? Yup, ol' Sin City — Amsterdam.

So far, so noir, so good, eh? Well, I thought so, too, but there are serious problems with this debut novel from Kirk Lake. Ray's incessant attempts to play both ends against the middle make him a less than sympathetic protagonist, and when he and Lisa come to a sticky end, I was neither surprised nor saddened. Lisa is never sufficiently developed as a character, though there are some intriguing touches (the collage of eyes she constructs above her bed; her sudden ability to bottle a guy to death). Queen Jane and Sweet Marie seem entirely dispensable — I was expecting their parallel story line to converge with the main plot in some ingenious manner, but it never happens, and I'm not very convinced by the notion of Dylan-worshipping drag queens anyway. I mean, Bob Dylan?! He's not exactly gay icon material, is he? Structurally, the book divides very neatly in half — London/Amsterdam — the latter half being considerably pacier than the former, which is slow to get going. But then the resolution is a mess.

The urbane, streetwise style of *Never Hit The Ground* places it in the modern crime fiction territory previously staked out by Elmore Leonard, Robert Campbell, and, especially, James Hawes, but Kirk Lake has some ground to cover before he's as good as any of these authors. I don't enjoy being negative about people's work, still less when it's their first novel, but I just couldn't get much satisfaction from this — sorry. But then, the book jacket is adorned with praise from *NME* and *Dazed and Confused*, so why should Kirk Lake pay attention to what I think? **Simon Collins**

GREAT TALES OF
136 **JEWISH FANTASY AND THE OCCULT**
JOACHIM NEUGROSCHEL (Ed.)
£14.99 / $22.95 724pp; US: Overlook

MY BACK PAGES
Classic Bob Dylan, 1962-69
ANDY GILL
£14.99 144pp; UK: Carlton Books
THE 'ALBERT HALL' CONCERT 1966
Bob Dylan & the Hawks
Sony/Columbia CD
GUITARS KISSING AND THE CONTEMPORARY FIX
Bob Dylan & the Hawks
Bootleg CD (no label)
THE BOB DYLAN TRIBUTE CONCERT
VH1
DON'T LOOK BACK
dir: DA PENNEBACKER, 1965

he apotheosis of Bob Dylan really grew out of the period where he electrified his music, and in the process, legitimised for rock music the sort of lyrical content that folk music had carried. Even though Dylan had already produced major electric hits by 1966, and in LA groups like the Byrds were already doing Beatlized interpretations of his songs, the sense of betrayal felt by his fans of the old era was still palpable at the Free Trade Hall in Manchester, on May 17, 1966.

This is probably the most famous bootleg tape of all time, and because the original tapes were somehow mis-identified, has always been known as the Albert Hall tape. It has been available for some time in an allegedly Italian pressing with the odd title of Guitars Kissing and the Contemporary Fix. It was supposedly dubbed from the same master tapes as Columbia's official release, which retains the old, misleading title. Columbia declined to send a review copy of the official release to Headpress, although they originally had agreed. You'll have to ask them why. You would assume that they have remastered the tapes beyond what the bootleg offers, but you never know. Of course, now that the official release is out, the bootleg is a sort of pirate disc, and it would be very wrong of me to suggest that you search the bootleg out and deny Sony their rightful legal share of your money, because Sony's deep love of the music and concern for Dylan's loyal listeners deserves to be rewarded fully. And coincidentally, the disc was released in time for Christmas too.

Whichever disc you hear, as recounted in Headpress 16, this is an extraordinary set. It marks the point where rock'n'roll music was finally transmuted into rock, for better or worse. This is where it starts to transcend the pop traditions, top 40 boundaries, and even, for a short while, the control of the hustlers and conmen who handled the money.

The two disc packages begin with Dylan's acoustic set, the Woody Guthrie Bob already shifting into something else. The second disc, with the group that would become The Band (apart from Mickey Jones replacing Levon Helm on drums) is a revelation. It's not just the booing from the crowd, the voice that yells 'Judas', to which Dylan replies 'I don't believe you' and tells the band to 'Play fucking loud'.

Dylan was used to this by now. At Newport in 1965 Pete Seeger had tried to cut the cables bringing power to his instruments. Al Kooper was so shook up after the crowd reaction at Forest Hills, NY (virtually Kooper's backyard) that he quit Dylan's band. So too did Levon Helm, who grew tired of the constant booing. But as Don Pennebaker's film of Dylan's 65 tour of Britain showed, he didn't really care. He'd adopted an attitude to deal with all this, as seen by his surreal snideness in mocking the press who interview him, and by his constant disparagement of the 'British Dylan', Donovan. Pennebaker gets great footage of manager

Artist unknown

Albert Grossman in action, conning the BBC, and also a series of really creepy-crawly shots of groupie-extraordinaire Bob Neuwirth. Although everyone, including Joan Baez, seems happy to bask in Dylan's reflected shadow, Neuwirth is like one of those guys who carries the heavyweight champion's belt to the ring. 'Yeah champ, you got it champ, whatever you say boss.' When he starts dissing the soon to be dumped Baez, you actually start feeling sorry for her.

All of this is covered in Andy Gill's My Back Pages. This is a useful reference book, but suffers from an anoraky tendency to miss the forest while concentrating on the trees, like a hippie on a trip studying every vein in that groovy leaf. Gill's source interviews, especially with Al Kooper, have provided him with great material, but it isn't distributed evenly: it's as if the book has been finished before all the interviewing could be done, and of course Dylan himself is only here second-hand.

Fortunately, Gill is strongest in the period we're concerned with here, the 65-66 transformation. It's also very thorough on the early folk albums, but tails off quickly after Highway 61, with the albums from Blonde On Blonde through Nashville Skyline getting progressively shorter shrift — which is a particular shame with The Basement Tapes and John Wesley Harding. I wonder occasionally about Gill's instinctive knowledge of Americana: the Bill Lee who played bass on Dylan sessions is Spike Lee's father, which is a cool piece of trivia. When Dylan sings 'his pointy shoes and his bells' he may be singing about a jester's costume, and he may also be talking about flared trousers, bell-bottoms in America, and often 'bells' in Sixties jargon. But that sort of nit-picking isn't the point. Gill cares deeply about this music, and it shows throughout. Who knows what the 52 page CD booklet in the Columbia release is like, but if you didn't behave legally and buy the official release, this book would surely make up for that loss.

The official Dylan tribute concert is old news by now, but it has been broadcast recently in the UK on VH1. It's sad. Al Kooper gets to sit in with John Mellancamp, whose backup singers do a full Vegas assassination of 'Like A Rolling Stone' while Kooper does his organ bits in obscurity. Kris Kristofferson reads off an autocue stuff written by the same kind of guys who write the intros to the Oscar ceremonies. A series of Chardonnays like Sophie Hawkins (Chardonnay=great white whine) drag Dylan back to 1962's Hootenannies. Sinead O'Connor tries to out-asshole a New York crowd, and they send her backstage crying.

There are a few good points. Richie Havens seems to have lost nothing in 30 years, and Tracy Chapman seems a bit like Havens reborn. But apart from Booker T & the MGs, the only people who appear to be enjoying themselves are Eric Clapton, who does a brilliant job as a sort of chairman of the board, and, in sharp contrast to Clapton's executive sleekness, Neil Young bounces around the stage like a kid set free by Dylan's Sixties brilliance. When Dylan himself appears, you realise how many great epitaphs he's already written. 'I Shall Be Released' (sung at Richard Manuel's funeral), 'Knockin on Heaven's Door', 'Forever Young'. You wish it were true. Bob's own performance is a letdown; I couldn't help but feel we were hearing that same sort of mumbling he used to put off the crowds back in 1966. Thirty years on, and that's what it's come to. Michael Carlson

Press, 1997; ISBN 0 87951 782 4; distributed in UK by Turnaround

NOW, THESE GOOD, WISE AND HONEST MEN WHO ASPIRE TO OPEN PEOPLE'S EYES, SO THAT THEY CAN TELL THE GOOD AND USEFUL BOOKS FROM THE BAD, FOOLISH, AND HARMFUL ONES — THESE MEN ARE KNOWN AS CRITICS.

from 'The Gilgul or The Transmigration'

So that's what it's all about, eh? Well, I'll do my best. I'm not going to pretend to have read all of this hefty beast (oh c'mon, it's over 700 pages long! I do have a life outside of Headpress hackwork, y'know). But I hope I've read a representative enough sample of the 31 tales collected in this volume to be able to give you a reasonable idea of what to expect. All of these stories are translations from Yiddish, and the majority are by 19th and early 20th Century authors, although the earliest pieces are anonymous and come from The Mayse-Book (1602), a compilation of the fables, parables and folk tales typically told at a farbrengen, a social gathering of a rabbi and his followers (maysenen is Yiddish for storytelling). The stories originate largely from Central and Eastern Europe — the ghetto and stetl cultures of Germany, Poland, Czechoslovakia and Russia — and offer a fascinating glimpse of a largely vanished culture. Those who have studied Cabbalism and alchemy (and I'm sure there are some of you out there who have), or indeed read the juicier and more poetic parts of the Old Testament, will know how richly evocative Hebrew imagery and mythology can be. Recurrent themes in the collection include matrimonial quests (in classic folk-tale tradition), conversations with (and visitations from) the dead, the wrong-righting and culture-defending deeds of 'wonder-rabbis', and, especially, the fractious relations between the Jews of the Diaspora and their frequently hostile Christian host communities.

One of the more famous tales presented here, 'The Golem or The Miraculous Deeds of Rabbi Liva' by Yudl Rosenberg, was a Yiddish best-

CULTURE GUIDE

137

seller when first published in pamphlet form in 1909, and subsequently appeared in several other forms, including a stage play, a novel adaptation, and in 1914, as one of the earliest horror films. It recounts the exploits of Rabbi Liva in 16th Century Prague, and the Golem (a sort of Frankenstein's monster made from clay and animated by Cabalistic invocation) he created to defend the Jewish community from the perennial threat of the Blood Libel — that is, the false accusation that Jews carried out ritual murders of Christian children at Passover to obtain blood for making unleavened bread. The Blood Libel has been aired again in this century, firstly in the notorious forgery *The Protocols of the Elders of Zion*, and later in low-rent Nazi propaganda sheets like Julius Streicher's *Der Stürmer*. As Norman Cohn and others have pointed out, the same accusations have been made throughout history against unpopular minority groups, from the early Christians of Imperial Rome, through the witches of the Middle Ages, to the 'Satanic abusers' of our own times.

The other well-known tale collected here is 'The Dybbuk' by Ber Horowitz (also filmed, in Poland in 1938, shortly before Hitler's troops set about removing Yiddish culture from the face of the earth), a story of a displaced evil soul, the eponymous Dybbuk, and its ousting from its host body by Rabbi Israel Baal Shem-Tov. Despite its subject matter, 'The Dybbuk' is more funny than scary (think *All Of Me*, not *The Exorcist*), and in fact, if I have any criticism of this collection, it is that I didn't find any genuinely creepy stories at all, in spite of there being

demons, witches, evil spirits, ghosts and Jewish werewolves galore. The stories are too pious to dwell on the dark side for its own sake, and goodness and order inevitably prevail. What you will find here in abundance are quaint, charming vignettes of mittel-European life, a poignant blend of pathos and joie-de-vivre, and, above all, the abiding commingled sense of faith and perplexity felt by people who considered themselves the Chosen of God, but found themselves dispossessed and cast adrift in an alien and hostile culture. **Simon Collins**

THE GAS
CHARLES PLATT
£6.95 180pp; UK: Savoy Books, 1980; ISBN 0 86130 023 8
(Available through Headpress, p.70)

> 'I LOVE YOU,' SHE WAS WAILING, EMBRACING HIM, PRESSING HER TEAR-STAINED CHEEK TO HIS CHEST, RUBBING HER CROTCH AGAINST HIS STOMACH. 'I LOVE YOU, DADDY!'

Although *The Gas* was first published in the States in 1970, it remained unpublished in Britain until 1980, when those naughty boys at Savoy (*Meng & Ecker*, *Lord Horror*, *Reverbstorm* etc) unleashed it as part of their campaign to aggravate the forces of law and order in the person of James Anderton of the Greater Manchester Police (see the Headpress anthology *Critical Vision* for further details). The novel has remained an underground classic of sorts, and copies of the 1980 printing are still available, albeit at a somewhat revised price.

The Gas relates the story of Vincent, a research scientist at a secret lab in the West Country, who witnesses an accident which releases an experimental gas into the atmosphere above Britain, a gas which provokes uncontrollable lust and aggression in those exposed to it. As Vincent tries to reach London, where his wife and children are waiting to flee to the hills with him, the country falls into increasing social disorder. Vincent, reunited with his family and travelling with a young hitchhiker, Cathy, and a renegade priest,

drives from London to Cambridge, where the book's Bacchanalian climax ensues in King's College chapel.

Whilst *The Gas* is not very well written, and is easily outclassed by the tales to which it may most easily be compared — *The Day of the Triffids* by John Wyndham, JG Ballard's *High Rise* and *Concrete Island*, David Cronenberg's film *Shivers* — Platt does score heavily in the visceral gross-out stakes, and there are several set pieces that linger nastily in the mind: the exploding Cambridge landlady, for instance, the panorama of perversion found in the engineering and medical labs, the incestuous orgy in which Vincent and his gas-happy family indulge, the demented coprophagous sci-fi fan and the dog-masturbating policeman. Philip José Farmer, in his not very illuminating introduction, also mentions the parachute sex and the postie shagging the letter-box, and indeed these and many other lurid interludes are both funny and lively, but I think Farmer is altogether too generous to the book's rather hamfisted attempts at satire. Sure, there are orgiastic nuns, randy vicars, mad scientists, and so on, but this does not make *The Gas* the equal of *Gulliver's Travels*. It is a scurrilous, scatological, puerile, silly book — and perfectly enjoyable on that level! The hilariously bad cover art is a fair indication of the unsubtle delights within. **Simon Collins**

LAND OF HYPE AND BORING
The Dance of the Voodoo Handbag
ROBERT RANKIN
£16.99; Doubleday
SCEPTICISM, INC.
BO FOWLER
£9.99; Cape Paperback Original
SUCKER
LANA CITRON
£9.99; Secker & Warburg

Voodoo Handbag is billed as a virtual comedy. In another reality it's probably funny. Is Lazlo Woodbine a private eye trapped in the evil world-wide web of Necrosoft, or is he being manipulated by the 1984-ish leader Billy Barnes? Mix Monty Python with *Little Shop of Horrors*, toss in some Terry Pratchett, and you've got a second-hand crazy-quilt

Photo © Will Youds

SNOWPONY

Snowpony live in Manchester, 16 January 1999

THE SLOW MOTION WORLD OF SNOWPONY
(CD, MCA/Radioactive) and
Snowpony live in Manchester, 16 January 1999

Showcasing their debut album (already out in the US but not yet available in Britain), Snowpony took to the MDH stage as glitter-eyed girls in the audience were awaiting the newest darlings of the Doc Martens set, headliners Mercury Rev. And out came the strange and uneasy whirlpool sounds of 'Easy Way Down', a cut-up piece that is maddeningly alluring. It opens the gig and also the album, and provides a good benchmark for the nefarious pleasures that lie at the heart of Snowpony. Would it be enough to win over the girls? Probably not, but the audience did take notice, and some probably went away wondering what it was all about.

One of several high points of both gig and album is 'John Brown', which incorporates a naggingly familiar Garage Punk riff (replete with vinyl scratches), a steel guitar, and a coda that provides the usually laid-back singer/songwriter Katharine Gifford with an opportunity to really flex her tonsils. But already songs from the album are being muscled out in favour of newer material — naturally, given that the thing was recorded and completed for a release back in June 1998. Furthermore, since their last Manchester appearance (with an 'ambient' Yo La Tengo), the band have completed a US tour and acquired a new dynamic in the form of a keyboardist/guitarist. The extended line-up has made for a more confident, more exciting live set, while 'Crumpled Ten' and 'Into The Heart Of Dalston' mark two new musical offerings destined for post-Slow Motion World release.

The set ended with a storming rendition of 'Bad Sister', its detuned horns made easier on the ear by some lively on-stage antics involving a bottle of Evian spring water. Joe Scott Wilson

story that throws out some great ideas (downloading your granny's subconscious?) but does nothing much with them. What he does do, when a line *isn't* funny (and that's most of them), is repeat it. When a line isn't funny he repeats it. Like that. It doesn't get funnier for me, but call me strange. Hey, strange! See what I mean? I have to confess I read this book in manuscript and when I accidentally started it over halfway through, it actually took me five pages before I noticed! Memorable, it ain't! Lazlo's Holy Guardian Sprout, named Barry, tells him 'the secret is knowing when to stop.' Too true, sunbeam.

The ideas flow also in *Scepticism Inc*, which is narrated by a supermarket trolley. In 2022 talking trolleys work in the St. Pancras Shop A Lot, next door to the Metaphysical Betting Shop, where Edgar Malroy runs Scepticism Inc and never loses a bet on metaphysical issues. He's sort of a cross between Statto and L. Ron Hubbard.. But soon he falls in love with a woman who thinks she's a messenger from God, and presto! it all starts to go wrong. So far, so good, and unlike Rankin, Bo Fowler's first novel features wry narration (from the trolley) and some humour.

Problem is, it's Kurt Vonnegut's wryness and Kurt Vonnegut's humour, and Vonnegut's been doing it better for the last 40 years. Fowler is one of the highly hyped and hugely advanced young writers whose pictures fill the glossy magazines. I suppose if you can win Turner Prizes for remaking Andy Warhol films on video and Bookers for redoing William Faulkner, he's on to a real winner. So it goes. Some British reviewers even called this original. Do yourself a favour and stick to Vonnegut.

Don't be fooled by the massive hype surrounding Lana Citron: she's a lot more photogenic than Fowler, in fact, an actress might kill for those eyebrows, but behind the glossy publicity stills lurks a first novel with originality, which separates it from rest of those bright young Oxbridge or UEA grads. Sadly, *Sucker* isn't about Monica Lewinsky, but it is impressive in the way Citron switches styles, playing with characters' voices in her shifting narra-

CULTURE GUIDE

tion, and playing games with the English language, something at which Irish writers have always loved to outshine their English counterparts.

On the surface, this is about four characters looking for love. But the way Citron shifts deftly between Bea (searching for true love) and Nonny (simply searching) and digs out the darker corners of their existence, separates it from mere sexual roadmapping. She draws her male characters, from shallow Brian to sugar-daddy Marcus, with similar heat-seeking accuracy, with a minimum of superfluous narration. She's more deft at defining the age barrier between Marcus and Nonny in one scene than Alan Hollinghurst was in the whole of *The Spell*.

This ability to use different styles to a purpose, rather than just showing off, and the fact that they are her own styles, should spotlight Citron as a writer to watch. And oh those eyebrows... **Michael Carlson**

PENNY IN HARNESS

PENNY BIRCH

£5.99 (+ £1 p&p) 259pp; UK: Nexus, 1998; payable 'Nexus'; Cash Sales Dept, Virgin Publishing, 332 Ladbrook Grove, London, W10 5AH

Penny in Harness.

From the wine label style 'Adults Only' warning to the tasteful b&w cover shot of the pouting blonde in PVC (looking like she's dressed for a Roxy Music album cover without realising that boat long since left the island), this wants to be sophisticated smut. Art Porn. It wants that title so bad that you can almost smell the *need* coming off of the pages. And, from the first line — '*There are few things more embarrassing than getting caught short in the middle of nowhere*' — to its promise of an insight into the 'bizarre world of whips and harnesses, of crops and restraints', you would think it's pulled it off with ease.

But, this is a plain and simple fuck book. Admittedly there's more imagination and eloquence on display than in your average top-shelf mag's space-between-the-twats filler, but when our heroine has a corn cob up her arse by page 8 you just know it's going to go all the way.

Employing a polite prose style, generously peppered with lines like 'After what seemed an eternity', Penny takes us through the initiation of a curious girl into the world of 'unusual' sex. From her first tentative fumblings in the woods through to her training as a Pony Girl and ultimately to her graduation as a fully fledged mistress, our heroine never quite manages to satiate her appetite or, more appropriately, 'Relieve the burning ache in her pussy.'

For your money, you get at least one major and one minor sex scene per chapter — ranging from eagerly delivered blow jobs to spankings, restraints, horsy rides, butt-plugs, dildos-a-plenty, blistering dyke action and some exquisitely detailed, well-lubricated, safe sex buggery. And all performed behind the lace curtains and on the private acres of toffs in Wiltshire. Posh birds going at it like you were always told in school they did, and I just couldn't help but picture Liz Hurley as Penny, particularly during her description of '*her boyfriend's cock against my anus, pushing, breaking into me and then sliding up my bottom with what must be the rudest feeling of all*'. Come to think of it, if this was 'Our Liz' then surely Hugh Grant wouldn't have had to trawl in the gutter for a horror like Divine Brown with which

to experience the seamier side of life. Just a thought. **Rik Rawling**

SCREAM, MY DARLING, SCREAM!

ANGELA PEARSON

£9.99; UK: Delectus; tel: 0181 963 0979

Being a red blooded male myself, I'm in touch with my masculinity to the point of being thoroughly and profoundly aware that all men, including myself are, in fact, *whipped*. I'm merely stating the obvious because everyone knows exactly what I'm talking about. Angela Pearson was thinking of something slightly more literal when she penned these comely vignettes of flagellation back in 1963. The six tales in this collection have been lovingly reissued in a facsimile edition quality paperback, complete with a contemporary photo of a veiled and cadaverous creature staring out from the cover with an air of utter contempt.

In the first story, 'I don't suppose you'll kill me,' a woman uses sexual blackmail in order to beat the bejesus out of her man.

In 'A Potentially Dangerous Situation' a girl and her friend use sexual blackmail in order to beat the bejesus out of a couple of strapping young bucks.

In 'A little Music while You Work', a prison warder's daughter uses sexual blackmail to beat the bejesus out of a trustee up for release.

In 'It's Time For Your Morning Caning', a maid in a country house uses sexual blackmail to... Can you guess? I think we're beginning to see a pattern here.

I always thought that this kind of material was peculiar, in that it exists specifically for a reason that has nothing to do with literary aspirations. Like car manuals, it exists in a myriad of forms, but only has one purpose. As erotica, I'd be lying if I said I didn't achieve minor wood at some of Ms Pearson's descriptions, so in that sense I think it's a success. We always know what's coming next — if you'll excuse the phrase — so the predictability takes some of the fun out of it. This is genre specific, and therefore probably taken best in small doses, like foie gras or religion. I think both men and women will find something stimulating in

Scream, My Darling, Scream!, but the entire premise of this flagellation business is already very familiar to me, if only in a metaphorical sense, and I think most men will agree: They have what we want, so we do what they want. **Mark Deutrom**

ROSEY THE BABY KILLER AND OTHER STORIES

BILL SHIELDS
£9 / $10 113pp; US: 2.13.61; ISBN 1-880985-54-3; distributed in UK by Turnaround

Bill Shields fought in Vietnam. Now he is a poet. His latest collection, from 2.13.61, one of America's leading fringe publishers, is a sortie across the mind of a real talent. His Vietnam experiences and their aftermath become keys to some dark, dark rooms in this collection. The arc is time, swarms of memories detonating in the present, terminating in these magazine-case poems, fired in rounds of written tracer-fire. Shields' incredibly economical style just tells you what happened, pretensions bleached, the essences of life-moments saturated to maximum vividness. (I recommend Ian McEwan fans tread this way.) A simple visit from a Shields relative — or anyone who was *not There* — is unwelcome, switching Shields' awareness into jungle-shreck mode. Moments trombone-zoom into years, whole lives are compressed into koan-like obituaries. The death of his daughter, the suicide of friends, his marriages, receding feelings — Shields doesn't blink, not once. Then there are the flashbacks to that sub-Eden horrorshow — the 'deep fried' villages, the children, all the casual daily Apocalypses. The myth of the Hero, so hungered for in American society, is savaged by this collection. **Eugene Carfax**

GOT TO GET IN LOVE (BY TUESDAY)

DIARY
£6.50 (incl p&p); DyscFunctional CD; Diary, 52 Stapleton Road, London, SW17 8AY; tel/fax: 0181 767 4657; email: jplant@cix.compulink.co.uk

'Christ on a bike, what the hell was that?' was my first reaction to *Got To Get In Love (By Tuesday)*, by cheeky cockney band Diary — a sort of Michael Caine sings Alexei Sayle in the style of a pub band from the Eighties. At nearly one whole hour long, Diary offer us the most grating back-bedroom rock that I have heard in a long time. It became more than challenging to sit through this recording. It became Zen.

Let me introduce you to the band: On guitars we have the teenage strumming of Nick Rowan. On electric bass we have the uplifting and distorted plucking of Tomoko Yamashita. The bouncy and student-like drumming is brought to us by Tony Bravado. Last and no means least, Diary's crowning glory, let's hear it for the most tuneless middle-aged man with no vocal talent you could ever wish to hear: John Plant!

The music is maniacally basic; the lyrics are nonsensical ramblings that lead to nowhere — I can safely say that this is not a good CD. **Will Youds**

WILL

CRISPY NUTS
Wrench Records 7" EP; Wrench Records, BCM 4049, London, WC1N 3XX; tel: 0171 385 1939; fax: 0171 565 2838

Fast and furious, short and sweet, this is Japanese hardcore packed with energy. Crispy Nuts manage to squeeze four songs into a seemingly tiny moment of time, helped by their 'Punk-Pop for the Nineties' non-majestic guitar sound. Yet another dimension is added with the vocals which seem to be played on the wrong speed whatever you set your record player to. The sum of these parts is a strangely listenable record. I say look to the future — for the future is Crispy Nuts. **Duke Fretscorcher**

SOLVENT BASSED PRODUCT

HEADBUTT
Suggestion Records CD; Suggestion Records, PO Box 1403, 58285 Gevelsberg, Germany

Headbutt are definitely (defiantly?) at the metal end of the industrial music spectrum, and this CD comes on strong like vintage Ministry at times. The opening track — 'Facial Towtruck' — steams in with power riffs, catchy chorus and a driving rhythm. This sounds like pissed-off music for pissed-off people, but to be honest without a lyric sheet it's hard to know whether Headbutt want to destroy the world or merely give it a gentle smack on the bottom.

The rest of the CD lacks the insistence of the opening number, but industrial metallists will appreciate the noise produced by a band featuring three bassists and two percussionists. There's an unlisted ninth track on the CD which consists of a loop of the singer screeching 'No!' again and again — which is as annoying as Al Jourgensen's looped squawk on one of the Revolting Cock's albums. **Pan Pantziarka**

DOES TIME AFFECT MEMORY?

VARIOUS
£10 (incl p&p); Double CD; Amanita; Amanita Etxeparia, 64240 Urcuray, France

This double CD spans weirdo music from across Europe and the States, most of it by people and bands I've never heard of. It's standard left-field stuff, from guitar-driven industrial, to jazz-tinged experimentation, and deranged electronics. The danger with this kind of compilation is that the dross outweighs the good stuff, making the collection either tedious and worthy, or else unlistenable after a couple of plays. In this case, though, the mixture of styles makes the whole thing listenable again and again. There are outstanding tracks from Phased 4°, Fin de Sciecle (remixed by Bourbonese Qualk), Trottel, Keukhot and Pest. Also worth a mention are tracks by Headbutt and Feuhler. Best title goes to the Splatter Trio for their track 'Base Five Curly Motherfucker'. All in all, this is definitely worth a listen — though the cover sucks. **Pan Pantziarka**

DEE SNIDER'S 'STRANGELAND' OST

VARIOUS
Coalition Recordings International CD

METAL ROCKS! At least that's what they tell me. This is the latest musical offering from Dee Snider (ex of Twisted Sister) made to accompany his film *Strangeland*. It does, indeed, transport you to a very strange land, one where I am not too happy, but a teenager with black bedroom walls may feel quite at home. Metal really does scare me. I once shared a field at Reading festival with thousands of Marilyn Manson fans, and while (thankfully) there were no human bones smoked in my presence, I still feared for my ribs.

This tape has a lot of big names on it. Anthrax, Pantera, Marilyn Manson, and, of course, Dee Snider. There are a few highlights, Kid Rock and (Hed)Pe being most memorable. Other contributors include Coal Chamber — they really are one ugly band. Nothing breaks new ground (there is the obligatory metal/rap cross over) and frequently the only musicianship mustered is just sufficient to knock out a basic beat. Accomplished it is not.

I've a sneaking suspicion that followers of this genre are mostly aiming for mum-shocking controversy — something this album would easily achieve. If you're into metal, *Strangeland* will nestle nicely in your collection. If, however, like me, you only occasionally like to visit Planet Thrash, then it is still worth a discriminating listen. **Duke Fretscorcher**

ABERRATION
dir: TIM BOXELL
New Zealand; cast: Pamela Gidley, Simon Bossell, Valery Nikolaev; cert 18; Marquee Pictures
Amy, a Cyndi Lauper wannabe with an annoying designer kookiness about her, moves into a woodland cabin for a winter break. Before too long, the generator packs in, green slime starts to roll down the walls, and things happen to make her think that she's got rodents or cockroaches. And if that cliché quota isn't quite high enough for you, how about the loopy local hicks who stop by? Turns out that strange lizard-like

creatures are on the loose and responsible for the bad stuff. They're also fast-moving with a taste for human flesh. Amy wants to kill them, but the local Marshall — who's a Biologist in his spare time — wants to study them. (The Marshall-biologist appears to be doing an impression of Bruce Campbell.) The creatures can adapt to almost any environment. When one of the things is thrown into a fish tank, it grows gills instantaneously. That's the film's only inspired moment. The 'drama' is needlessly protracted by a psychotic ex-boyfriend (Valery Nikolaev) who ventures into the plot to track Amy down, only to be eaten by the little monsters.

PERVIRELLA
dir: ALEX CHANDON
Great Britain; cast: David Warbeck, Eileen Daly, Emily Bouffante, Sexton Ming; cert 18; Screen Edge
HOMEBREW
dir: TOM MOOSE
Great Britain 1996; cast: Adrian Ottiwell, Robert Taylor, Tom J Moose; cert 18; Screen Edge
I watched these two as a double-bill, and you'd be strongly advised not to do the same. Looking at the list of movies Screen Edge distribute, it's difficult not to feel that these are the worst of the bunch. I'm all in favour of home-grown talent and British movies, but ultimately there's a finite amount of goodwill I can bring to anything, and these both outstayed their welcome.

Pervirella is perhaps the more disappointing of the two, as it clearly has some kind of budget — although the African and Asian scenes are obviously not shot on location, as is intimated in the cover blurb. There's not really any sex, no nudity beyond toplessness, and certainly no laughs from this corner. The only good things I can say about it are that Emily Bouffante, the actress who plays Pervirella, is easy on the eye, and there's one scene with Billy Childish and Thee Headcoats. That's it. Oh, and the orgy scene towards the end is watchable, looking convincingly enough like a Sixties movie party scene. Films which try self-consciously to be cult artefacts usually fall flat on their face, and this

one's no exception. I can't even say it's a good effort — it's not, and should be avoided by anyone who values 90 minutes of their life.

During *Homebrew* there's at least the sense that the cast and crew (no distinction here, really) were having a good time — if some friends of mine had made it, it would have been fairly enjoyable. As it is, it's a fairly substandard take on the *Bad Taste* genre — at times more sickening, but less inventive than Peter Jackson's debut; more like *The Return of Billy the Kid*, but more puerile (I know it's hard to believe...). Lots of shitting and puking, Nazis (always good for a laugh), and the worst computer FX I've *ever* seen. But the film works, at least on one level. The director (who, typically, plays about a third of the roles in the movie) is quoted on the inner jacket as saying that he wanted to turn peoples' stomachs — well, mine was certainly turned. Scenes involving one zombie shitting into another's mouth, another puking up his innards, and limbs being lopped off all vied with each other to sicken me more and more, but none of it could compare to the terrible Eighties synth score. I didn't think they made music like this any more. Ultimately I suppose I'm the wrong person to review this — but I suspect that the target audience is too young to watch it legally. **James Marriott**

BLEAK FUTURE
dir: BRIAN O'MALLEY.
USA 1997; cast: Frank Kowal, Wendy Newcomb, Brad Rockwell, Rob Cunningham; cert 18; Screen Edge
Set in the 'not too distant' future, this, O'Malley's fourth feature (the previous three being video projects), makes use of locations in the Californian desert to reveal — yet again — that after global genocide the earth is a barren place of sand, rock and feuding mutants. The main character here being 'Slangman', a man of knowledge. *Bleak Future* is this man's episodic journey to salvation (only to find himself possible alien fodder).

In this vision of the future, everyday objects from pre-millennium times are either sacred or feared (a Coke can is passed off as a hand-